How to Figure Out a Woman

Also by the author
How to Figure Out a Man
Soulmates: Poetry for Lovers

How to Figure Out a Woman

The Games Women Play

joella Cain

COOL HAND COMMUNICATIONS, INC.
BOCA RATON, FLORIDA

ISBN: 1-56790-118-2

First Printing

COOL HAND COMMUNICATIONS, INC.
1098 N.W. Boca Raton Boulevard, Suite 1
Boca Raton, FL 33432

Printed in the United States of America

Book design by Cheryl Nathan

Illustrations by Stephen C. Left

Cover and inside photos by Michael Davidoff

Creative concept by Peter Ackerman and joella Cain

Cain, joella, 1944-
      How to figure out a man : the games men play / joella Cain ;
   [illustrations by Stephen C. Left].
         p.   cm.
      Title on added t.p. : How to figure out a woman : the games women
   play.
      Two works published back to back, inverted, with separate title
   pages.
      ISBN 1-56790-118-2 : $17.95
      1. Man-woman relationships. 2. Men--Psychology. 3. Women-
   -Psychology. I. Title. II. Title: How to figure out a woman.
   HQ801.C263 1994
   305.3--dc20   93-46072
                                                            CIP

This book has been written because my brother, Robert T. Cain, insisted I inform the unfortunate men in the world who have been clipped, duped or possibly castrated by a Tarantula, Showdog or Femme Fatale International. I hope the exposure and case histories will better forewarn and arm you men. Better still, the information contained within might assist you in finding the right woman.

Contents

Special Acknowledgments

I think it quite appropriate that a man discovered this manuscript, another man edited it, and still another man published it. However, it's even stranger that all three published *How to Figure Out a Man* too!

It proves they are fair men because they could have refused to even acknowledge or include the *Man* book, which exposes all of men's tricks. But that is why I respect these three men at COOL HAND Communications. A special thanks to Allan Weiner, who found both manuscripts; another man I'm totally indebted to, Gerald Shaw, for cleaning them up with his trusty red pen; and the last "main man," Chris Hedrick, without whom they wouldn't have been published.

Introduction

This book is written for men who continually become involved with the wrong women or leave a good woman for a bitch. Women should also read this little exposé about the categories of conniving cuties who are out to capture, steal or entice *your man*.

Since the Neanderthal Male, men have been exasperated by the fact they couldn't "figure out a woman." That is precisely what certain women wanted them to think.

Yes, you can figure them out. However, I haven't met one of these "trickster types" who wanted a man educated to her wily ways. Sorry fellows, it's this simple: when you associate with "Tarantulas," "Showdogs" and "Fatal-Attraction" types, you are far out-matched. You guys are the recipients of many well-learned games handed down through the centuries by crafty women who are masters at manipulating and deceiving men.

I found these women in action fascinating to watch, and observed in amazement while viperous vixens played their tunes and you, the unsuspecting male, danced.

It's somewhat of a dichotomy because while you were dancing and scratching your heads in wonderment about how to figure out these species, the music got faster and you hopped higher.

After so many years of observation and being privy to firsthand secrets of my underhanded feline sisters, I decided to categorize these groups—so you can figure out a woman.

This book is long overdue and the subject matter has perplexed most men since the birth of Adam, who incidentally was conned by a woman. I imagine the poor fool is still baffled as to why and how he was thrown out of the Garden of Eden. The bookstores are stocked with an overabundance of literature (wrong classification) for women on how to catch, seduce, marry, love, capture, expropriate funds from, divorce and ruin a man. Much to my dismay, there are none written for men on how to protect themselves against such well-disguised vampires who prey on the male's jugular vein and, of course, his pocketbook. These maniacal manuals are written with the same saccharine sweet premise—manipulation of the unsuspecting and unknowledgeable male. Better still, they should be titled, *Take Him, He'll Love and Reward You for It.*

Let's face it, bub, most of you love getting clipped. Unless you educate yourself and develop a sense of awareness about the game, where you aren't one of the players, it will continue.

What's wrong with honesty between the sexes? Do men find dishonesty more feminine? If so, have you ever wondered why? We are all taught as children that honesty is the best policy, but not where male-female relationships are concerned. Just listen to dimwit and her mother talk and I'll take bets Mother isn't stressing that daughter be honest with hubby. If Eve had been honest with Adam and informed him that she wanted to eat that apple, maybe the ol' boy would have substituted a pear and talked some sense into her clouded, greedy brain, thus preventing both of their posteriors from being exiled from Eden. Another interesting check into the history of women reveals that Eve didn't give a damn about the consequences for her or Adam—she just wanted the goods.

For centuries the male has been the manipulated instrument through which some women have gained his riches, kingdoms and, yes, sometimes even his life. You'd think from man's evolution through the ages, time and knowledge would have produced more aware and intelligent males when it came to dealing with the "weaker" sex, but it just isn't so.

The only difference between Cleopatra and the brunette in the typing pool is that Cleo exerted a helluva lot more imagination when she rolled her well-proportioned body up in an oriental carpet just to entice Caesar. Today's typing pool brunette just applies a little Maybelline to her eyes, checks out your hot-button and starts the tricks. Men have sold out.

They are as easy today as they were in the beginning of history. A woman's goals remain the same and men have complied: hook, snag, catch, whatever adjective suits you, but God forbid, don't play the game straight. But men should accept partial blame for a certain female's dishonesty. Maybe you men haven't appreciated those honest women. There are some, you know. Maybe you have fallen for Ms. Muffett perched on her silk tuffett for a reason.

It's about time the male faced, with total objectivity, his own inner self. Maybe by accepting those phonies and their games he's subconsciously condoning that type of behavior. He might benefit in future relationships with a bit of knowledge on how the cunning, deceitful and mercenary female operates and also by asking himself why he's buying it.

I believe both sexes will benefit from this knowledge. It might prevent a disastrous marriage or ugly divorce. For some men, it could even prevent a hitch in debtor's prison for not paying Cinderella's outlandish alimony payments.

This is a book for the male of the animal kingdom. Wise up, pal, maybe you have been guilty of playing a few games yourself; but do you always want to be the loser?

—joella Cain

Historical Women and
Their Fascinating Tricks

Women have been strategically controlling men for centuries through a myriad of brilliantly contrived tactics. Just go back in history and you'll find many original Showdogs, Tarantulas and Queen Bees (the type of woman you may run into).

George Meredith, a great admirer of women, once wrote that women would be "the last thing to be civilized by man."

Robert Neville stated in his 1929 book, *Women of Some Importance*: "Extraordinary powers of fascination in the female do not seem to go with great intelligence, the vast majority of beauties not having been remarkable for brain power, though in their own particular line many of them were clever enough. The truth is that the average man is apt to mistrust erudite women, not caring to find himself in a position of mental inferiority as regards to the opposite sex for which reason in matters of love, a pretty but brainless girl will generally eclipse her more learned sisters. Courtesans in particular are apt to be deficient in mental power, the proof of which is that though their lives are crammed with adventure they very seldom have any interesting or amusing stories to relate."

Famous women who attained wealth, power or station in life throughout history aligned themselves with powerful men. They possessed a main goal or goals and all shared a common thread that ran through their carefully woven fabric. That was they devoted their entire concentration, attention and love on that particular male.

The only exception was Eve. She, the immortalized female "master manipulator," was a true Queen. When God and Adam informed her not to eat the apple, she did exactly what she damn well pleased.

My research revealed some interesting and hidden insights into how some famous women attracted, pursued and, yes, ruled their powerful men. A closer look will give you men a better education about the female species and also women could learn a trick or two.

Surprisingly, most were no raving beauties, but had refined their clever techniques to perfection. Many took their assets and parlayed them into a fortune.

One of the finest examples of a Showdog-Tarantula-Queen combination at work on her prey was Cleopatra. Cleo was creative and innovative in her quest for ruling Caesar and then Marc Antony.

Plutarch says of Cleopatra: "Her actual beauty was not in itself so remarkable that none could be compared with her, or that no one could see her without being struck by it; but the contact of her presence when one got to know her was irresistible. The attractions of her person combined with the charm of her talk (voice) and the distinctive character of all she said or did, was something bewitching. It was a pleasure merely to hear the sound of her voice." You'll notice this is a predominant quality in all famous women including Miss Jackie O. Cleo was proficient in many languages and could easily shift from one to another. She spoke fluently, without an interpreter, Ethiopian, Bedouin, Arabic, Hebrew, Syrian, Parisian, Greek, Egyptian and Latin. Cleo wasn't dumb.

Marc Antony was mesmerized by her total image, but didn't fall in love with her until six years after their first meeting, even though she bore him three children.

Mr. Antony was a philanderer and was married when he met the Queen of Egypt. He needed money for his battles against Octavian and knew she could capitalize this venture. She had one child by Caesar, a boy, who was the heir to the throne of Rome. Antony used this to secure her trust, proposing to take the child under his wing and assure her the boy would inherit the empire.

His first meeting with Cleo must have thrown him into orbit. (Remember, first impressions are lasting ones). She arrived at their designated meeting spot via ship, which was draped in purple gauze and decorated with candles. Some of her handmaidens were dressed as sea nymphs. Antony had been invited aboard for dinner and a banquet was placed on deck. He spent a fantastic evening being entertained by the best.

Antony and Cleo met periodically and she became pregnant with twins. He, in the meantime, divorced his wife and married his arch enemy's sister, Octavia.

After a three-year absence, Cleo decided to bewitch him during their next meeting. Again their romantic union took place on her ship. This time she carpeted the entire vessel's salon with roses so thickly packed that they formed a sort of sweet-smelling mattress. Cleo, a Showdog to the inch, knew how to choreograph a love tryst. Marc was totally enchanted.

Her line of action was quite clear—she would have to excite his admiration for her regal power and her boundless resources of wealth, and at the same time win his actual love.

She was ambitious, scheming and unscrupulous. But no one recording of her history denies that she was brilliant, energetic, courageous and tenacious.

She wowed Antony with fabulous parties featuring intellectual and artistic guests, and provided him with enormous delight and entertainment.

Again, she was clever and became his constant companion. She was with him at every turn and let him escape her neither by day or night. She played dice with him; drank, hunted and partied with him, never leaving his side. (Many women of history captured their men by becoming habit.)

Even though Antony was romping around Egypt with Cleo, he was still married to Octavia, who was caring for their children, running the estate in Rome, remaining faithful and entertaining his friends. In short, she was the perfect wife, a worker bee. She was prettier than Cleopatra, but dull in comparison. She didn't possess the sex appeal that radiated from every pore of the Queen.

Eventually, the siren's call of Cleo won. Marc Antony married her and the marriage was recognized by Egyptian doctrine but not Rome's. He didn't bother to divorce Octavia, as yet.

However, by the time he turned 51, he divorced Octavia and fell madly in love with Cleopatra. He also became totally emotionally dependent on her. No doubt he was experiencing "male menopause."

When the battle of Actium began, Antony was so possessed and obsessed with the Queen of the Nile, she accompanied him to the battle site. This was to be his downfall. His heavy drinking, their constant quarrels, and his total obsession with her caused the mighty warrior to lose the war.

The night before he was to battle Octavian, Cleo and Antony had a horrendous quarrel. He continued drinking until early in the morning and both were not speaking. They had previously agreed she would be on her ship ready to leave if he lost to Octavian. She was to wait until the end of the night before making a decision to sail.

But while Antony and Octavian were in the middle of a hot confrontation at sea, Cleopatra decided to hurt her lover even more and leave for Egypt immediately.

Marc Antony, seeing Cleo's vessel being prepared to sail, left the battle scene and followed her. He overtook her boat—and spent three days on deck because she locked him out of her cabin. Throughout the journey back to Egypt she refused to speak to him.

They finally arrived in Alexandria, estranged. Cleo retired to the palace and Antony retired to a shack by the sea. He lived like a hermit for awhile.

After several months, they reconciled and awaited Octavian's entrance into Alexandria and their deaths.

While Octavian was capturing the palace, Cleopatra fled to a small building located in the courtyard. Antony stayed in their bedroom in the palace and, as Octavian moved closer, plunged a sword through his chest. Cleo followed with a similar suicide within hours.

Cleopatra's life was a prefect example of a Showdog-Tarantula-Queen Bee combo in action. Who knows, if Marc Antony had stayed with Octavia the worker bee, history might have been different.

Cleo wasn't the only Showdog in the annals of history.

Madam Pompadour was King Louis XV of France's "main mistress." He had many—before, during and after Pompadour—but she lasted twenty years. Why? She was sharp enough to ignore his dalliances and smart enough to run interference with them, without him being the wiser.

In fact, she befriended some of them and treated these flings with such kindness in public that his display endeared her more to the king.

She kept him entertained with her music ability and artistic talents. And, like Cleo, she was extravagant, throwing balls and banquets so he wouldn't get bored and go in search of another mistress. She surrounded him with arty and intellectual friends. Many of the famous writers and artists of that day were continually invited to the palace. Always her main goal was to please him and further her political interests.

Once she found him helplessly entranced with another female, so she went on a diet and counseled with a friend. The advice was, "render your company more and more to him and be gentle. Do not repulse him in his fond moments because the chain of habit will bind him to you forever." This hint she followed to a tee. It worked until she was replaced by Madam Du Barry.

Now, La Pompadour was entertaining, amusing, and a marvelous confidant to King Louis XV but Madam Du Barry was a "sexpot."

In fact, during his long liaison with Pompadour, the king often accused her of being cold and sexually frigid. Du Barry was a much welcomed change as she learned her skills as a prostitute at the house of "La Gourdan" where she was known as "The Angel." Her clientele were again writers, artists and intellectuals whom she befriended and brought into the King's court to further stimulate their social circle.

Du Barry also threw lavish balls while residing at Versailles. Like all Showdogs/Queens, she could spend a quick buck on clothes, jewels, entertainment and decor.

She was the last official mistress of Louis XV and when he died, she struck a deal with the powers to be to tell all about the secrets of the state, thus blackmailing them into installing her in grand style, at the palace in Licennes. But this lifestyle was to be short-lived. The French Revolution was in full swing and, because of her extravagance and court enemies, she lost her head to the guillotine.

Marie Antoinette, married to King Louis XVI, was such a Showdog/Queen that she informed the starving French citizens to "let them eat cake." This ignorant remark didn't endear Marie to the French revolutionaries. While France was in the midst of turmoil, she was entertaining lavishly at the Palace of Versailles. Finally, the revolutionaries ran her and the King into exile. However, they were so incensed with her spending, they wanted her head. She was guillotined in 1793.

A modern-day mistress who achieved a "rags-to-regal" story was Wallis Simpson. Wally had been married twice when she set her cap for the soon-to-be King Edward VIII.

This gal was a Showdog personified. Her Duke spent millions on jewels, designer duds, homes, plus rare antiques, all for his tiny Duchess.

The Duke of Windsor became King for a short while, but because he couldn't marry a divorced commoner, he gave up his throne for her.

She was furious. She didn't want to marry him—she wanted to be mistress to the King of England. When she learned of his decision, she begged and pleaded with him to remain on the throne. He wouldn't hear of it.

They did marry and she became the Duchess of Windsor. She catered to him, waited on him hand and foot, but could scold him and put the Duke in his place quite quickly.

She was conniving, scheming and brittle. Rumor has it she even stole her own jewels just to collect the insurance. This little nobody lived better than most Queens and was treated as a pedigreed Showdog.

This was just a little history lesson you can use for your own protection. If one you really don't love has become a habit, it could lead to an unwanted wedding.

It's plain to see there are some common traits these famous ladies shared, including a very seductive voice. They concentrated on the "main man" in their lives—mothering, catering and acquiescing to his every whim. They were all proficient in the art of seduction and sex appeal.

They became a habit by always being there for their male. Men are creatures of habit, most desiring a permanent mate who will cook and care for them, without causing too much friction. A smart woman knows this and uses this technique to the hilt.

None of these women, as Robert Neville states, were "mental giants" because the average man doesn't want to compete or feel inferior to a brainy female.

A man doesn't mind or isn't aware that a woman can be clever, conniving, manipulative and scheming—especially when it comes to her chosen man.

Pabulum and Pubertese

From the moment a female child is conceived, some poor man's problem is just beginning. Do you know why? Because that bundle, swathed in blushing pink, eventually grows up and marries some unsuspecting male who's not prepared—but, brother, she *is*.

Her preparation begins the minute "Little Ms. Delicate" emerges through the birth canal. She is immediately fawned over by her mother, DaDa, proud grandparents and adoring aunts. They handle her with kid gloves, oohing and aahing over her every movement. Her bottom is wiped, oiled, powdered and perfumed, while loads of frilly clothes are purchased just to adorn the dimpled darling. She is literally placed on a silk cushion. If she's smart, she'll remain there until the day she dies.

Regardless of the obstacles she has to overcome, she'll make it. Since early childhood little girls are nurtured on the belief that it is their right to be placated. Even the toys they play with are indicative of their pseudo-femininity. While little boys are playing with Tonka trucks, little Ms. Muffet is dressing the perfect couple, Barbie and Ken, or emulating Mommy by playing house.

If big brother or the neighborhood bullies happen to incite her, off she goes wailing to mother, throwing a much perfected temper tantrum that would put Sarah Bernhardt to shame.

She's also perfected a few manipulative tricks of her own; her first victim being good ol' dad. She learns quickly by practicing modulating the tone of her voice usually to resemble "Chatty Cathy" when trying to soft soap the gullible guy, while climbing on his lap, hugging and kissing him. These tactics never fail.

As she grows older, the same tricks apply to boyfriends. In high school, Ms. Puberty found a way to a man's heart during football season was to know the game. She bought a rule book, learned everything about it and went to the game with what her date thought was an abundance of game knowledge. She loved jumping up and down to squeal, "Holding, holding". Of course, she didn't know what they were holding, it could have been their crotches. She abhorred the sight of blood, passed out at the sound of body contact and couldn't stand the smell of perspiration. But she continued the act. The game was being played off the field as well as on.

Take Jenny for example. All through puberty she took on the personality traits and attitude of any males she dated. While still in high school, Harry, who embraced the hippie movement, transformed Jenny into his own personal flower child. The once studious, introverted Jenny became wild and raucous. Harry's middle name was "trouble" and of course Miss Chameleon rode right along on the waves of disaster. After boredom set in and her parents stopped cajoling her, Jenny dumped Harry.

Enter William. Bill was a polar opposite of Harry: college student, worked in a bank after school, didn't smoke, drink or carouse. Immediately our conforming Jenny fell right into step. She enrolled in college and gave up her wicked ways for the role of "Miss Priss."

When she became bored with that fake image, a flamboyant Greek entered her life just in time and swept Jenny off her feet. He wined and dined her like he was Onassis. Needless to say, "Miss Class" herself became the social butterfly. Gone was the once studious, ex-pot-smoking-slob-turned preppie.

After Mr. Extravagant faded into obscurity, Jenny finally met the love of her life. Jim was stable, earthy, outdoorsy, cheap and into the au natural. He was the type who would take her to Vegas but make reservations at the KOA campgrounds. She gave up the high life for a simple existence. Her extravagant wardrobe was replaced with one pair of khaki pants and hiking boots. Their engagement was spent hiking across the Grand Canyon, eating bean sprouts and trail mix. She pretends to be excited about her future austere existence. However, the day might come when the real Jenny will have to stand up.

By the time Baby Jane has blossomed into puberty, she has perfected her skills in every manipulative mechanism useful in controlling the poor unsuspecting lug. Society has assisted "baby precious" in refining these controlling attributes. Many little darlings learn to use it by age three, smiling and showing their dimples to the judges to get the title of "Little Miss." When puberty hits, if she smiles larger and bigger she can take home the title of "Miss Teenage America." By the time she's twenty, she can wiggle her fanny at the right judge and become "Miss World." She obviously has the world in her hands if she employs the tricks handed down to her. After all, it worked for Mother.

Beware, Tarantula Approaching

The first lesson in figuring out women is they are not all alike. Some are tall, fat, thin, short, blonde, brunette and so on. One important point to remember is their one common trait—brains. None, I say, are dumb. So brother, never underestimate a woman's intelligence. If she acts like a trained seal, observe closely and you'll find it's only an act—for your benefit, of course.

Women have always used their intellectual "inferiority" when it was to their advantage, throwing their opponent—you—off guard. Not once did God create a dumb female. Au contraire, they're not able to balance the checkbook, but they can always run a complete D&B on guess who? Men shy away from intelligent women who aren't afraid to show it. They feel it destroys their macho image. The gross mistake here is that every woman is smart when it comes to getting what she wants. Most men will choose the dumb, helpless piece of fluff, only to find out too late. The helpless one has buried his ego, squandered his money and made off with his worldly possessions—tying what was left with a pink ribbon and stuffing it all you know where.

If you don't want this to happen to you (or if you're tired of getting buried, ripped off and stuffed), then know your opposition inside and out. Forewarned is forearmed. You never hear a woman say she doesn't know a man. They pride themselves on this attribute. You will always hear a man say, "If I could only figure out a woman." It's easy, you just have to know their games. We are going to categorize several different types of women and expose some of their game plans.

In your future search for the perfect mate you will have the ammunition to protect you from entering the bonds of matrimony with a mistress of disguise and deceit.

And you'll need all the protection you can get when you meet our first category, the Tarantula. Now, a tarantula is sometimes very attractive with slow, deliberate moves. If you're allergic, it can be poisonous.

The female Tarantulas I am referring to come in all sizes, shapes and colors, and possess a varied ethnic pedigree ranging from the Jewish Princess to a Sarah Lawrence Debutante. Much like their namesake, they find the weak spot of their victim quickly.

They also know where your hot button is, so they can push the hell out of it for future gains. With this immediate knowledge, they eventually weave you into their web and you never realize how you got there.

The Tarantula is super analytical, unobtrusively. She uses the male's weaknesses to reinforce and strengthen her already strong position. Her main goal is to overcome her future breadwinner and charge account provider—you.

The first and foremost weakness most men possess is ego. Second is guilt. Tarantula Tillie is very aware of the male ego syndrome, so she plays—or shall we say preys—on this vulnerable spot. Wham! You've been had. You ask how? My dears, as Browning would say (Elizabeth that is), there are so many ways it would really take me days. But let me have just a few minutes and you will be better informed.

There was a Tarantula (Jewish Princess variety) who operated so diligently she almost poisoned herself. Marriage was her main goal. After a year of devoting her time and master tricks toward her prey and he still hadn't proposed, she decided to give him the full treatment. She set the stage and the play was on. Shakespeare couldn't have written a better one.

One evening her male target announced bluntly that he was having dinner with a friend, a female. Distasteful, yes. He was playing his own game. But no man is a match for the Tarantula. She discovered they were dining at his apartment and decided to cause a scene.

Unfortunately, he had left his young playmate there to cook dinner while he bounced down to the local singles bar for a drink and a quick look at the local action (never said all men were angels...quite the opposite sometimes). The Jewish Princess followed him to the bar and proceeded to read him the riot act. After she accomplished that feat, she dashed to his apartment and, owning a key, barged in unannounced. She demanded the playmate leave pronto.

She knew he would be furious, so she devised a game plan—the guilt caper. Frankly, in this particular case both were guilty of the games people play. She proceeded to gulp a handful of his thyroid pills and immediately slid into a "coma." He arrived shortly after her suicidal swan dive and called an ambulance. When she "came to" he felt like a heel. He was. But games have a way of boomeranging on the players. She felt elated. Sure, she was faking it, but she had his full attention. He was guilt ridden and humble as hell.

While she was "recuperating," his attention was undivided. Gifts, daily flowers and total devotion were showered in her direction. The Tarantula felt smug and secure in her web. She brought up the subject of marriage constantly. She bemoaned the fact that if he had been married to her this horrible incident wouldn't have transpired. Also, her birthday was just around the corner and the rat felt so guilty he gave her a surprise party and a full-length mink coat. She had been hinting at one for several months.

If he had any backbone, he would have leveled with her and severed their destructive relationship. Instead, he made her feel inadequate as a woman by flaunting his cute cooking companion in her face. He could have prevented his future enslavement plus saved both of the them unnecessary financial expenditures. There is nothing worse than a woman scorned, especially a Tarantula, as you will soon see.

Now the princess had him on the hook and every time she didn't get her way, the rat thought she would try another suicide attempt. She played this to the hilt. She started seeing a head shrinker twice a week at $50 a crack and cried a lot. As the ol' Bard puts it, "What a hell of witchcraft lies in the small orb of one particular tear."

If you are the game-playing male, it never proves fruitful. Both parties were game playing and the futility becomes evident. The man never wins, so why play? Buddy, you're out-matched, out-witted and out-vindicated when it comes to dealing with the Tarantula. On with the fairy tale.

Christmas rolled around and the boyfriend wanted to go home for the holidays, but the princess wasn't invited. A tremendous outburst of temper tantrums ensued so he canceled his trip and spent it with the princess. Another plus for the Tarantula.

She was expecting a ring from Santa, but received an expensive pair of leather boots and a hot roller set instead. Remember, Tarantulas are possessive and love material goods. She was quite perturbed, to put it mildly. You'd think receiving a mink a month before would have quenched her materialistic thirst. (That's more than most women, who are honestly working for it, ever receive).

New Year's arrived. A partying princess and chained-trained chimp, or shall we say chump, went out for a night on the town. They were sitting with friends in an exclusive club waiting for midnight to arrive. The boyfriend was obviously eyeing every blonde that came in the door (the princess is a dyed redhead). She kept her cool so long, then reached over and smacked him in the jaw.

He was mad; she was mad. He didn't call her and she became panicky. Her control was slipping. She had to create the coup de grâce. Remember, she was playing on his ego and guilt feelings. He had two more weaknesses. He was impressed by social prestige and money. She had both. She didn't get it by scrubbing floors. She chose the right parents. He was honest with her in the past to inform her that he didn't love her enough to marry her. Now with marriage her main goal, you would have thought she'd have told him to take a long walk on a short pier. But Tarantulas love a challenge. They also adore being top dog and having the last laugh.

January was his birthday so she immediately planned the most opulent and ostentatious affair. Get the picture? The web is being woven again. She knew he would be impressed and feel like a heel because he hadn't called. She invited his friends from all over the United States, rented a huge banquet room at the Yacht Club and had a menu that read like a dinner staged by the Queen of England. She collected all of his childhood mementos and had baby pictures printed of him for place cards. She even contemplated hiring a blonde to jump out of his huge birthday cake, but thought better of that near-mistake.

Finally the big day arrived with much pomp and circumstance. With the aid of a friend he was sidetracked into stopping at the Yacht Club for a drink. The Tarantula had even informed the friend what suit her boyfriend should wear because she didn't want him to appear tacky.

Tarantulas think of everything. He was surprised, to say the least, and also guilty, which she knew he would be. His ego was inflated to think the little darling had exerted that much effort and expense on his part. You guessed it. She got him back—lock, stock and infidelity. The Tarantula had him hypnotized. As of this writing, he's "Mr. Jewish Princess" and she sits on the throne, spending his hard-earned money, even selling his stocks whenever she feels the need to decorate her newly acquired marital web.

Let's do a quick analysis of this situation. The problem was a lack of honesty. Both parties were game playing. The Tarantula didn't realize why she wanted the rat. She just had to have him. She certainly didn't love him for the right reasons.

He didn't love her either. He was playing his own sick charade. He obviously wasn't a match for our Tarantula. Their relationship was less than mediocre at best. You must remember when dealing with Tarantulas, they don't care if the union is idyllic. They are interested in getting their way and ownership.

Tarantulas are treacherous. They are selfish, egocentric, demanding and cunning. They will go to any length to achieve their goals. Emotional leaners, they have not been known to be the givers of society. Observe a Tarantula and you'll find her gowned in courtly clothes and baubles from Tiffany's while surrounded by expensive furnishings. They are label buyers, even when it comes to a man. One of the first questions a Tarantula will ask you about is your occupation. The reason for this question is to mentally calculate your income. They love money and social status, and want a man to provide both.

Tarantulas aren't interested in the honest reasons that coincide with a relationship. They have a rather ego infested desire to possess and own a man.

More often than not, Tarantulas are impressed with being impressive. They migrate to all the "in" places where all the "in" people will notice them. Watch a Tarantula in a group of people. Notice her actions and reactions pertaining to other people and women in general. They are usually overly sweet and catty and make snide remarks. They must be the center of attention. They don't handle female competition graciously.

If you suspect that you're dealing with a Tarantula, let her spin a web for someone else.

Test & Review

Simple ways that may help you detect a Tarantula and
make her spider legs crawl.

1. Hide her make-up and invite her out to dinner to her favorite
   place. (Allow her one tube of lipstick). Brother, she would rather
   risk losing you and replacing you with another sucker than being
   caught without her eye shadow. It's one way to find out whose
   ego she is interested in.
2. Tarantulas, in general, hate the out-of-doors. It smells of nature.
   Let's face it, the trees won't be too impressed with her Dior fishing outfit. Plan a camping or fishing trip. Don't make it unbearable or impossible, but don't check into the motel or lodge (a
   Tarantula can handle that). Remember, they love an audience.
   Watch her respond to nature. If she roughs it well and doesn't
   complain, give her a plus. It's a good test.
3. Accept an invitation to a dinner party or important event. Go extremely casual. Clean, but dressed down. Tarantulas can't bear for
   their men to look underdressed—it reflects on them. Seldom do
   they look beneath the attire.

Is That Southern Belle Ringing Your Bell?

Let us move on to another male maneuverer: the sweet Southern Belle. She will feed you more Bull Durham than corn bread. This is a difficult category of male users, or shall we say abusers, to expose. They are master game players and less obvious than their Tarantula sisters. There is the Southern Belle and the Northern one. (Mutations in every species). These Belles lie and con so sweetly they convince you, with eyes fluttering, that you're the wrong one. So convinced are you that you are low man in the hominy grit pit that you place this corn pure cutie's rounded arse on top of the Mason Dixon Line. They win top price for "Best Vindictive Vixens," although it's hidden under the sweetest pecan praline coating.

The Southern variety has it all going for her. She can over-emphasize her ignorance, pseudo-sweetness and super-dumbness. Not only do men love it, they buy it. Amanda never raises her voice; that's downright tacky. She's totally dependent. Of course, those traits only apply until Amanda decides to divorce you. Then she is capable of ferreting out the most unethical lawyer in town. She is also capable of taking honey-bun straight to the financial cleaners. You feel obligated to pay because little Scarlet hasn't lifted a finger to work your entire marriage. She was quite adept at spending money—yours. She can call you a son-of-a-bitch and it sounds like she just announced the magnolias are in bloom, honey.

It has always amazed me how the South ever lost the Civil War. If they had drafted the Southern Belle they wouldn't have. She would have executed her sugary charms on the Northern Yankees, as she still does, and walked away with the Union, lock, stock and bank account. La Belle would have lured him across the line with her professed purity. Virginity is her calling card. But she would have saddled him with ten children. The stork just happened to deposit them on the doorstep, causing the poor entrapped sap to hock his gun for a plow just to keep the brood in food.

Once the Belle, Northern or Southern, has her manicured talons into your flesh, there is no escaping unless you're willing to use your jockey shorts for collateral just to borrow enough money to get out of town. She plasters him to the homestead with all the syrup and honey she can spread around, and if that doesn't work she keeps him broke. How does she accomplish this feat? She employs the same basic techniques as her Tarantula sister, only she spins them much more intricately. She has added tricks to her circus performance that maybe the Tarantula should learn.

Children are a prime pawn in the Belle's master chess game. She uses them every time it's convenient, and mister, that's all the time. Afternoons will find Ms. Turnip Green napping because the children have gotten to her. She must leave you home with the children or a sitter so she can shop, preferably in the evening, for the young ones just act too tacky and naughty in public. And God forbid you should ever spank one of Mommy's little darlings. You will be classified as a brute and a mean ol' ogre. She is too delicate and so are they.

You can't win for losing with La Belle. When you've had enough of this phony posey and want a divorce...suffer. You couldn't leave her. What would her family say? The neighbors? The society set? Besides, the children need a daddy, what for I haven't the foggiest. Maybe to pay the bills. Dear ol' dad can't reprimand them, play with them, or educate them. Dad is just rough, stupid and not smart enough for La Belle's charges. But the kids are only something special when it's to her advantage.

You wouldn't dare leave Miss Delicate anyway. She would convince you she couldn't cope. She needs tons of alimony and child support because she couldn't possibly go to work. The children, now your responsibility, need constant attention. You'd feel like a real clod leaving this damsel in distress. She couldn't possibly fight her way through life's traumatic pressures.

Let's take a look at some of these calculating cal-a-lilies in action. One molasses-dipped cutie had the world conned, especially her husband. She was the perfect example of the all-American girl. Naturalness was her middle name. Attractive she wasn't. In other words, you would be hard pressed to pick her out of a crowd of two.

Ms. Molasses was an airline stewardess based in Atlanta where she and her devoted hubby lived. One weekend our little orange flower had a two day "layover" in Miami. She and several friends scouted the singles circuit one evening. It seems Miss Perfect liked to cross the color line when she was out of town. Not only was she blatantly committing adultery, but tasting the forbidden fruit. Even if her friends had been the vicious type, she still would have remained the untainted one. Her image was already established with family, friends and husband. Not a soul would have believed it. But true it was. They're phony like the Tarantula, although the Tarantula has more class. Belles, Southern or Northern, only talk about breeding; they really don't possess a pedigree.

They are the most accomplished actresses that the dear Lord ever created. They conned Him into that, rest assured. Are you getting the picture? If not, you better. Once waylaid by La Belle, you'll be living your life in black and white, while Miss Orange Blossom is living it up in Technicolor, and guess who's paying for the film?

However, her social image of the perfect wife, lady and hostess is impeccable. Never, and I mean never, will she utter a profane word. She dresses basically, uses minimum war paint and is a natural brunette. Just the type you'd take home to mother. Sweet as a Virginia baked ham…glazed in honey. You know the type.

Another case history of a La Belle in action is quite interesting, although she employed a little more pre-planning. Unfortunately, it didn't make the history books. A Birmingham Belle, divorced with one child, decided she needed a regular paycheck and a man to bring it home. She was working in a local dress shop. Enter a male with quite a substantial income. He was a dress manufacturer's representative, with five Southern states as his territory, which netted him a fat paycheck.

The curtain went up and act one of her perfected play began. He wined and dined her royally during their affair; and she somehow remained virginal and pure as the white driven snow. La Belle, Southern or Northern, always remains pure until marriage (even a second or third marriage). Another prime marketing trick to get you to the altar. You'd never suspect they have been touched by human hands. You think you're getting a prize and buddy you are—the booby prize. Three guesses who the boob is, and the first two don't count.

He married her and sent her child, from a previous marriage, to an exclusive private school. These Southern status seekers differ little from their Tarantula counterparts. They love home, maid, kiddies (for their own manipulation). They are more basic in their status symbols, but still materialistic. Their security lies in the suburban syndrome. They enjoy impressing the corner grocer, next-door neighbor, girlfriends and your business associates. You are their financial security and, brother, they will make sure you hold up that end of the bargain.

This particular honeysuckle proceeded to have a custom-built home designed in the most exclusive area of Atlanta and purchased expensive furnishings and paintings. With the one child out of her hair, she joined hubby on the road selling...herself. She learned the business quickly and at times could overshadow Hubbo.

She was well on her way to financial security. She had already conned him into adopting her child, so with two people depending on him and having to cater to her astronomical financial demands, the ol' boy had to work harder. He acquired several extra manufacturer's lines and was seldom home.

Finally, his salary was at its peak. Madam Belle was totally secure and slapped a divorce paper under his nose. Not only did she take everything—house, car, furnishings, support, alimony, savings—she took one of his top dress lines, the most lucrative, and proceeded forward. She didn't miss a beat. He was so devastated he was close to suicide, a completely broken man.

She had convinced him throughout their relationship that she was unable to survive alone and without help...poor little dependent Southern Ms. Muffet. Let me tell you, she survived very well. He didn't. This case is a prime example of what a dedicated well-trained Belle can do to a man. She was a master game player. Obviously, he didn't know the rules. He didn't take the time to see through her Southern facade. He bought the corn bread and black-eyed peas routine. Quite an expensive dinner.

Let's take one more Southern Susie, if you can stomach it, and follow her game plan. Susie was born and supposedly bred in the Deep South. After one semester at Vanderbilt University (they never acquire a degree because they aren't after an education, only a man) her family moved to Chicago. Her one goal was to net a big fish who could bring home the bacon and bacon fat. She took a job, knowing it would be temporary, and cultivated a stronger Southern accent. Northern men are sheer suckers for the developed and contrived helplessness.

Well, "I'll swan," as they say in the South. One day Mr. Right just happened in the door. Now Susie worked as a receptionist for an employment agency, which gave her access to all the particulars about their clients. Mr. Right was sent out for a job interview and landed the job. He was off and running. What he didn't realize was someone was out to catch him. He evidently liked what he saw because he invited her out to dinner later, and being the actress she was, she had him in the palm of her hand.

Now this Mr. Right had just experienced a crisis in his life, which had left him extremely vulnerable. She quickly zeroed in on his weakness and became Miss Understanding of the Year. Dumb they aren't. They dated several months and Mr. Right stated marriage wasn't his prime goal. However, it was Susie's. She conjured up the old baby trap game and conveniently became pregnant. (Mr. Right still claims the child wasn't his, but notice he pays for it.) She called him at work one day and announced he was to be a proud papa. In the meantime, Miss Helplessness had arranged for a doctor, altered birth certificate (keep that image pure) and all the trimmings. All for a grand total of $3000…some package. They will spend any amount of money (yours) to retain that untarnished image.

Trap him she did, and the child forever remained her pawn in the marriage game. She immediately demanded a home and got it, the checkbook and got it—and being a "good" Southern Baptist—demanded he didn't drink, smoke, enjoy hobbies or his friends, unless she OK'd it. Bad went to worse but Darlin' Susie kept acquiring houses, antiques, charge accounts and another child…just to keep Mr. Right. Dad kept changing jobs in order to elevate his salary and to elevate her status quo with friends.

Every time she felt her marriage faltering, she bought a new house, had a false pregnancy, conjured up a new illness or cried and wrung her dainty, well-manicured hands. He felt guilty every time he contemplated divorce and she knew this, so she worked on his weakness. She also had help from his mother, who was more than willing to assist her with the guilt program. The situation became a vicious circle.

After ten years of "wedded bliss" he finally got the gumption to ask her for a divorce and mean it. By this time she had all the assets hidden or sold, and the game was on. The divorce trial resembled a TV soap opera with her in the starring role as the weeping victim; and she received a huge cash settlement and quite a chunk of child support. Also, all outstanding bills were to be paid by him. Believe it, they were outstanding and plenty of them. Remember, Belles never let go. After the divorce was final and she had taken him to the cleaners, she still called him daily to come watch the kids, move the furniture, fix the car and so on. He went. She said "jump," he said, "How high?" It takes two to play the game. These Tarantulas and Belles know their victims; and, if the victims were smart, they would cease to be one. You'll find La Belles unmercifully use the guilt program and children to play up their pseudo-helplessness, allowing them to snag and keep their opponent. They have one hand on the Bible and the other in your wallet, laughing all the way to the bank.

Test & Review

1. Whip the silk cushion out from under her arse and cut her charge accounts in half. Inform her money is tight and see the reaction. If she offers to take a part-time job just to help out the financial lack, she isn't a true Belle.
2. Send the children away for a week and spend every available moment with her. Inform her she is not to mention the children even once. Plan romantic things to do. If she resists and objects to the idea or talks incessantly about the children (her security blanket), you've got yourself a true dyed-in-the-gingham Belle. Get the kids back and find a good divorce attorney.
3. Every time La Belle whines and wrings her hands, don't weaken and give in to this act. Stand up for your rights and ideals. Tell her no more than yes for two weeks and observe the outcome.
4. A Southern Belle wants what she wants when she wants it. However, they don't want to pay the price.
5. If she's constantly getting "the vapors," brother you've got a true blue Belle.

CHAPTER

Showdogs

Every man should own a Showdog, just once. That way he can compare the outrageous kennel costs with the price of a handling an appreciative companion.

A materialistic mongrel must have her diamond collars shined and polished for every outing. And you, the proud owner of such an expensive pet, must comply with her wishes...lest you get bitten. (Showdogs get mad and throw temper tantrums if they have to wear an old chain).

Showdogs don't work. If they do, they play at it. They can be found decorating the house, socializing daily, sending the children off to their private schools and pushing their husbands to make more money.

Their "free time" is devoted to furthering their status in society, improving their self image, and attending benefits and functions under the guise of improving the environment for the less affluent.

A day in the life of a Showdog is as follows: Aerobics class in the morning, lunch and gossip with the other doggies, maybe a hair or nail appointment in the afternoon, then back to the kennel for a nap (Showdogs' schedules are hectic). In the evening the Showdog adorns herself in the latest creation for dinner, of course at the best French bistro...show time!

You can spot this type of narcissistic person in a second. She is a label buyer, always spouting where the little diamond bracelet was purchased, what part of town she resides in and the name of her private clubs.

Showdogs ramble on incessantly about nothing. "I hope the weather is cold Friday, that way I can wear my mink. Johnny bought it for me at Saks for my birthday." (Actually, Johnny bought it so she could be "top dog").

"Oh, I'm going to wear that red sequined gown you admired this year to the Heart Ball. You remember the one I bought at Bloomies?"

Borrrrrrring best describes these cranked up canines. They have nothing to talk about except department stores (the most expensive), fashionable boutiques, the new sports car, the nail girl, parties and the Weatherbys' latest divorce.

Showdogs love to entertain. Showtime again—that's the focus of their existence. They purchase freshly ground imported Brazilian coffee, have fresh flowers delivered weekly, serve only the finest wines and champagnes, and sleep on D. Porthault sheets.

Dogs love to travel. One stunting Showdog friend of mine who was six feet tall with ultra-white hair (had it done in Europe) use to fly from Scottsdale, Arizona, to Beverly Hills for the day, just to shop on Rodeo Drive.

Twice a year she and her owner would hop the Concorde for London, not to see the Queen, but—what else?—to shop. Their twin girls wore designer togs since their diaper days. No pampers for these mini-show-dogs.

Showdogs make great mommies because their puppies are a direct reflection of their image. Another Showdog baby, yes ultra-platinum, bought her son a full dress tuxedo when he was five. He attended dinner parties and social functions dressed to the nines with all the other adult dogs.

His father was a developer of sorts, and when a certain development was completed the Showbaby wanted an exact replica of the model home, built to scale, for his playhouse. The father paid his carpenters overtime and plane fares just to fly to their home and build the puppy his own identical miniature model. This playhouse came equipped with a computer, TV and private phone. You can bet he'll marry a Showdog and have his very own Sycophantic Schnauzer.

The Showdog species couldn't exist without men around who can support them. The purchasers of this breed are perfect counterparts. They complement each other.

Showdog owners are hyperkinetic androids with a strong motivation to be successful. They possess a strong desire to win. They love beautiful women. His counterpart, the Showdog, offers him no competition in business and is a great showpiece. She is content to sit in their winter home in Jamaica planning their next social wing-ding.

Occupations of Showdog owners vary from celebrities to Mafia chieftains to entrepreneurs big and small. But anyone can be a Showdog owner, even people who like being a big fish in a small pond.

Husbands and boyfriends of Showdogs live in the fast lane and expect their pedigrees to accompany them. They tip lavishly and dine in the right restaurants. Sometimes you can find them at the race track or shooting craps in Las Vegas, Nassau, Costa Rica, Monte Carlo or Atlantic City.

Once a Showdog owner, always a Showdog owner. Johnny Carson has been a Showdog owner for years. He spoils them and beds them in the best kennels in Beverly Hills, Malibu or New York. When he wants to trade them in for a younger, prettier Showdog it costs him a fortune for their alimony payments just to sustain their "royal arse" in the manner they became accustomed.

Men who are attracted to Showdogs demand their undivided attention. That's why they don't like for their pets to work. What if their peers thought they couldn't afford the boarding fees?

Showdog owners are very macho and extremely proud men. They are overly protective toward their little pooches. They are generous with money, praise, love, sex and affection.

I've dated several Showdog-owner types and, believe me, life was never boring. Many times I would hide just to recuperate, and I'm an overactive type-A personality.

Showdogs must be prepared to live in the fast lane. Many Showdogs I've known take Vitamin V (Valium) regularly. If you're already an A type, you'll love it.

Showdogs aren't mental giants and their reading material consists of *Town & Country*, *Architectural Digest*, numerous gourmet cookbooks and possibly two of the top fashion magazines. They never read anything intellectual or philosophical. In fact, they think Ayn Rand was a rare disease.

But don't let me mislead you. Showdogs aren't dumb when it comes to getting what they want. They can be genius material when it pertains to acquiring the goods. Their degrees are usually in home economics, the arts (God forbid they actually paint or sculpt), fashion or interior design. They use this information to create a class image for themselves so you, darling, wouldn't think of asking them to shop at Sears.

Some of these "precious puppies" come from upper-middle class to wealthy (highly bred) families, many having some training in the social graces. And occasionally you'll find one or two who attended Stevens College or were sent to Europe for their schooling. But generally Showdogs have created their own image of pedigree-ism.

The most blatant case of pure Showdogism is when these dogs come from very poor families but develop the attitude that they deserve the very best. And, brother, they plan on marrying it. Do you think they would work their preened fannies off to pay the bills?

I've been privy to first-hand knowledge on how these doggies get the blue ribbon and trophy. Two secretaries I employed were perfect examples of mongrels turned pedigrees. Both were blonde, broke, needed a job, loved glamour and hated work.

After a couple of months on the job and observing how eight hours a day of hard work cut into their beautification routine, both became engaged and set the wedding date quickly.

The first one whined and moaned to her fiancé, who was twenty years older and financially set, that she was "tooooo" tired after work to go out, cook dinner, have sex or even get out of bed.

She informed him her life's goal was to take care of him and possibly dabble at writing the great American novel. He bought this garbage and offered her the same salary to stay at home.

Up until this time money was a sore spot, as it hadn't been discussed how much she would get for an allowance when they married.

She quickly accepted his offer, stayed home, slept till noon and who knows if she ever wrote one word.

The second secretary came to me begging for a job. Her boyfriend, a Showdog owner, left her destitute. She worked her fanny off for a grand total of three weeks. Boyfriend reappears.

She started showing up at work around ten in the morning and taking three-hour lunches. These consisted of getting her nails done, taking an aerobics class and shopping—all the time collecting a paycheck from me. She finally quit because her future Showdog owner wanted her to travel with him.

These mongrels turned pedigrees were both from a middle class environment and probably drank out of plastic orange juice cups as babies. They weren't silver but you'd never know it from their newly acquired image. They had enough jewelry to stock Tiffany's.

More importantly, these Showdogs didn't have to be born with a silver spoon. They were smart enough to seek out the type of man who could afford their developed tastes, and the Showdog owner variety enjoys showering gifts on his pooch. Upkeep on this breed is costly, so Joe Average can't afford the ante. That explains why you never see an authentic Showdog dating or marrying Mr. Average.

Speaking of upkeep, be prepared to spend a fortune just on clothing and jewelry for these extravagant animals. Costs run from $300 per week (this is a cheap dog) to $4,000 per month (now we're getting to a pedigree). Oftentimes it can run to well over a million annually. This is a Showdog.

I knew an average but authentic Showdog who spent about $4,000 a month, excluding her travel allowance which was horrendous. She had visited more than 50 countries in less than two years. Of course this was without "Daddy Dog," who detested traveling.

Remember when Jackie O was married to Aristotle Onassis? He could well afford the cost. However, she spent $1 million the first year of marriage on rags to cover her rump, giving even Ari a near heart attack. This is one of your top Showdogs. In fact, her spending habits became so outlandish even Ari, then the richest man in the world, decided to bail out. Of course he died before the divorce could be culminated and Jackie O, an International Showdog, moved back to the states with $20 million in her kick. Not bad!

Another famous Showdog was the third wife of Johnny Carson. Now Johnny was no novice to Showdogs, so he was preconditioned to her demands. But even Johnny wasn't prepared for her astronomical desires when they approached Alimony Alley. One of her monthly costs in her alimony list was $5,000 per month for gifts. Another illogical request was $2,000 and some change for "Puppy Support." Now this puppy was well over 21 and already sired by a previous breeder. The topper was, after they were separated Mrs. Carson purchased her annual Christmas gift, spending $100,000, and had the bill sent to Johnny. Showdogs are ballsy. They have to be, as they never know when another owner will show up.

There is another type of Showdog. The working breed. I like this type! In fact, I could easily become a working Showdog. That's my goal. Right now I'm just a working dog.

Joan Collins is a working Showdog. She spends money on all the trappings, but there is a distinct difference. She worked for it. This breed is the polar opposite of the Showdog. They know there is no "free lunch" for independent ladies. They are willing to pay their dues for the Buena Vida.

They love the finer things in life and spend the money they've earned freely and lavishly. They most always buy expensive presents for the stud in their life. This usually causes a reverse problem. The Gigolo. Let's hope Joanie learned an expensive lesson from her association with Peter Holm. He asked for $80,000 a month in alimony.

Elizabeth Taylor is a beautiful example of another working Showdog even though she always married Showdog owners, with the exception of Eddie Fisher. Joan Crawford and Gloria Swanson were working Showdogs. Bette Davis was just a hard working dog.

How do you know if you've got a Showdog on a leash? Well, Showdogs are usually platinum blondes, striking redheads, or sexy but classy brunettes. John Delorean was a typical Showdog owner and had a beautiful sultry brunette wife. Of course, when the millions ran out she left and immediately married another Showdog owner.

Showdogs don't look like the girl next door. These pedigree primpers are always attired in the latest "haute mode." Their watches are Piagets or classy Rolexes. They sport long acrylic nails and many have opted to have their busts improved with implants. They always have one, possibly two, large diamond rings that hubby or boyfriend bought them after he "made it."

Showdogs love to show off and be noticed, if you've got an authentic "Prima Pooch." They drive a sporty Porsche, Corvette, Mercedes or Rolls. They reside at the best address and have it professionally decorated.

Their designer duds are closeted in at least two walk-ins and the furs, never fake, are housed in "cold storage." We are talking about the real dogs, not the nouveau type. They are faking it until they make it.

Test & Review

1. How can you tell if you've got a "real" Showdog on the leash? This is easy. Check her watch, car and clothes, how she lives. If it all checks out, and the watch, car, clothes and home are for real, you've got an authentic Showdog. If you're going with the poor man's answer to a Showdog you'll have to do some shopping. This one suffers from delusions of grandeur much like the "Tara Syndrome" in the Southern Belle chapter. This type must play the game on a much smaller scale, but nonetheless, she's playing the game. She is more phony than a true Showdog. She will try and impress you with the family background, where she went to college, label you to death, and cop a snooty attitude.

2. How to obedience train your Showdog. Tell your pampered pooch she can't take the Concorde to Paris this time. Money is too short and she must take a regular flight. You will see a frothing at the mouth where you think she has distemper.

3. How to get even with a Showdog? Forget her birthday. Brother, she won't talk to you for a month or sleep with you until her next birthday.

4. If you are really a Showdog owner, don't apologize. Track down that real Showdog. And for God's sake, don't marry a Liberated Lena. You'll be miserable.

CHAPTER 6

Liberated Lena

There are those women who like to think they are liberated, trying desperately to be independent, but who are actually supported by men. Fathers, husbands or boyfriends make it possible for their pseudo-liberated lifestyles.

Liberated Lenas want to be successful in their ventures and give the impression to their "sisters" that they indeed are on the road to total freedom.

Upon closer scrutiny, these Lenas who are always professing, "I'd rather do it myself," are doing it with someone else's money. Now that's fine, but there are usually several men in the wings of this theatrical production—something you should know before you become a financial backer in her operation.

One such Liberated Lena started an elaborate health spa on the west coast of Florida. Daddy bought the property, borrowed the $1 million to erect the facilities, and plunked several hundred thousand dollars of operating capital in her bank account. She promptly went about decorating on a grand scale, traveling to other spas (research, silly) and going through money like a princess attacks Saks.

Daddy came up with more funds and she hired a male consultant. Now she planted her newly toned body behind an elaborate desk in an elaborate office, dressed in her elaborate workout duds.

Every day she would feed the media on how this was her original concept from the ground floor and, of course, her background was in the health field.

Behind the facade was Daddy funding the entire operation, her consultant making the decisions, her instructors instructing, and she was starting divorce proceedings because her husband couldn't stand her new "liberation."

Now please. This is not what I call liberation. The Lenas do. They play at freedom having a grand old time when someone else is paying the bills.

I could play you this scenario many times over. That is why, in reality, Liberated Lenas aren't truly liberated.

When push comes to shove and the stove gets hot, they call in a man to help. This modus operandi is predetermined. Women can only go so far in business because of our knowledge of the game.

Liberation, in Webster's terms, means "free." I don't know one totally free person in this universe. There are always inter-connections with other people.

Men have always depended on each other. They have business associates and support groups in the form of associations and they help each other in business. The powerful magnates align themselves with the right people.

How can a group of women be liberated in a world that isn't free? Even in a so-called democracy like the United States, we aren't liberated. If you think so, just miss a tax payment and you'll have a warrant out for your arrest from the Internal Revenue Service, pronto.

Society isn't free. We are controlled and governed by the system. And it's becoming more rigid. In fact, while they were exploding fireworks over the newly renovated Statue of Liberty, more stringent laws were being enforced on "we the people."

If you think you are liberated, in the true sense of the word, you're full of crap. You can't even make a decision to wear a seatbelt or not— you must because Uncle Sam says you will. That is not being liberated.

While the minority groups are freeing themselves from each other, "Big Brother" is enslaving all of us. So what's all the loud noise about liberation?

Women think if they fight harder and bitch louder they will be free. Free of what, from whom?

Face it, whether you are a man or woman you will never experience total liberation. Not in the purse sense.

If it makes Liberated Lenas feel better and more in control to pick up the drink tab, call you for a date, and/or pay half of the rent and expenses, let her. She'll find out what men have always known. That's not liberation; all that responsibility is imprisonment.

We now have a certain segment of society where these liberated women are dying of heart attacks, their cholesterol counts are higher than the national debt, they are running to seminars on "how to avoid stress and tension" and the topper is that many are sleeping alone.

I am not advocating women abandon their quest for success, but they better realize the price tag attached to that attainment. Female entrepreneurs are learning the difficulties involved in running their own businesses, especially alone.

Men have been aware of the problems surrounding "the entrepreneur" so they know how to offset and handle upcoming chaos.

It ain't easy, Virginia, but face it, it's less nerve racking for men. They have been conditioned to bring home the bacon; we've been trained how to fry it.

So if you guys think you've got a Liberated Lena on the line, you'd better really do some in-depth research. A second look might enlighten you to the fact she is, in truth, a Dependent Donna.

Test & Review

1. You can tell if you're dating a Liberated Lena when you call for a date and she's available any night of the week and, of course, the weekends. A worker bee would have to check her appointment book, rearrange her schedule, and possibly set a date for the following weekend.
2. She owns her own business and the business car is a Mercedes with a phone. Ask to meet her family. Bet Daddy isn't a blue or white collar worker. Watch out, if you marry this one, you'll have to work your ass off to keep her business going.
3. Lenas are always dressed in the latest "haute mode," want to dine at the finest restaurants and live at the best address. A little bit of Showdog here.
4. Lenas usually have one child, if that. Many have no children. They don't like competition either. Most, not all, have adequate divorce settlements of sufficient alimony payments.
5. They are always attending parties, for business you know, or entertaining clients. They are quite similar to the social climber, but they are classified as the business climber. God forbid they make ten business sales calls a day like all professional people do. They feel that is beneath them.

The Madonna Syndrome

This category of cunning, beguiling and deceitful females is the most difficult of all classifications to detect and expose. Why? Because they fabricate a perfect persona for the public when in truth, they are calculating, manipulative, phony mantraps.

In the beginning, men find them irresistible, especially if they are looking for a wife and mother image. The Madonna is an excellent choice, they think, and just the type you can take home to Mother.

These megalomaniacs possess a contrived exterior that borders on sainthood. But in reality they are the direct antithesis—more like a "she-devil" in disguise. They are mercenary masqueraders who use every psychological ploy in the book in order to control their mates. Transference is their one coup de grâce.

A very calculating captivator with a flawless image managed to hoodwink her husband for thirteen years. Only after she divorced him and took the house, car, kids, savings and a hefty monthly support check, did he finally realize he was duped by a professional. Even to this day, it's virtually impossible for him to accept his prized angel was a manipulative bitch who scratched her way through divorce court.

Madonnas usually refrain from any "sins of the flesh." They rarely smoke, drink, cuss and are into formalized religion (this is part of the act). Modulated tones help perfect their image, that is unless it's time to talk turkey to their attorneys. They possess a cool and contained facade.

Most generally, they are not passionate, exciting, emotional, compassionate, understanding or the least bit interested in your problems—although they might attempt to act the part if it serves their purpose. Madonnas are self-contained and never attempt to communicate on anything deeper than the weather. Most never lose their temper or shed a tear about too much other than a sad movie.

They are the proverbial "ice maiden" even down to their Clairoled looks. But never make the mistake and think the bleach has seeped into their brains and destroyed any cells. They can outmaneuver Jung, Adler and Freud; all in one fell swoop when it comes to out-psyching their opponents.

As I said, transference is excellent ammunition that Madonnas find indispensable when playing one-up-manship with their spouses. And to further explain my premise, follow this little scenario.

A particular Madonna used the children as her wedge against the husband to further gain control, power, money and then her freedom. She knew her husband was a better-than-average father and worshipped his children. She, realizing this fact, continually used this against him by exploiting the children like a pawn in her chess game. She used transference to the hilt, constantly harping that her husband worked too hard and didn't spend enough time with the youngsters. Now, what she hesitated to mention is he had to work overtime because she wanted the big house, a new car, the finest furnishings, designer fashions and four trips a year to Vegas.

She was aware that by complaining he was a bad father, he would try harder to prove to her he was indeed a good one. He played right into her hands and spent every waking moment with them, which gave her free time to shop, play golf, socialize with her friends and high-tail it to Vegas for her little respite.

Now she could sleep until noon while he transported the children to school, Little League, etc., and she got her beauty sleep and maintained her "lily white" image by taking them to church every Sunday.

She possessed another under-handed trick that was used frequently to perpetuate her social appearance. This was to put him down and erode his self-esteem while at the same time elevating her somewhat insecure one.

This misanthropic malcontent never missed a beat when it came to faultfinding and depleting his self-worth. She even had the balls to attack his pride and integrity in front of his employees, friends and family.

When it came time for her to make the big move (divorce) after she had her phony image intact, hired an expensive lawyer and premeditated every strategic move, he still wasn't entirely convinced she had been underhanded. Such are the ways of the Madonna.

How can a man avoid this treacherous type of female? It isn't easy, as this category doesn't play any game, above board. You have to be Sherlock Holmes in order to detect this type in the beginning.

However, one way is the minute you realize someone is working overtime at eroding your self-esteem...beware. Take a closer look at the perpetrator.

Steer clear of oppressive personalities; they aren't healthy. They prey upon unsuspecting, innocent, happy people who they can crush and tyrannize. And remember that a person who is inferior often covers this malady up by developing a superiority complex.

Never allow anyone, including your spouse, to malign your positive endeavors. Know your own worth and be man enough to defend your position and opinions. Create a positive viewpoint about your beliefs and guard them against any adversary who would rob you of these attributes.

Communicate, communicate, communicate. Observe, pay attention. Don't stumble through life with your head in the sand like an ostrich. You leave this earth with exactly what you come into this life with...nothing. However, the trip is the important factor here, and you might as well plan to live it with a tremendous amount of self-worth, integrity, personal satisfaction and goodness. It doesn't matter if you win or lose, it's how you played the game.

CHAPTER 8

Queen Bee vs. The Worker

There is an old cliché, "Give to the givers and take from the takers." Now the Queen Bee has developed her own philosophy: "Take from the givers and take from the takers."

She's a master at this game. She learned it from the hives. The Queen sits on her throne and the Drones supply her with honey while the Workers scurry around flitting from flower to flower collecting her glucose.

The Drones die and the Workers are exhausted. Not the Queen. She is busy training a new group to run the hive.

You men love a Queen Bee because you think you have just that—a queen. She has created this image and you think you've got the pick of the honeycomb.

Even if your love should wane, you'll find it terribly traumatic leaving the Queen because she is proficient at making you feel guilty. After all, what would the Queen do without you—the Drone—to supply her with honey? You don't mind being the Drone/Worker combination.

Poor Queenie, she might have to hoist her fat ass off the throne and gather her own sugar. Now, if you are married to a Queen Bee and she works, you can bet she has a throne at work. And a couple of Drones. Queens always have a court with ladies in waiting and a couple of knights to do their bidding. The castle never shuts down.

Usually, Queens are created by doting and overprotective fathers. Sometimes mothers are responsible for placing these burdens on the male species. Daddy probably called her "Princess" as a child and Mother was picking out Prince Charming for her in high school. You can see why this untitled royal "pain in the ass" wants a castle on the Rhine. She thinks she belongs there.

Now the Worker is the direct antithesis of the Queen. She usually comes from middle-class America or from a poor family. The Worker had to work after school in a store, baby-sit, or help her working mother with siblings and the housework. She earned her way throughout her early formative years, thus possessing a good sense of reality about life, love and pursuit of happiness. She realizes there are no "free lunches" and, better still, doesn't expect any.

Unfortunately, you men don't migrate toward the Workers and fail to see that they make excellent wives and partners. They are used to working and sharing, and will pitch right in to accomplish mutual goals. Maybe they are too realistic, therefore losing the "glamorous aura" the Queen seems to possess.

Most generally, the Worker doesn't ask for alimony, child support (and if they do, it's a realistic figure and fair) when they get a divorce. However, they are always the ones who get taken when the chips are down—usually by men.

I think their independent attitude and strong efforts for survival must be a major turn off for you men.

Queens are demanding—much more so than their counterparts, Jewish American Princesses. JAPs can be very demanding, but if they want something or, better still, someone (usually the gentile man who has been a no-no), they won't sit on their butts and expect it handed to them. They will go after it and yes, even pay for it.

A Queen won't. If she wants something she expects someone else to get it for her. There is a difference. You will never find a real Queen paying a man's way or laying out any cash for a piece of romp. Never!

I have known several Princesses who gladly "pay to play." I knew one who met a man at Club Med in the Caribbean. After they returned to the states, she flew him all over the Western Hemisphere and then took him back to the Caribbean for an extended holiday. Of course there is always a catch. He was too stupid to know how to play the game and Princesses are very possessive, especially when they are paying. He flirted with all the stewardesses and other females.

After awhile the Princess got hopping mad and dumped him for a new conquest. This same procedure happened to another Princess friend of mine, only she seemed to be a glutton for punishment as she repeated her mistakes with several in a row. It would be a cold day in Hell when a Queen Bee would buy a man a Coke, even if he were hot footing it across the Sahara Desert in the middle of summer.

Often you have to discern and observe closely for awhile before you are absolutely sure which category you're dealing with. Forewarned is forearmed.

Are you noticing some similarities among some of these categories? Well, there are some salient approximations. For instance, the Tarantula has a little, maybe a lot, of Queen in her, as does the Southern Belle. The Showdog is a breed apart. The Jewish American Princess would like to be a Queen; that is why she practices diligently at being a princess. The Southern Belle doesn't even practice—she thinks she is a Queen.

Now Queens don't do windows. They most always have maids, or would like to. If they can't afford one (and of course that's your fault), you'll do the cleaning. I know many Queens whose husbands work all day and clean the house on the weekends or evenings. Even if she doesn't work she will not lower her queenly body to do mundane housework.

Queens aren't usually into fitness. However, there are exceptions to every rule. They must be surrounded by a court, most generally women friends who are impressed with their pseudo-station in life and are not in direct competition with the Queen.

I know one Queen, at least she thinks she is, who manages a dress shop in Southwest Florida. She is one overbearing bitch. There is no substance to this woman, but she has many peopled fooled, including her husband. This Queen is extremely rude, unnecessarily so, and what she doesn't realize is that her breeding, or lack of it, and her tremendous insecurities show up like a sore thumb. The old saying "You can dress them up but you can't take them out" certainly applies to this Big Queen in her very little court.

Queens are usually married to successful men. Naturally, few poor slobs can afford Queenie and her entourage.

But even if this breed succumbs to a middle income existence, they never lose their Queenly ways. I once knew a businessman who owned a graphics company. He frequently stopped in the middle of projects to take Queenie to the doctor, bring the children to school, run to the grocery store, etc. What was Queenie doing with her time? Sitting on her large rump, and I mean large, watching Donahue. That's all Queenie did, except poke her nose in his business and cause him to lose numerous clients. Now this is the case of a poverty-stricken Queen, but a Queen nonetheless.

One Queen, who was married to a surgeon, would wait until he came home for lunch and a rest, then she had him grocery shop, run errands and plan the evening meal before making his rounds to see patients. What did she do all day? Play bridge.

Many Queens can hardly find the nearest restroom by themselves, or so they appear to be that queenly. They know someone will do it for them. One Queen I know couldn't make a plane reservation. Her husband usually did it and if he was out of town she was lost. Once when I asked her to call the airport and check on our reservation she retorted, "How do I do that?" I snapped, "Try picking up the phone and then dial." It became so complicated that finally I did it to save time and to make sure we got on the plane.

Queens are really a mess if they are part Southern Belle. God, what a combination. One of these mutations is married to an attorney. She watches TV all day and when he comes home from the office he vacuums, dusts, and picks up the apartment. When she visits her family in Georgia he does a thorough house cleaning from drapes to carpets to upholstery. The "castle" is ready for her re-entry.

He thinks she is great because she can cook and decorate. Sure, he gripes and groans about her lazy habits, but he would never leave her. "How can she make it?" he asked. "She's totally dependent on me." He shouldn't flatter himself. When they were separated for a brief period, she snagged another fool to cart her lazy behind to a health spa in California. Her husband had only been gone three days but she climbed right into the saddle to hunt down a King Arthur so she could reign supreme.

The Worker is another story. Very few men appreciate or even respect a Worker. She will sacrifice for her mate, children and even the dog so they may enjoy a better life—all the time being tromped on by her mate, the children and the dog.

Workers will toil right along with their husbands so life can be better. Many times, more often than not, these husbands will leave the Workers high and dry. They know the Workers will make it. They don't feel guilty leaving her with the mortgage payments, the children's orthodontic bills or the dog's Alpo tab.

I've known Workers left with three small children, a home, tons of bills and no alimony or child support payments. They have worked two to three jobs, put themselves through college, then turned around and made sure all three children had college educations.

I've known Workers to support their husband while he was getting a college degree or becoming a doctor. After his practice or business was going "great guns," he would leave her for a cute little nurse or his secretary who was a Queen.

There is not much more to say about Queen Bees. They are boring and very seldom do they read anything deeper than *House Beautiful.* Remember, "the castle" has to be perfect, because this is the setting and surroundings where the queen feels most comfortable. Her image would crumble without the trappings of royalty.

Queens aren't bad (no category of women is) some are just better than others. You might like a Queen. They offer no mental competition, are easily entertained (costly) and certainly don't demand much excitement, just a tremendous amount of attention.

Test & Review

1. If you're dating someone you think might be a Queen and need confirmation, try this one. Tell her you want to spend a weekend away with her but she must make all the arrangements. You are going to pay, naturally, but you don't want her to use a travel agent. She must call the airlines, hotels, etc. Everything must be done firsthand. If she passes the test, she is just a princess.
2. Queens generally don't like sports, are not athletic and are rarely adventurous. Plan an outing, something where she has to pitch in and work as a team (sailing for example, not motorboat). It must be an adventure where she has to do something other than sit on her silk pillow. If she doesn't gripe and complain and really goes the extra mile on this one, you really don't have a Queen Bee.
3. Suggest you go exploring the Mayan ruins in the Yucatan (no first-class hotels for three days, really exploring). If she balks at this idea, you do have a Queen.

CHAPTER

9

The Sexatary

As the girl who climbs the ladder of success on the boss's lap, the Sexatary is one gal to be reckoned with. No one is tighter with the boss. She's closer to him than his wife, spends more time with him, knows him better and has studied and mastered his thought process. She is more indispensable than a wife. If she is left to her own devices, she can run your company or run away with it—and you.

By her own admission, Helen Gurley Brown was a Sexatary. She married David Brown, then editor of *Cosmopolitan*, and the rest is history. She became editor, didn't she? In fact, she wrote her first book, *Sex and the Single Girl*, while she was just a little Sexatary. And she certainly advocated getting more than "chummy" with the boss.

Many secretaries have an eye on the boss's job. However, the boss is kept in the dark about this secret goal. These girl Fridays become essential to Mr. Head Honcho. They screen his calls, appointments, information, etc., all under the pretense he's too busy to be bothered (but all the time their brains are working overtime). This protective ploy allows them to weed out the competition and, of course, eventually know more about the business than you (watch Jennifer on *WKRP in Cincinnati*).

Many times I have been greeted on the phone by Priscilla Protective or Nancy Know-It-All. They are a classic pain in the ass. When they ask why you need to see Mr. Big for an appointment, you, like an idiot, tell them.

The typical dialogue goes something like this: "I would like an appointment with Mr. Moses please."

"And what is this in reference to?" she answers curtly.

"I am with *Parvenu* magazine and would like to talk to him about his promotion and advertising for the next issue."

"He's not interested at this time," she immediately decides for him.

When they give me this routine I immediately ask if he's received the materials that I sent. The usual answer is, she can't remember; it must be in the pile on his desk. This is a dead giveaway. If "Big Brain" hasn't even seen the materials, how can she know whether he's interested or not? You're usually going to have to continue dealing with Ms. Cretin so you can't call her a liar. And once you're on the wrong side of "Super Sexatary," you're through.

Now what you should have said, in a very confidential tone, is "I need to talk with Mr. Moses about a very confidential and personal matter." At least you might be able to talk with him personally even if it is on the phone. You'll have a better chance of getting through, but there are no guarantees.

A Sexatary is like the media. She can make you or break you...period. She holds the power, the key to the vault in the business world. I have seen more Sexataries climb the ladder of success quickly. They don't need an education, degree or even knowledge of the industry. They are at the right place, always at the right time, and have the needed contacts.

Many Sexataries in ad agencies are promoted to media buyers or account executives. More often than not, they stink in their newly found positions, but nonetheless they are there.

There is a resort corporation in Florida that employs more than 2,000 people and half are Sexataries. The average age is 24; bust, 44; I.Q., 4. Many of these cloned bimbos have made it to assistants to the V.P. of marketing or public relations. None can make a decision. All are at a level of total incompetence, but every year they get raises (often for giving them).

Sexataries can be managed. You have to use a little psychological charm and a lot of savvy, possibly popping for a gift or two in order to accomplish this feat. But if you want the order or job, it's worth it.

First we have to analyze why Sexataries are so difficult to deal with. Let's face it, they aren't really in control and know it, so they have to justify their position. They do this by *acting* like they are in control. In a sense they are—of your appointment.

Men are in an excellent position with female Sexataries. All they have to do is sling a little charm, a lot of bull (complimentary), and make her feel like Queen Nefertiti. She will do their bidding, joyously.

Women who depend on her to "Open Sesame" to Allah's chambers are in for quite a challenge. It might take awhile, but it can be accomplished.

But women should never make the mistake of looking too good when dealing with a Sexatary who has pseudo control. Micro-minis and sexy clothes are a no-no. I have made this mistake more than once and have been shot right out of the box. Check out the story about the department store assistant (see Women vs. Women chapter).

You must remember the Sexatary prides herself on being closest to the boss. If she thinks Mr. "B" might find you attractive, you'll never enter the inner sanctum. If you have long hair, wear it up.

Many times if you have an impressive position and the Sexatary knows this, the jealousy is immediate. She doesn't realize the sacrifices you've made to attain the position; she only knows you have it.

Men are also possessed by the green-eyed monster when a woman calls and she has a good title. Men, supposedly professionals, do a number on professional women that borders on evil. Always try to play down your position and title. If your ego can handle it, it's much safer.

I had a friend in the fashion trade and worked with him when we were both starting out in the business. Many years passed and we re-established our friendship. He had an assistant who ran his showroom for him while he was on the road. He paid her a meager salary (she was worth less) and she literally controlled his life. Little did I know that they had dated seriously for several years. After they broke up, she remained with him as an assistant secretary.

She was born in England and, of course, kept her accent current. She had aligned herself with a few titled people and used these contacts to the hilt. Coupling her accent and her friendships with "British Royalty," she managed to convince my friend and anyone else who would buy it that she was very well-bred.

Now this Sexatary was really insecure. She worked for an ex-lover, made no money and was menopausal—a real mess. But she could make life hell for anyone who needed to deal with "the boss." She was rude; he thought she was proper. She lied outrageously; he believed her. She was actually nuts; he thought she was high strung and conscientious.

She almost broke up a friendship which had endured for many years. If I had known they had been lovers I could have played the game. Instead, I was just being myself, and brother, she hated that.

One time I was shot down by a Sexatary who guarded the gate to a writer in Key West I wanted to interview for a magazine. Little did I know he was a sought-after bachelor on this little island and the women who lived there were overprotective. Ha! Insanely jealous might be a better term.

Needless to say, I didn't get an interview or an answer.

The point is, research those Sexataries as best you can. They hold your future in their hands. It's how you play the game that determines how you climb the ladder when they own the rungs. This applies to everyone in a position that's dependent on a Sexatary's authority, acceptance or assistance. You can't afford to offend the little people because they open or close the door to the decision-makers.

Test & Review

1. You can tell on the phone if you have a Sexatary or a legitimate secretary when you ask for an appointment and she acidly replies, "And just what is this appointment in reference to?" After you explain and she's still reticent, you have a Sexatary. Be prepared for the "challenge." If you get the appointment on the phone having not met Miss S, you're probably OK.
2. If you happened to "just drop by the office to leave materials" and she gives you the once over and the impression she's in control of the situation, you know you have a Sexatary.
3. Sexataries can be mean, conniving and down-right witchy. I've left or sent materials and they've destroyed them. I've called and left messages and they've destroyed them. I've called back for answers and they've destroyed me. The real challenge is the Sexatary who dated the boss and he dumped her but she still runs the office. I have been in the middle of this one before and didn't come out unscathed. If you're aware, stay out of the line of fire.
4. Know your Sexatary. She is your opponent and the fight will be all the way to the boss's office. Hope you win!

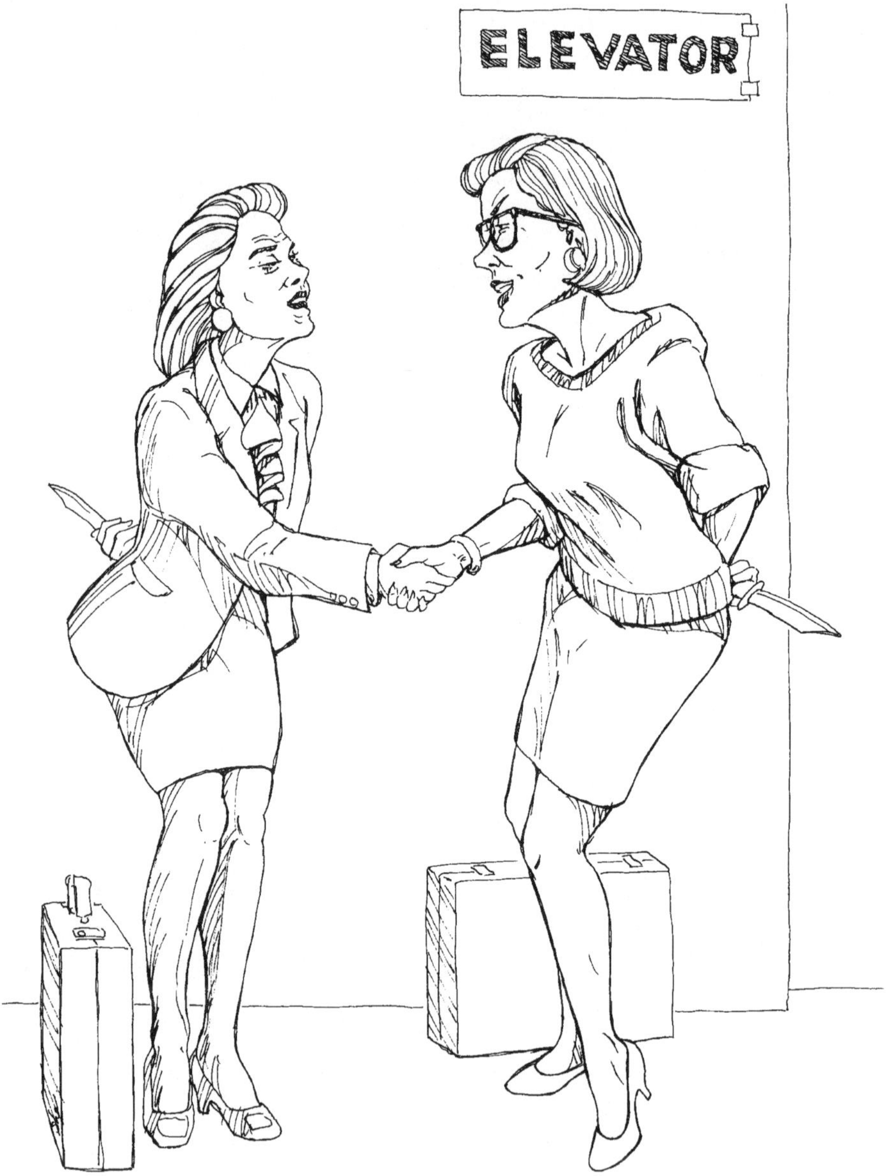
ELEVATOR

10

Women vs. Women

The female species can be cunning, vindictive and viperous. If you don't believe this, just observe them dealing with each other. This is why the "women's movement" is such a joke. Women don't network with each other the way men do. Sure they give lip service to networking, forming ladies' groups of women in business for the sole purpose of assisting each other in business. However, networking is much more than exchanging business cards at a breakfast or cocktail party once a month.

Networking means just that. Helping each other attain goals, sharing contacts, purchasing another woman's products, frequenting her business and so forth. Men know how to help each other and they are genuinely interested in their fellow compatriot's climb up the ladder of success.

Men support one another. Women don't. They act as if they are afraid their female associate might get the edge up on the climb to success. In fact, if they have any power in their positions and a woman is in need of their assistance, they generally won't extend themselves.

Call it what you want, stupidity, naiveté, jealousy, power head-trip (remember, women invented games) or just plain meanness. I know from firsthand experience what it's like to deal with this portion of the female species. Tough, if you need them.

Hell, they don't give each other the time of day. Why should the world bend over and kiss their asses reassuring them? Yes, Virginia, there is a Santa Claus. This is the complete dichotomy of what "liberation" means. Women should have advanced light years ahead of where they are now. Simply put, they should have emulated the businessman by noting how he conducts business with his associates and the professional manner in which he conducts himself.

Men place other highly successful men as role models on a pedestal following their ascent up the success ladder. They are impressed when one of their peers makes it. They are supportive. Maybe they learned this as children playing team sports.

Women like to blab about equal rights but when it comes to getting off their rumps and giving one of their sisters a boost, they usually try to make the climb more difficult by breaking a few rungs. Figure that one out.

Why do you think the book *My Mother, Myself* was written? This is about mothers and daughters in competition with each other. Take sister rivalry. This should really clue you in. They can't even tolerate their own blood-relation if she is a female. If you put these "bloodthirsty" bitches in power, you're in for it—unless she is an unusually secure individualist.

Women never cease to amaze me. First they piss and moan about "equal rights," then march to Washington, silicone breasts flopping in the breeze, fighting for recognition of their equality. However, when they are given an opportunity to assist a fellow patriot in accomplishing anything, what do they do? Put a knife in her back and then twist the hell out of it.

Men have always been supportive of each other. They loan money when the other guy is in need, form investment groups, share contacts, and enjoy a camaraderie in both their personal and business lives.

Many times you'll see men investing in another man's ideas, thus catapulting them all toward financial security. You never hear of this type of partnership where women are concerned. Until women learn to interact with each other, first on a one-to-one basis, they will never reach the pinnacle of success that men attain.

For example, I gave many women in business a chance to support a magazine that was designed to promote women and their achievements. The total concept and editorial slant was for and about women. This was the first localized woman's magazine of its kind in the United States. Now there are forty.

When I started this publication I expected my support to come from women. Wrong. In fact, they did everything possible to sabotage the project. I am talking about potential advertisers, female business owners and women's groups. The average woman reader was very supportive, generally speaking.

Women business owners, female marketing directors and ladies in advertising agencies could have helped make the magazine better, thus promoting "the cause." They weren't helpful at all. In fact, they were often detrimental. Why, you ask? Who the hell knows that answer? Dealing with some women isn't logical. They are like the government and enforcement agencies; nothing they do is rational.

Bimbos in business, they are a trip. They have no concept of professionalism and allow their insecurities to invade the little amount of pea-brain intelligence they possess. Women profess to stick together. Forget it!

Until women are willing to be honest in their personal relationships and professional in their business lives, they will continue on the treadmill of defeat. A recent survey summed it up where women vs. women are concerned. A higher percentage of women surveyed said they wouldn't vote for a qualified female presidential candidate. The majority of men surveyed said they would vote for a qualified woman.

It isn't only the business bimbos who have a problem with other women. Watch a wife operate against another fellow female if she thinks her property and possession, a man, is threatened. When women are insecure, they will stop at nothing. They don't even fight fair. They are down right lethal. That is why they make great mud wrestlers.

I've observed women really tear into another female if the husband shows the tiniest bit of interest. I have watched them pull unsavory tricks, unbeknownst to the spouse, so the wife really looks like a first-rate twit.

Study women when they are in a group where they outnumber the men. They all start jockeying for position. It's better than the horse races.

I had a British girlfriend who lived in the United States since age eighteen and spoke English with just a trace of a manufactured accent. However, when she was in a group of women and had a male audience, the accent got so pronounced that I accused her of attending Berlitz. She would put on tremendous "airs" about her background; private schools in England, royalty in the family, you know. This was all a crock of crap, but the men loved the accent and it worked. She always held the rapt attention of any and all men in the room.

She also believed in reincarnation. Sure. She thought she was a revived Queen Nefertiti from Egypt. She played this one to the max. Men bought it. They adored her act. After four divorces and four settlements, I'll call her a surviving Queen. Read more about this type in the Femme Fatale International chapter.

Many of my professional friends who are women and own their own businesses seem to share my same lament. They all claim not to have the support they need in business from women.

One of my friends, a photographer who does numerous social shoots where women hire the photographer, is always losing jobs to male photographers. She's as good and has the female approach to these functions, but she's usually third in line behind two males.

If women won't support each other they are no better than the men they call chauvinistic pigs for promoting their male buddies over qualified women.

Test & Review

1. How do you know you're dating a reasonably secure female? Watch how she interacts with women within her own circle. Is she genuine and supportive or does she always find fault, constantly berating and putting them down? Often women feel secure with women they know or they don't consider to be competition. Now place her around strangers of the female gender. Make sure some of them are knockouts. How does she react now? This is an immediate telltale sign.
2. Watch how she responds to your female coworkers. Take her to the next office gathering. There is always one femme fatale at every party. Get her reaction. If she takes it pretty much in stride, she's secure. If she's chomping at the bit, ridiculing and being negative about a "looker," she's dangerous.
3. I am a woman and love men. I love beautiful women, children and animals. Unusual, maybe. If an attractive woman enters a room, I turn right along with the men to admire her. Why not? We all have our own personal beauty and what God didn't give us we can buy from the best plastic surgeon. I love to watch other women watch attractive women. It's a dead giveaway. Just observe their reactions. The whole truth is right in their expression. Never fails.

11

Femme Fatale International

Now, members of this category can be any nationality in the world, except American. They are the best at what they do...snagging a man. They are the masters, the crème de la crème when it comes to the manipulation of the male, preferably American. Why? Several reasons, chump.

Number one, they all have accents. Men are suckers for accents. It makes them (the Femme Fatales) seem vulnerable and cute. This deception brings out the protectiveness in the American male—much like our Southern Belle or the cute little flat-faced virginal blonde all men want to protect.

Usually the international females possess a much higher mental capacity than their American counterparts. They are more mature and advanced in the art of seduction. More often than not, they speak several languages fluently, so if they can't entertain you they can certainly confuse you...and you just love it!

Let's take the South American señorita. She is probably one of the sharpest of the Latins. Perdone, the Cubanas run her a close second. Classy, aristocratic, gorgeous, sensuous, and yes, sexy. This Brazilian or Argentine bombshell can play havoc with your libido and pocketbook.

These South American señoras can really spend the bucks. Regardless of their class status they must have a maid, regular visits to the hairdresser, a weekly massage and the latest haute couture.

The Cubans learn at an early age to marry up. They are much like their American duplicates, the Jewish American Princesses (only they're CAPs instead of JAPs).

In spite of their Catholic backgrounds they marry several times, always upgrading their spouses. They, like the JAPs, have tremendous family support. This support system gives them a certain amount of security that the average American male doesn't have. This might explain why they feel they deserve the very best and get it.

The South American female is striking, even if she isn't a beauty. She knows how to dress, handle the help, entertain and keep hubby happy in the boudoir.

It's easy to see why and how an American male would fall for such a delectable dish. I have several Latin girlfriends and adore them. They are irresistible and if you are going to get involved with the Femme Fatale International, you'll never be bored with this group.

In fact, if they are treated with "kid gloves" they make great wives and excellent mothers. You'd better have lots of stamina because they like to sleep late, nap in the afternoon and party at night.

If you have to work for a living, skip the señoritas or find one who has been working for a living. She'll be a little easier to handle en la noche! Don't get me wrong. They aren't lazy, they just like "la dolce vita."

But keep in mind that divorcing one is a different story. She'll win every time. After all, there is always "child support." This includes the maid and/or nanny and, of course, it takes time and money (yours) to relocate and acquire the right environment that "su señora" has become accustomed to.

Plan to take it in the shorts with this one. Ditto for most Femme Fatales. Just talk to Sly Stallone about Brigitte Nielsen. This Danish strudel took him right to the bakery and turned the oven on high. First she bamboozled him with her six-foot bleached blonde frame and manufactured bust. However, what really capped the deal was her Nordic accent. Innocence personified.

Because ol' Sly had just been taken for one of the highest divorce settlements in history, he had Gitte sign a prenuptial agreement (very generous) giving her an allowance of $300,000 per year, plus any monies from her movies that Sly placed her in, and of course all gifts he bestowed on his international beloved.

Well, it seems she was one "hot piece of Danish" and after the Italian Stallion got wind of what was common, and I mean common knowledge, she received $3 million plus another mil or two for agreeing not to talk about their personal life. Not too bad for a novice and a foreigner at that.

Let's take this in reverse. Joan Collins met her Waterloo in the form of a Swede. One look and you wonder what Joanie saw in him. I'll bet his accent was adorable. Peter Holm ended up without a home but he made out like a bandit with a few shekels in his designer jeans. And Ms. Collins was a few pounds lighter in the pocketbook.

I knew two sisters from Canada who pulled the ultimate "Canadian Caper." You'd have thought they were the Royal Mounties after a victim, and darlings they were. Guess what? They caught two of them.

One happened on to an island known for its resort atmosphere, and lack of men I might add, and immediately captured the resident available millionaire.

After number one sis tied the knot, built a palatial beach house and bought a yacht, she started socializing with hubby. Of course, they were all of hubby's connections. She found out that the local merchant, also a millionaire and richer than her own catch, was about to be divorced from his wife.

Not a minute had passed when she was on the phone to her sister in Canada, informing her to get her "bloody ass" down there quickly.

She immediately threw a cocktail party to introduce "Sis II" to the local gentry and invited Mr. Available. Sister was introduced to the old codger with tons of money and pronto, they were married. Take note, Canadians aren't cold or slow!

There was a small fly in the ointment. He wasn't as generous as his brother-in-law. In fact, he was a stingy, tightfisted bastard.

Not to worry. Sister II is still trudging along and manipulating him to the hilt. Occasionally, she sports some new jewelry, gets the house (an old one) redecorated, and dons a new outfit. She is usually seen having cocktails at the local golf club while he is at the store counting his cash.

The sister act plays well to Americans. I once observed redheaded twins from England play another self-made millionaire to the living end. He married one and inherited the other. They were inseparable, and off they romped through the Caribbean on his captained yacht. This pair was lethal.

They ended up in Haiti using Voodoo, drugs and weird sex on the poor unsuspecting soul. One day he sobered up and wanted out, but his wife informed him it would cost him at least 12 big ones. He stayed.

Now this guy had been straight, normal, looking for a companion, and had made his money honestly, the hard way.

I ran into him at a private tennis club in Miami one day and he begged me to sail to the Bahamas on his yacht for the weekend. Of course, I declined, but I felt sorry for the guy. God knows he's probably sailing the Caribbean still, with the British Bombers keeping him in suspended animation so he won't defect and leave them penniless.

The best example of the Femme Fatale in action was a French woman I met in Mexico. She had married a Mexican several years younger than herself and bought a resort on an island in the Yucatan. Husband carried sod, brick, adobe, and helped her build this insulated haven where even movie stars stayed.

All was well until Señor eyed a younger señorita and decided to have an affair. Well Frenchie found out and decided to divorce her Mexicano and take the mucho dinero. Mind you, this is Mexico and you can't own property unless you have a Mexican partner who owns fifty percent or more, which her esposo did. And, of course, Mexico is a difficult country to acquire a divorce.

Viva la France! She got a lawyer in Mexico, divorced him and took all the money, property, condos, and left him with nada. She is still at the resort moaning and groaning about "leeving" without a man. "Ees impossible to leeve without a man, no?" No woman should be without one was her motto. When I last saw her she was actively hunting for another fool to help her improve the resort and do some expansion.

Since World War I, it has been fashionable for Europeans to marry Americans, just to get to America. It still is and you guys aren't any the wiser.

These Femme Fatale Internationals can really turn on the charm. They come by this naturally and are the masters of the sexual game. Sex is their tool, the hook for attainment of their real goal. And that is whatever you have, they want. Money, fame, prestige, citizenship, you name it.

They are hard to resist because they appear dependent and not a threat as American women do. Possibly in the twenties, thirties, and forties, American women possessed this same type of dependence, but now they are so busy being Superwoman and creating an independence aura, they find it difficult to play the game. However, there's one American breed left that can outmaneuver and manipulate the Femme Fatale International, and that is the Southern Belle.

Now you've already read about the Southern Belle. But she also warrants an award and mention in this chapter. La Belle, who was so correctly depicted in the many plays by Tennessee Williams, uses her accent to the hilt on any and every man.

I had a business acquaintance who called me up about a new sales executive. His description was she was a Texan with a cute accent. "Has she any sales experience?" I stupidly asked. He dismissed my question and continued. "She looks great, and has this Southern accent." I again asked, "Can she sell?" After many references to her cute Southern accent and numerous questions from me about her selling ability, finally I said, "Well, can she sell?" He retorted, "Hell, I don't know, but that accent sold me." As my male Italian friend always says, "There you have it."

I had a Southern Belle acquaintance inform me that an accent and sexual experience could take you a long way in a relationship with a man. I asked her what happened after the sexual circus became boring. Well, she innocently replied, "Y'all still have the accent." Touché.

Test & Review

1. If she speaks with an accent, you have a Femme. Lucky you, now the fun begins. Do you really like this foreign piece of fluff? If so, cest la vie.

2. You have a Femme Fatale that has just baited you and you want out. These Fatales are brutal and difficult to eradicate from one's life. However, as I informed you, they all want something; money or citizenship or both. Play the poor soul. You lost all your money and she will have to work to help out with the monthly expenses. If she doesn't balk and is a citizen, you might not have a Femme Fatale. You're in the clear and probably have a decent working relationship. If she isn't a citizen but goes to work, tell her you can't marry her until she becomes a citizen. Then if she goes to school and to work, brother you've got a gem, keep her at all costs.

3. Now if you really want out and she won't cooperate, threaten to turn her over to the authorities. If she doesn't buy this one, steal her "green card" and/or passport. If she still won't budge, call them. Hey pal, it's a hell of a lot cheaper than alimony.

A Bitch Is a Bitch Is a Bitch

Bitches aren't discerning. They will spew their venom on both men and women (women being their favorite victims when a man is at the center of their desires).

Usually Bitches show their hand and come out of hiding when a man is involved if there is another woman in the picture. They are masters at putting down another female if she poses a threat to her in any way.

Bitches have no conscience, ethics, morals, principles or honor. They throw caution to the wind in order to attain their goals. They will cut their own mother's throat if she stands in the way. They are the most dangerous of all categories.

Personally, I've been subjected to their antics and knew their game. However, I let them play it to the hilt, just to see how far they would go. They were none the wiser, which proves they sometimes underestimate their victims.

Bitches, like all con artists and game players, think they are clever and that their prey is stupid. Usually a woman can figure out another woman's program. A man isn't as quick on the uptake.

What do all Bitches have in common? Insecurity. That is the reason they are who they are. An extremely well adjusted secure person doesn't have to resort to bitchiness.

Bitches come in all sizes, shapes, forms and nationalities. They are easy to detect if you are aware (and a woman). Men usually don't realize they have a Bitch in tow until it's too late.

Study these case histories and maybe you'll be wiser when it comes to dealing with "La Bitch."

As I informed you earlier, women can really turn on the "bitch routine" when a man is in the picture. I'll never forget the woman who, after I fixed her up on a date with a male friend of mine, proceeded to put me down in front of him. It was probably meant to make herself appear smarter and more attractive. It didn't work and quickly backfired on her (first of all, I never offered to introduce her to another person). We met at an art gallery opening, both my male friend and a date. She started out making a cutting remark about a cape I had worn and continued the entire evening trying to impress her date by knocking me.

These types of tactics never work in the long run, but bitches think they do. She not only lost a friend, the man wasn't interested in her either.

Bitches always have a hidden agenda. Honesty is not in their vocabulary. And if you think they are wicked toward their sisters, you ought to see what they can do to a man who has excited their wrath.

The story goes something like this (and it actually happened to one poor unsuspecting guy I know): The first time he breaks up with her, she takes the rent, pockets it, flies the coop and moves in with his best friend.

The scenario continues. He forgives her, they re-establish their commitment. Well, *he* does anyway. She starts staying out late and causes a general disturbance in the relationship before taking the rent and moving out again.

Bitches are the perfect counterpart for the male species we women call Bastards. In both categories honesty isn't one of their virtues.

Frankly after researching numerous Bitches and Bastards, I think they are mentally deranged. I mean that. Their underhanded tactics, horrendous insecurities, and conniving and manipulative ways are all reasons to stay far away from this species.

I have met many in my travels. They are the prima donnas, the egomaniacs who constantly cause a disturbance just for the sake of attention. Nothing is ever right. A real joy to deal with. Of course I am being facetious. I've had several working for me and they are exhausting.

When they use these tactics on men, they wear him down so they get their way. When they are dealing with another woman and she's onto their dirty tricks, they just get fired. Who needs it? Life is too short and too tough, at best, without these Negative Nellies creating havoc.

Insecurity is usually at the bottom of a Bitch's problem. However, there are some people who attract and even like disruption. Dump them or you'll be the loser.

I once knew a Southern Belle Bitch, an expert at nagging. She married a friend of mine who was a fun loving guy and pretty positive. When she got through with him, he didn't associate with any of his male friends. She didn't like them. And, of course, he couldn't see any of his female friends. She hated them too. His law practice was moved into their home so she could keep an eye on him day and night. Finally he became a recluse, only going out with her just to keep peace.

She monitored his every move, including all the finances. And, brother, could she spend the money. As he got older he was convinced, or shall we say she convinced him, she would take care of him in his old age. Actually, she'd put arsenic in his martini before he'd have a chance to get old.

Bitches just like to bitch. It's a habit they acquired when they discovered it worked on men (who are often brought up to feel guilty). Bitches perpetuate this inbred guilt, and he thinks he's right at home. I never blame the Bitches. I find it's the object of the bitching that needs the shrink! It's the same with women who tolerate Bastards.

Bitches use all kinds of tactics to get their way. Temper tantrums, sulking, sexual retraction, fear, even threatening to turn you into the IRS for cheating on last year's income tax.

That same Southern Belle Bitch once found a cashier's check for $20,000 that her attorney husband had hidden. It really belonged in a trust account. She refused to give it to him until he gave her $1,000 cash on the barrel head for clothes. He acquiesced.

When a female starts with the guilt and head trips, she's not far from playing stronger games like blowing your head off if she doesn't get her way. Get lost immediately, if not sooner, because your life is bordering on Hell.

Women will play their bitchy games on other women without batting their false eyelashes—especially when a male or a job is involved.

Put Bertha Bitch in any position where she has a smidgen of power or control and kiss your sweet ass bye-bye.

Men have a saying about bitches: "All she needs is a good lay." Wrong, Charlie Brown. If this were true, you'd have to stay in bed 24 hours a day just to keep their mouths shut.

I warned you that Bitches are deceptive. You might be living with the all-time great Bitch, yet your friends think she's Ms. Congeniality. Sure, you bowl with the boys. But they don't know she hid your shoes and ball and it took you a week to locate them because she didn't want you bowling with those slobs.

You bring your friends home for a game of poker and Ms. Nice serves little snacks and retires to the bedroom to watch TV. "Hell," you hear from your friends, "I wish my wife would let me bring the guys home." What they don't know is after they've gone, she screams that she won't tolerate those low lifes littering her house, and then she won't sleep with you for a month.

Now here is the dichotomy. Men will migrate toward insecure women because they think there will be no competition. They are under the mistaken theory that intelligent, secure women are competitive.

This is so wrong if you would think it through. If a woman is secure she doesn't have to compete with you or anyone else. Also, she is happy with her lot in life and can afford to assist you on your climb up the success ladder. Secure women won't lower their self-image to put down another female. They don't have to.

This is why you jokers usually get in trouble with relationships because you insist on perpetuating the wrong ones. Wake up and smell the java, Bub. I'm not talking about secure women. Beware the pseudo-liberated ones who come on macho to the hilt. Forget this group. They are the Bitches.

Test & Review

1. If you are already married to a Bitch, you certainly have our sympathies. But try this one. Don't follow my suggestion if you are not going to follow through, because you are doomed then. Plan a week cruise. Get all the brochures and leave them around the house. When she asks what you are planning, simply say a trip...alone. Why? Because you need a rest from all the nagging. Now, if she can be a sweetie for one month, you'll consider taking her with you. Of course, she could really turn the tables on you and make your cruise a living hell. However, you can always retaliate by throwing her overboard.

2. Every time she bitches about something, continue doing it, even if it incenses her. Inform her the minute she stops bitching you'll consider rectifying the problem. Then if it's reasonable, do it. It's like training Pavlov's dogs. Ring the bell and when they start to salivate, feed them. You can train Bitches to be more human, but it really takes time, effort and balls. Do you have the energy to do all that when you could turn her in for a better bet? One consolation—you won't be bored.

3. If you aren't yet married to a Bitch...don't. If you are seriously dating one, don't continue unless you are a masochist.

4. If you're madly in love with a Bitch and can't leave her, lots of luck!

13

Widow's Roost

As a woman approaches thirty, her chances of marriage become less than half of what they were at twenty, according to recent studies. Women between forty and infinity really have it rough. This wasn't always the case, but enter another problem. Men who are forty won't be caught dead dating a woman their age. The twenty-year-old is in demand these days, which leaves many women out in the cold. This really creates competition at its worst or best.

Never before in the history of our civilization has the female been forced to use her bag of tricks more, and then some, to snag her trophy—a man. There are few eligible bachelors left and the only ones who are, have no interest in women of a certain age. The fight is on and brother, it's the show of shows. It beats late night TV.

Plastic surgery has never been more in demand. Women are flocking to aerobic classes and the fitness craze has even bitten the senior citizens. Grow old gracefully. Are you kidding? As the cosmetic commercial states, "I don't want to grow old gracefully, I intend to fight it every step of the way." Girls start fighting the aging process in their twenties. By the time they hit forty, they're donning pink boxing gloves and fighting it tooth and manicured nail.

Society is in a hell of a predicament. The problem of men dying ten years sooner than women has created a world of Amazons. Most of the money in the world is controlled by women. But who do they have as companions to enjoy all this wealth? Old wealthy grande dames have resorted to living with and keeping homosexuals so they at least have an escort to the next ball.

We have a large segment of women between thirty-five and seventy-five living without men, unless, of course, they resort to the younger male who might, and usually does, have designs on her money.

Many of my friends and female business acquaintances are dating men several years their junior. These women are attractive, vibrant, intelligent (supposedly), and yet they are bedded down with beach boys, surfers, bartenders and loafers. Nothing against any of these occupations; it's just a tremendous dichotomy because these women will not be seen with their sexual partners in public.

I once invited a girlfriend of mine to a cocktail party and asked her to bring Bennie, her sexy surfer. She screamed, "Why, I couldn't possibly bring Bennie, he's totally socially unacceptable." Now Bennie was OK in the sack or all right to wash the car, change the tires, and share a pizza with. But take him out? Are you joking!

Another reasonably intelligent college educated friend of mine fell madly in love with a heel. He was great in bed and terrific when it came to stealing her jewelry, money and even her car. He was several years younger than Dumb Dora and even left her making the rest of the payments on the car he stole. They finally caught up with him and found out about his chosen occupation—taking women. Older ones.

Now both of these women are in their thirties. What is the problem, folks? They both should be able to find a suitable male within their age range who is on the level.

Take the older, well-silvered (with money that is) widow or divorcee. She is great prey. Just watch the pilot fish swim circles around this type. Palm Beach is loaded with this type of shark. They used to call these men gigolos. Now there is a nouveau type of escort...the "gay blade." The gay populace, with tuxedo in hand, has infiltrated the socially prominent.

They can play the game better than the gigolo and end up with more loot because for some reason these wealthy women don't suspect they're gay. The women know they don't want their body. They are oftentimes creative, fun, good dancers and socially acceptable. I know of one gay man in Palm Beach who makes it a full-time job escorting and traveling with older, wealthy women.

When they go to the "big charity ball in the sky" he inherits mucho dinero from these desperate dames. But the price tag is high for this type of inheritance. He waits on them hand and foot and is constantly at their beck and call.

The shortage of eligible men in Palm Beach is at epidemic proportions. Many women have been left with tons of money and are still ambulatory and active. They will kill for a male.

The reason: There are more than 60 balls a year to attend and numerous social functions where an escort is needed.

If he can stand upright for any length of time and has a tuxedo, he's acceptable. Many married women watch their spouses like hawks. It seems in this town anyone is fair game.

Women aren't bashful about calling a man, married or not, to escort them to a charity function or a cocktail party.

There was the ménage à trois that took one old gal for more than $500,000. It involved a gay person who befriended an old wealthy widow. She was heavy into the bottle at the time of their meeting. He played at being her confidant and friend, thus helping himself to funds, a place to live and a Rolls to drive.

After several years of this charade, he decided he wanted to become a "total woman" and talked his companion into putting up the funds for the operation.

After "operation petticoat" was successfully completed, the old crone's new companion was a woman. Well, the doctor was an artist, to say the least, because this former male was a stunning female—a six foot tall, sultry brunette with a new vagina and fabulous bust.

Now the "Femme Fatale" could wear all of her victim's furs, jewels and designer clothes. She took over the financial end of the widow's existence, pilfering funds daily from her unsuspecting benefactor.

She moved them into a "swell house" after selling the crone's old one. "New woman" had a real estate license and placed the new house in both of their names.

Ms. Gay Liberation decided to date…men. And bye-the-bye she married one. So they both lived with "money bags" and were siphoning money from her trust fund by the thousands. They would forge her name while keeping her drunk and doped up with pills.

One day they forgot to keep her locked in her bedroom and she escaped. Gay libber and her lover shot out of town like two rockets with the money.

At last hearing, relatives were suing the banks and trying to find the Fairy Princess and her Prince. But they had left no trace after they abdicated their thrones.

Sad? It happens all the time. The basic human is a lonely soul and will do most anything for companionship.

Many is the time some old goat has been taken by a pretty young thing. Does he care? Hell no. He thinks it was worth it. After all, didn't he have a romp or two with someone half his age?

I've asked many twenty-year-olds if they had ever dated an old goat. Some replied "yes," for a short time and for money only. Others replied "Are you kidding?"

Men constantly need their egos boosted, as women do.

However, men are in a better position to bolster theirs by pursuing younger conquests. Women look foolish when they date younger men. It only magnifies their age.

Now a fifty-year-old woman can be a knockout (Joan Collins and Elizabeth Taylor have already hit sixty). But she is still fifty and a man her age is more interested in a woman half his age.

The merry widow isn't so merry anymore. Not too many years ago this type was a much sought after commodity.

Now, the merry widow better be damn young if she wants to dance, because if she's mid-forties, she'll be sitting on the widow's roost twiddling her thumbs.

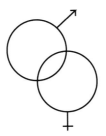

14

Menopause, Yours or Hers

God how you've changed....I don't know you at all anymore. Gold chains around your neck, shirt unbuttoned exposing sparse hair. You never dressed that way before.

I understand from your friends you don't date women over thirty; they're much too old. You never used to be that bold.

You seem to be remote lately, dissatisfied and hard to reach. I heard you traded the wagon for a Porsche and got a place on the beach.

What happened to the guy I used to know? Responsible, secure and almost as pure as the driven snow; on your way toward success in the corporate climb, never relaxing, working all the time.

You neglected your wife, the children and even yourself, never giving a damn about your health. Now you pop vitamins and jog every day. You work very little and just play, play, play.

There was a time we both wanted the same things and if we had talked, our lives could have been rearranged.

But you are a stranger to me now....God you've changed!

If you're single and experiencing "male menopause," it's not as devastating as it is to your married buddy. Married menopausers have many problems, especially if they are actively coming out of the closet.

They have two options: Stay married and drive the old lady nuts trying to figure out what the problem is, or dump the little woman, kids and suburbia. Either way, it's tremendously trying on one's emotional system. That little Sexatary with the big bazooms and no brains looks mighty good to you when your pseudo-secure world is crashing around your newly permed head.

You can't win, buster. If you stay married, and many 'pausers do, you might decide to enter into adulterous clandestine affairs. With this decision you run the risk of wifey knowing and initiating a divorce, then taking you to the cleaners. You're miserable and so is the family.

If you decide you want out and start divorce proceedings, you have the guilts and give her more than her share. No one told you life was a day at the beach.

It doesn't make any difference how the cookie crumbles, there is always another little cookie out there who knows just how to bake your bread.

Many young nubile things love "menos." I've asked plenty of them why they dated older men. One answer, Charlie—MONEY!

If these out-to-lunch loonies dated men closer to their own age, chances are they'd be picking up their own bar checks. Loony they might be, stupid they aren't.

It never occurs to Barbie and her sisters they should work for a living when Charlie the well-heeled tuna picks up the tab. They were weaned on the Miss Universe Pageant and *Dallas* and *Dynasty*. Where's the dough, Joe?

Fort Lauderdale is a Mecca for Melvin Menopause and his Madonna look-alike. Take a Saturday stroll around Pier 66 where all the yachts are docked. You won't find many gray-haired beauties in their skirted Jantzens gracing the bows of those floating flop houses.

The strong bikini-clad figure on the bridge isn't Charlie's daughter down for spring break. Wanting the prettier things in life isn't bad. But you guys are cruisin' for a bruisin' if you don't know the rules of this game.

Now if you stay married and you're both going through menopause, God help you. Between her "hot flashes" and your "hot affairs," things should be cooking. In fact, they should be burning up.

Maybe you're one of those overly secure men who bypasses the big M and truly loves his wife. Brother, when she approaches her middle-age crisis, watch it. She might use it to the hilt. If so, any sane woman will look good to you...even your mother-in-law.

I once knew a gal who married a very wealthy older man. Since he had been married many times and was in his late seventies, he thought all this menopause nonsense was past. Wrong, Charlie Brown. She was in her prime and married him solely for his money. Enter her menopause.

One particular year she had overspent her monthly, yearly and future annual allowance. She convinced him she didn't get "hot flashes" or nausea if she were cruising—of course on a bigger ship, not a tiny one.

She had a doctor in on her schemes because the doctor bills were in excess of $7,000 for her menopausal malady. So hubby was convinced that cruising was cheaper than the medical payments.

Do you really think I could have made this up? Every time she had a menopausal attack, she ran to her travel agent and planned a month's cruise. She'd been to more than forty countries before he wised up. It wasn't menopause. She just couldn't stand to be in the house, let alone the same country with the old codger. I loved her action, it was first class all the way.

Her menopause left rather quickly and somewhat suspiciously when he filed for divorce. I am sure she has a new idiot and I'll bet her "hot flashes" are hotter than ever. I love it! Men will buy anything but the truth.

Another one of my most brilliant friends acquired a rather early menopause. She even fooled her physician as he put her through extensive expensive tests, finding nothing. She would tell her husband that terrible ol' curse was making her depressed—hormone drop, you know. However, when she shopped her depression would leave and she became happy and secure, she gave the impression of being a blushing bride. Well, hubby was so elated that she was again her sweet self that he gladly paid the MasterCard, American Express and Visa. He even helped her store many unopened packages. The last time I talked to them, he was building a special storage room to house the backlash of her many shopping sprees. She's happy, he's happy, so what the hell.

See, it never stops. Women fly out of the womb, instinctively knowing that from the cradle to the grave they've got you. If it isn't their period, a backache, headache, assache, the children, the in-laws…it's menopause!

There are ways to handle the mid-life crisis and profit from the experience. First, realize that when you reach a certain plateau in life, there might be some re-evaluation needed.

As we take steps toward maturity our desires and goals change. This doesn't mean you have to take drastic measures like acquiring a nineteen-year-old girlfriend, divorcing the wife and trading in the little castle for a bachelor pad.

The mid-life crisis is so difficult for men and women because they think it's the other guy's fault. You must delve into your own faults, attitudes, actions and reactions. You are a product of your thoughts. It's your attitude and thinking toward the problem that makes the difference in success and failure.

Improving your health and appearance and buying a Porsche is all positive, if you happen to like Porsches. However, if it's to round out the image of a "kool kat" when you're feeling insecure within, forget it. You're icing the cake when the batter is bad. Won't work. You just change stages and the actresses in the play. The playwright's the same. So is the script.

Instead of looking to the other person as your mirror image, look within.

However, if you and your wife never got along and the marriage has progressed to the point of no return, get the hell out. Life is short and everyone, including her, deserves fulfillment instead of frustration.

A word of advice: Take this time to improve yourself mentally, physically and emotionally. Many men make the mistake or replacing the old with the new immediately. This is a gross error in judgment because at this time you're a sitting duck. And we know the hunters. They are up before dawn, gun cocked and ready to snag that much coveted mallard—you.

At this point in your life, you aren't a match for Doris the duck hunter extraordinaire. She's been planning her attack and you've just escaped from the cage of another huntress. You better lie low, pal, until you have your feathers unruffled.

Take this time to build a better self-image. But create it through your own achievements and self-improvement regimens. Then you'll be better equipped to evaluate the next encounter.

Date women you like, admire and respect. If you have been working on your improvement program, she will return the admiration. Don't ever, and I mean ever, date a woman because she makes you look good. What does that say about you? Granted, packaging is important. I am not saying don't pursue a beautiful woman or girl, whatever your preference. Couples should compliment each other in every category.

But stay away from the obvious daddy-daughter syndrome. This will make you look weak. You see, you always thought that dating a much younger woman gave you a macho image with your peers. Quite the contrary. They wonder what she sees in you (and, of course, they know), and another more suitable conquest won't get near you because she already knows you've got a problem.

Test & Review

Are you and she menopausal?

1. Do you start dressing up when your daughter, who is a cheer-leader, brings her friends over to practice in the garage, then move the car onto the driveway, raise the hood and start tinkering? Instead of tinkering you sneak glances at their high kick numbers and salivate over their young bouncing boobs. Know you are becoming a D.O.M. (Dirty Old Man) and taking the first step toward M.M. (male menopause).
2. Have you started wearing gold chains around your neck and they aren't your St. Christopher's medals? This is a dead giveaway. You're in trouble.
3. You just purchased a *Miami Vice* flowered shirt and leave it unbuttoned to mid-chest. Ugh! Why not wear a flashing neon sign: "I am a 'pauser!'"
4. You have this tremendous yearning for a Porsche, Corvette or Trans Am when you've got six kids, two dogs, three cats and a parrot—oh, and a budget that's over-extended. The Big M is tugging at your heart strings.
5. She gains weight in places you didn't even know she had. Her metabolism is changing and she's sitting on her ass longer than she used to. Start exercising together and ask her to place you both on a low-fat diet. Make it a team effort.
6. She is constantly hot, but not in bed. Take her temperature and whether or not it's normal, convince her it's 98.6. She'll believe you. Women are often easy to placate if you take the time. Also, install a fan right over the bed....she'll have to spend more time there to keep cool.

15

Sugar Mama

Sugar Mamas have been in existence for some time, that is how gigolos flourished. Recently, Elizabeth Taylor became a "Mom's Moneybags" to Larry Fortensky, and gave this type of woman a new dimension. If Liz can do it publicly and society accepts the fact she is paying to play, other Sugar Moms will come out of the closet.

These women are pathetic because of their blatant lack of self-esteem. For one reason or another they feel unworthy of acquiring love without paying a financial price. They are the opposites of the Gigolettes (see next chapter). Suffering from extreme low self-worth, they attract and keep the object of their affection by one commodity—money.

The Sugar Mommy forms a symmetry with a man whose main goal is to be financially kept. She possesses no confidence in herself as a worthy person and resorts to using money as a tool. Secondly, she is aware that buying someone also gives her the power in the relationship. So she gladly doles out the money and goods in return for a person she can manipulate.

Unfortunately, as the arrangement continues, these monetary mistresses get jealous, possessive and begin to want the real thing—love. In the beginning they delude themselves into thinking this man really likes or loves them. However, as the money keeps dwindling, they begin to face reality.

A vicious circle begins with their "Boy Toy" becoming perplexed because he knew the game and the rules and assumed she did.

Of course, both are playing a game. He, like the Gigolette, used flattery and false love to get into her knickers and checkbook, and she was more than eager to have him in her pants and wallet.

Many parsimonious pursuers resent their moneyed mommies because any man, regardless how weak, hates to depend financially on a woman. It is psychological ego castration. They know they are bought and paid for and really have no independence or control other than sexual. This is their only tool. And most use it to the hilt.

The other partner in this convivial coupling is also resentful because she knows in her heart, if he weren't paying, he wouldn't be playing...with her.

It is a partnership based on fear and mutual distrust. After all, he could meet a woman more attractive and wealthier. She could find a smarter, sharper, more attractive man. Insecurity abounds in this type of mating.

There are exceptions and professional male escorts do have their purpose, especially in a society where women far outnumber men.

Older women who are along but still active don't want to take the time combing the singles bars finding a suitable companion. So they hire one for dinner or dancing. Many men even agreed that this was acceptable.

However, the relationship with Sugar Mommies is a masquerade with both parties professing undying love for each other. And if love isn't a prerequisite, then faithful sex and attention are.

They are living a lie, but since both are guilty many of these relationships stand the test of time. Many end in marriage. Of course they usually see a divorce lawyer after several years. Just enough time for "Baby Boy" to collect alimony.

Why are these women so generous with their money? One main reason, they didn't make it the old-fashioned way; they divorced or were widowed by a monied man. He worked for it, now she can spend it on another man. You can bet your bottom dollar there are no Sugar Mamas who had to work hard for that buck.

Test & Review

1. When the bill for dinner is placed in front of you and she constantly beats you to it, you have a Sugar Mama.
2. You decide to set up housekeeping with her paying most of the bills. You have a dyed-in-the-wool Mommy.
3. She buys you a car, but it's in her name. You can keep the clothes, wallet and watch, but large items are in one name only—hers. That way you can never run away unless you want to hitchhike.
4. Mamas become possessive, and the way they keep you on the straight and narrow is to pay for you. That way if you have one shred of decency, and I doubt if you do or you'd pay your own way, you feel guilty.
5. Sugar Mamas are prey for gigolos, so if you're being kept you now know what you are!

16

The Gigolette

A Gigolette is the female counterpart to the male gigolo. They play for pay, using every female stratagem and sexual skill to gain the goods. Years ago they called them prostitutes, call girls or mistresses, but now an eighteen-year-old who has been programmed by print and the electronic media believes sexual favors are to be sold.

One young man, a landscaper, frequented single's bars and when the object of his advances asked what he did for a living, he was ignored. Possessing an ingenious mind and after many put-downs because of his occupation, he had cards printed to advertise he was an attorney. Never again did he experience a put-down. In fact, he made out like a bandit.

Gigolettes will date a man whether he is eighteen or eighty; their one prerequisite is financial stability. Gigolettes, like the gigolo, aren't going to waste precious time if they aren't paid for their performance.

Calculating, cold and self-centered, these capitalist cuties can turn on the charm, which is a contrived and much perfected act, when the money is there.

Totally devoid of ethics, principles, morals or self decency, they use flattery and sex just like the gigolo to extract financial payment in return for this ego boosting of the weak male.

In actuality, one can't feel sorry for the Sugar Mama or Sugar Daddy, because they are getting what they paid for. The paymates couldn't survive without a playmate to bolster their own deflated self-esteem. Each fills the other's need.

One wampum woman in her thirties was introduced to a retired Army general and of course he was immediately smitten. However she, being a professional cabbage collector, informed him before she could commit to a serious relationship he must buy her a car and deposit some money in her bank account. The stupid fool did both, and then she dated him for a short while only to inform him they weren't compatible. HELLO!

He is several thousand dollars poorer, she is richer, and everyone is happy. She, by her own admission, will not waste time, effort or energy on any old goat who refuses to pay for her presence.

For fun and games she dates men her own age but when it comes to a serious endeavor, she's cruising for monied men. How does she ferret them out? While on the golf course. She took up the game when she found retired men with money, divorced, maybe widowed, played. This Gigolette can be found pointing her nine iron at her next victim at least three times a week.

Gigolettes, like gigolos, usually come from poor families, are uneducated, lack the social graces and class, but are proficient in sex and possess an overabundance of street smarts.

They are somewhat like homing pigeons possessing an innate knowledge of who and how to maneuver into a "using" relationship. There is a sixth sense that enables them to quickly discern who will pay for their talents.

According to Jung, and many of his peers, there are three types of people on this planet. Givers, takers and a combination (supposedly the psychologically sound) of both. A giver needs a taker and vice versa. That is why feeling sorry for a victim is useless. The recipient of abusive behavior realizes, consciously or subconsciously, he is being taken and uses no precaution to alleviate this action.

Takers, the gigolos and 'ettes, are bought and re-purchased repeatedly. This action reinstates their worth to themselves. That is why these takers of society never become emotionally involved. How could they? Their self involvement is enough to quench their insatiable appetite.

Their bag of tricks include charm, flattery, intimidation, sympathy (for them) and demands. They are assertive, never embarrassed to ask for what they want.

Gigolettes, like their male counterparts, always have a back-up. If money, goods, love and attention aren't coming to them forthwith, they can shift to another pawn without missing a beat.

In other words, they protect their best, similar to playing the numbers of a crap table. Always keeping many balls in the air, they can juggle several suitors at the same time. It is easy for them as they are inner-directed and never love anyone more than themselves. Callous, shallow and insensitive best describes these users of society.

One attractive Gigolette could collect more money from men in one night than some people could earn in a week. Her ploy? Sympathy.

She always used the hard luck story. True, she did have a seven-year-old daughter at the time and was divorced. However, this gal couldn't spell the word work, let alone do any. But she used the same tale night after night and could collect several hundred every evening from some unsuspecting sucker.

When she entered a lounge, usually a first-class club, she'd size up the men at the bar and sidle up to her victim. The story would be about how difficult it was to make ends meet, a single woman with a young daughter to raise, and how the child was being expelled from her private school because "Mommy" didn't have the funds to pay the tuition. Well, you calculate a couple of hundred times seven and you'll know what she brought in. Please, could I make this up?

This was many years ago and I am sure she's using the same bait. The old axiom, don't fix it if it isn't broken. Pride isn't one of their virtues. Balls is. Even the old Biblical saying holds true for these types of takers, "Ask and it shall be given to you."

Humility isn't in their vocabulary. Self-importance and arrogance are. All possess an inflated opinion of their attributes, thus believing they deserve money—yours.

Test & Review

1. The first words out of a Gigolette's mouth will be, "What do you do for a living?" Her first thoughts will be to calculate how much money that profession is worth.
2. A Gigolette knows her time is worth something, so she will sell it to you. In other words, buster, you'll pay through the nose.
3. If you live in better digs than she, plan on having a long-term roommate. The reverse might be true, but her mortgage is high, and guess who will pay—you.
4. You might find yourself in love with a Gigolette. If so, then pay the ante and shut up. If lust is the only thing you have in common, you're still going to pay and shut up.

CHAPTER

17

Bimbos and Bimbettes

This will be the shortest chapter in the book. No doubt you can guess why.

"Bimbo" is generally used to describe a brainless female. Just the word can conjure up a mental picture of a big-busted blonde who thinks *The Exorcist* is a movie about Jane Fonda.

There are Bimbos and Bimbettes. There is a difference, you know. A Bimbo can be anywhere from twenty-five to eighty. A Bimbette is eighteen to twenty-five. In other words, a Bimbo is an older version of a Bimbette; or a Bimbette can be looked at as a baby Bimbo.

Now these shallow gals might be mentally deficient when it comes to world affairs, historical facts or naming the current President of the United States, but they aren't stupid when it comes to gathering the goods.

Many men who date Bimbos defend them by saying, "I don't want to deal with another intellect or compete with a female executive or her career.

"When I socialize, I want to relax with someone who has a respectable appearance—as long as she isn't stumped for an answer when someone asks her name. I don't want to exhaust myself competing with another woman away from the office."

The "B" girls I've observed in action weren't doing so badly in the department of gathering baubles and designer clothes, having their rent paid and acquiring other perks. In fact, they fare better than their mentally astute sisters.

One Bimbette had three men on the string, all at the same time and all paying the bills. Intellectual she wasn't...smart she was.

What is more surprising is that all three men knew about each other. She collected money, clothes, furniture, trips, dinners, lunches and God knows what, and they thought she was the cutest thing since sliced bread. Bimbettes are easy for men to handle. Pay the ante and she'll keep her mouth shut for awhile.

Bimbos are easily impressed with the male prowess, more so than an intelligent career woman who really knows the score. A woman who has fought her way up the same ladder as the executive male has received the same treatment or worse.

Bimbos and Bimbettes play on looks to carry them to the bedroom, bank or altar, whatever their goal. They think by playing cute, sexy, coy and dumb, some male will put their "asses" upon that silk cushion and keep it there.

Bimbettes are sexually provocative and non-competitive. These two attributes account for their appeal to the male species. Bimbettes, usually devoid of ethics, morals and principles, most generally have several men doing their bidding all at the same time.

They are master manipulators because men make the mistake thinking they are not smart enough to create that type of unscrupulous behavior. Wrong, buster. They can and do keep three balls in the air at the same time. No pun intended.

Bimbos work overtime perfecting their "dumb act." It has to be contrived because, believe me, no one on God's green earth can be that stupid.

Bimbos/Bimbettes will win hands down against the sophisticated, mature lady. They come on as uncomplicated, cute, helpless innocent, vulnerable and approachable. What man wouldn't fall for this? Oh, and one more thing; they just love and adore their men.

Their main and only goal is to get, keep and use men for their financial security. They have no career pursuits. This is what makes them intriguing. They bring out that "protective urge" that most men need to fulfill so they in turn feel needed.

Bimbettes and Bimbos have been weaned on *Cosmo* from the time they were sixteen and learn at an early age "what turns men on." Bimbettes have replaced the "mistress" position of the thirties, forties and fifties. The only difference is mistresses had brains, sophistication and often breeding. Today those attributes are unnecessary. Stupidity coupled with a healthy attitude toward sex gives you a Bimbette in residence.

Test & Review

1. If the woman you are dating giggles a lot and hesitates when you ask her a simple question (like, "How are you today?"), you have a dyed-in-the-wool Bimbo/Bimbette on your hands.

2. Bimbettes aren't stupid when it comes to their game. However, they will buy any line a man wants to hand out...as long as he pays for her to listen to it. So the next time you are doing your best to impress a female and it's costing you $200 for dinner but she's hanging on to every word, you possibly have a Bimbette on the string. Take her to McDonald's and see how enraptured she is with you.

3. Bimbettes are in awe of labels and trends. They are totally unoriginal. Don't take her shopping at K-Mart, she'll dump your ass like a hot potato.

4. If it takes you more than five minutes to know whether you have a Bimbette or not, brother, you're in real trouble. Stop reading and place the noose around your own neck.

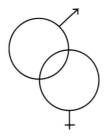

Two Cardboard Boxes, One Pair of Holey Pants and $1.98

Here's some advice for those men who've found themselves out in the cold with only the above possessions. But it will also be helpful to those of you who suddenly realize you're all alone and need a push to get you jump-started. What are you going to do? Develop a bitter, negative attitude, barricading yourself in a depressing apartment so that you can feel sorry for yourself?

Well, if you do, you're the only one who will sympathize with you. No one likes losers—especially a freshly divorced one who keeps carrying the past around.

Hey, we have all been down, dumped, canned, conned, abused and misused. But we don't have to advertise it.

When the going gets tough, the tough get going. You must immediately forgive yourself and your ex-wife regardless of the circumstances that caused the divorce. Possibly you married a Tarantula when you needed a Southern Belle. This is for you to psychoanalyze. And brother, you had better do some intense soul searching so the mistake isn't repeated.

Regardless of the reasons, you must re-enter the single life as a total man—not some half-assed gooney bird that craps on every woman he encounters.

Experts claim men take divorce more personally than women and find it more difficult to rearrange their lifestyle. Hell, if you can slay dragons in the business world, why not the same in the romantic area? Take a positive approach toward being single and plan to make it an exciting adventure.

First, you must take inventory of yourself. What hobbies would you like to pursue? Is your education in need of improving? How are your living quarters?

Plan a self-improvement program, including your environment. If your work and home surroundings are pleasant, you'll want to spend time there.

Too many men make this mistake and they resent their new mate, taking out every past problem on her. This is called transference and it means death to any relationship.

If you have worked out all the kinks and can stand yourself, this means spending time alone, then maybe you are ready for an emotional involvement.

How do you get in the swing of dating again? First you have to be where single girls are and then plan to make the first move. You will have to be assertive. Women love aggressive men. Don't buy all that bull about women liking the role of initiator. Many aren't naturally aggressive and really shouldn't be. This trait is usually a turn-off to most men.

All women I have talked to from eighteen to eighty agree they want the man to make the first move. You just have to be aware and ready to make the first approach. You cannot afford to be shy when meeting women. Opportunity knocks but once. Women can be found at the grocery store, restaurants, bars, airports, bookstores, the office, jogging, on planes, tennis courts, golf courses, the beach...anywhere.

Many men are afraid of rejection, so they won't make a move. Well, you can't expect the woman to if you're after a "class act."

Remember, you might get seven rejections from your advances and the eighth attempt might be a winner.

What do you care how many or how long it takes? Your goal is to meet the right lady.

Don't be blocked. Have an open mind when you are researching the field. Many men make the mistake of labeling a woman if she makes a wrong remark.

It takes time to know someone, so plan on allowing enough time for her true personality to emerge.

Plan on entertaining. Women are sucker bait when men invite them over for dinner by candlelight.

Enlarge your circle of friends. This is a great entree for introduction to a potential mate. Plan outings to the theater, museum, art gallery, picnics, sporting events.

Don't be a recluse. Learn several activities where you'll come in contact with women. Travel, even if it has to be short four-day jaunts. Travel alone at times. It's a great way to meet women also traveling alone.

If you are at a bar, hotel lobby bars are classier than singles' bars. But regardless of where you are, send a drink over to a possible new date mate. Women are flattered, especially in this day and age when men have become less than inventive and romantic.

I have observed a bar with attractive men conversing and several tables of attractive women just waiting for those men to make the first move. They don't. This always puzzles me. Times have changed and the dating game has become boring. Maybe this is society in general. If it isn't handed to you, why work for it?

I notice that men will start a conversation with a lady at the bar and talk for hours and never offer to buy her a drink. Women notice this and you are a cheap son-of-a-bitch. And you are, if you don't even offer.

Men need a brush-up course in pursuing women. They are out of practice. Women want romance. Why do you think those romance novels are best sellers? Take a lesson and you can have her eating out of your hand.

This doesn't mean you should come on like Rambo in training. Don't be domineering. This will surely label you as Mr. Macho. That isn't what you're trying to accomplish.

When approaching a potential lady you're really interested in, don't use the standard lines. Don't underestimate women. Most of them have heard it all.

Be sincere. Start slow. Be assertive but not blatantly aggressive. Invite her to lunch, to a party, the beach, a picnic, somewhere that isn't too intimate.

Be creative. Everyone loves this approach. Save the standard date of a couple of drinks, dinner and then to bed, for later. You'll be her favorite "date mate" when you come up with the unusual.

Become as well rounded as you can. Learn to dance. If you know how, then get off your rump and ask someone to dance. This is a great ice breaker and you'll be a much sought after male.

Why do you think women travel to Mexican resorts so frequently? These men never allow a single woman to sit out a dance. They are assertive, but in a pleasant way.

European men have always been more aggressive than their American counterparts. This, I am sure, has to do with our customs. However, women travelers have always been impressed with the European male.

Take a lesson from these movers. Don't be afraid of rejection. Dating is like sales. If you call on enough people and give a good presentation, someone is going to buy your product.

Some psychologists believe the woman's movement created a boomerang effect on both sexes. Now women are saying, "We are tired. Where's the little cottage with the picket fence, the kids and the husband?" She's bored with the assertive, aggressive role that brought her money, prestige and a title. Loneliness is the by-product.

Biologically speaking, men and women have become fish out of water. We are creatures of habit and have evolved with certain characteristics that are dominant within our personalities. The pendulum may be swinging back as many people yearn for marriage, children and the basics of life.

Gentlemen are back in vogue. Manners and politeness aren't labeled as "weak". Now men can allow their true assertive natures back out of the closet.

Test & Review

1. So you're single. Your social life is next to zip and you've got the blahs. Get with the program, Charlie. You are the master of your own ship and it won't sail without a captain. Think of two activities you've always wanted to enjoy, then do them. Regardless of the hobby, enroll in lessons that will push you toward accomplishing your goal.

2. You might love the cultural side of life. So, what's stopping you? Join the friends of the museum, take a painting or sculpturing course, go to poetry readings. You'd be surprised at the women you'll meet with similar interest. You will also become a more interesting partner.

3. Plan a four-day trip somewhere. It's exciting to travel alone. Try it, you'll like it. A four-day cruise can be a hoot if you don't sit on your duff and wait for something to happen.

4. Formulate a one-year goal. Write or type it on a sheet of paper. Copy the list. Seal the original.

CHAPTER

Man, Know Thyself

If man really bothers to take the time and interest to know himself, who and what he is, where he wants to go in life, what he truly desires to accomplish, and how he intends to achieve these goals, he will be happy. He will never be caught in the corporate trap, the marriage trap (assuming it was unhappy), or live a life of quiet desperation.

But man is often lazy. He wants the brass ring, regardless of the circumstances. That is why it is so easy for women to play games and create illusions just to snare men into their net. You, my dear, are a pushover.

You see, men have always set the stage and wrote the script. Women, hopefully, would follow the roles men created for her. Well, they couldn't come right out and honestly tell you that your script stank and there must be a better way, God forbid. So women, because they couldn't be honest for fear they might upset the "male ego," created a myriad of roles and facades.

Since God took a rib from Adam and made woman, man has been in control, or so he thought, of the play. But woman, being the ingenious creature she is, decided to add the role written for her and even elaborated the play. This maneuver totally confused the playwright.

That is why there is no honesty between the sexes. Man, who doesn't know himself, isn't prepared for that equality. So in the process, he has trapped himself and his counterpart.

Women made an error, a very bad one I must admit, by baring their chests and running off to Washington with their gravy-stained wrap-arounds on, crying "women's liberation." This sudden outburst of equality scared the hell out of most men and, in fact, created a cavernous gully between the sexes. The backlash is now beginning to haunt women, especially those twenty-five to fifty.

This so-called liberation caused other problems between men and women. Impotence, anger, anxiety, frustration, insecurity, a rise in divorce, loneliness and other debilitating difficulties.

OK, it's time we face the facts. Biologically, men and women are different. Men have evolved since the beginning as the bread winner, warrior and indeed the king of his castle. (Sorry Libbies, you know better than to mess with Mother Nature—or you should, now.) Women, hormonally, were best suited to nest. They kept the home fires burning, bore children, baked bread and were the queens of the castle.

Everyone was moving along quite nicely in their obligatory roles until the late thirties and early forties when World War II became a reality, and men were away fighting for freedom while the women had to work in factories and raise children.

After the war things seemed to return to normal, and even as late as the fifties, women were still longing to get married, have babies and run little white cottages with picket fences.

But during the sixties something happened. The flower children appeared with their hallucinogenic drugs, free love and sex, and women found independence. Ya-hoo! Then came the mother and oracle of Feminism...Ms. Betty Freidan. She, of the *Feminine Mystique* fame, convinced women we were unfulfilled, unhappy, and to trade house dresses in for a pin-striped suit and briefcase. And if it wasn't enough to contend with this windbag of wisdom, we had other feminist gurus. Ms. Gloria Steinem and Bella Abzug were both blowing smoke rings up very uneducated and unprepared asses.

Believe me, women weren't prepared for liberation any more than men. And after twenty years of this nonsensical movement, women are running to shrinks, dying of heart attacks, popping Librium and Valium, attending stress management classes by the hundreds and literally falling apart at the seams. Now they are really unfulfilled and they can't even get a date! Of course, Ms. Steinem can.

During this liberated movement, men began to retreat and some even began seeking the company of other men. Don't you love it? Never before in the history of mankind has the divorce rate been so high.

Neither men nor women were ready for this turnabout in roles. Men played with Tonka toys and women with tea sets and Barbie dolls for eons. Women didn't, nor do they now, have the foggiest idea how to prepare a P&L statement, apply for a large business loan, or how to play hard-ball in negotiations and network properly. Men acquired these attributes in business by osmosis; it is just second nature.

I've always said, "Behind every successful business woman there is a man." She either has a rich daddy, husband, a huge divorce settlement controlled by an investment firm, or she has a damn smart male partner. Check Liberated Lena if you doubt my observations.

For those women who must work because of extenuating circumstances or who prefer a career, "Women's Lib" has indirectly made it tougher for them. I know, I have been one of them.

When a man has to work with a woman on his level or a step above, God help her. He'll make it as impossible for her as he can.

If women are stupid enough to start their own business (I was) and depend on male suppliers, they'd better be related to a sharp attorney who has their interests at heart or they'll be paying padded bills forever.

Like a jackass, I believed all those positive thinking books. Ideas are money; just believe in yourself; you can do it. Yes, Virginia, you too can be successful. Work hard, avoid evil, and thou shall be rewarded. Well, that advice is true if you're dealing with people who are honest and sincere and realize their success partially hinges on yours.

Women are prey for men in business. I have been taken by attorneys, printers, graphic companies, printers' representatives, bankers, multi-millionaire clients, corporate presidents, car mechanics, handymen, painters, carpenters and yardmen. You name it, I've paid dearly for it. I now have a purchase order for everything, including sex.

When I started in business as a publisher of a woman's magazine with virtually no capital, tons of guts, a good attitude, loads of dreams and a total commitment to work, little did I know what I really needed to succeed was a penis. (Ms. Friedan didn't tell us that).

When I published my first magazine (by the way I never used the title of publisher, always managing editor—more feminine, less threatening), an advertising agency, owned by a typical "blue suede shoes" disguised in a three-piece suit, took me for more than three thousand dollars.

I had just started *Arizona Woman* in Scottsdale, Arizona, and literally trusted everyone. I was too ignorant to acquire his clients' signatures on the contract.

He collected all the monies for this advertising from his clients up front, which was legally our money, and then refused to pay us. He used some lame excuse that he didn't like the slant of the magazine (a lie, because he knew the tack we were taking with this issue). Of course it was all a guise so he could keep the money. Not only did he take the publication for its money, he clipped the clients for the commission and art production costs.

Anyway, I went to school and have found the way around these vultures, even though the degree was terribly expensive. It almost put me out of business before I even got started. I soon learned many of these types of activities were to be a part of my quest to be the female entrepreneur, and they always involved a man.

Many of my female friends who tried their hand at business were taken by men. A girlfriend of mine, whose father was a millionaire, went into the development business with a male partner. She was taken by the partner, banker, her attorney and a few city officials.

By the end of her ordeal she was filing for bankruptcy, selling her Porsche and changing her lifestyle. She was lucky—Dad was there to help her out of this mess. But she'd been trying to create an independent living and obtain a career in the wonderful world of business. No, Virginia, you can't go into business without a large pair of brass balls.

Her partner, an accomplished crook, didn't lose a dime. In fact, he made a bundle taking his female partner for everything through kickbacks to bankers and officials. He kept all his stolen money in an offshore bank and started another business in the same city.

One episode involving a shady magazine representative in New York cost me in excess of $2,000 and several hundred dollars in long distance phone calls, overnight letters, etc. Without going into detail, it also cost me and several other women accounts with a major company.

Another man cost me thousands of dollars in newsstand monies and the loss of some accounts. The final bill was so padded that I confronted him when I showed him a copy of the bill, mind you on his letterhead, and he informed me he hadn't sent me that bill, it wasn't his. Unbelievable! He had cheated me on the paper for the magazine by using an inferior European brand while all the time I was paying for American stock. He lied, cheated and almost punched me in the face as I was leaving. It would have been different if I had been a man. C'est la vie!

It was a no win situation. After I realized this fact, I decided to sell the publication and one prerequisite was the new buyer had to be a man. I knew he'd make it. My girlfriends and female associates in business, when they are subjected to a male superior or men in power, have all experienced similar situations.

Women are not in the same ballpark in business as men. They aren't even equipped to carry his briefcase in the real world of commerce. Not unless she has plenty of capital to keep going to school learning from these costly mistakes.

There are many women who are good in business, but they don't get a fair shake and that's a shame, because the world loses when we don't have qualified, fair people in positions that count.

The big lesson here is it would pay all you men handsomely if you took the time to find out what your bottom line is—not only in business, but in personal relationships, with your children and marriage. Maybe if you start dealing from the top of the deck everyone will react accordingly. Try it, you might be pleasantly surprised. Now you see why man must know himself.

Alimony Alley

Alimony, according to Webster, means to keep alive, nourish, give food and support.

This is why alimony was created by the judicial system. It was to assist a man's wife in establishing a new life for herself and children while in the transition period between marriage and the single life.

As usual, unethical people found a way to bend the law to suit their needs and get away with it. Enter Alimony Alice, the Cinderellas of the divorce court.

I once knew a gal, now a seasoned woman, and I mean seasoned, who was an Alimony Alice spelled with a capital A. Her only occupation was collecting alimony. From the time she turned eighteen she married, divorced, then collected her paycheck.

At last count, she had managed to corner four suckers I know of into marriages that lasted two years. She then divorced them and collected $30,000 for her two-year stint. The amount was always the same. Thus far, she has $120,000 in cash in her designer jeans for doing nothing.

That's just the cash. During her brief marriage charades she amassed furs, jewelry, condos and cars, always in her name and tax free. Also, in the interim between "job opportunities" she always dates men of means who give her money to start her own business.

This modus operandi has been continuing for thirty years and I'll bet it will continue as long as she can attract a chump. One benefactor gave her $60,000 cash to open a facial salon. The only thing she knew about beauty was where to buy it. She promptly bankrupted this toy. Meanwhile, she drove a Cadillac, lived in one of his homes rent free, bought a new wardrobe and played tennis everyday.

Her last union netted her another $30,000 and a tennis shop, which she bankrupted. I know it sounds boring, but why change when it's working?

She is now in her fifties and back in circulation again so she can con another idiot out of a cool $30,000. You must remember all the material goods she collected on the way probably places her net worth at over a half million. Not bad for doing an honest day's work.

This Cinderella with the many fairy godfathers hasn't contributed one positive thing towards society.

She's not alone in her quest for "easy money." There are many piranha lurking around the sea of matrimony.

There was a Southern Belle who migrated to Chicago with her family because welfare was higher and easier to get up north. Well, as you can imagine, her upbringing and values weren't too principled.

This one went a step further to insure her income through marriage. She would immediately get pregnant, divorce the jerk, and ask for alimony and child support. She did this three times and again never worked because of the children. Also, she would always buy a new house while married and, of course, the judge would award her that because of the children. She used the same lawyer for all three "job changes" and never missed a beat.

Now the children are about the age where child support is dwindling and her child-bearing days are over. Hope she stashed plenty of cash because this broad hasn't worked long enough to collect Social Security.

I have nothing against alimony when it's needed, but it seems to be the "free lunch" for lazies.

This can also work in reverse. I have an acquaintance who is paying $2,000 a month to an ex-husband she employed in her business. When they divorced, he asked for, and received, $50,000 from her for lost salary.

This was her business. She started from scratch, placed him on the payroll, and is now still paying all the expenses of running a business plus his $2,000. This doesn't seem fair.

Some women use alimony and community property laws as a hammer to hold over the head of their spouses to deter them from divorce.

This is an old game that still works. I know many men who would leave the "ol' lady" if it didn't cost them an arm and a leg.

They are at the age where the business is making money, life is easier for them and they don't want to walk out with nothing.

Men usually assume this attitude beginning in their middle to late forties. These wives quickly size up the situation and instinctively know what buttons to push. Forget the groin. They threaten to hit him in the pocketbook, then they are assured of always having a meal ticket around. Another plus to this type of head tripping is Ms. Button Pusher can spend money until she is blue in the face.

If hubby happens to scream about the MasterCard being over the limit, Ms. Pusher simply smiles demurely and informs him it could be worse.

It's like Pavlov's dogs. She rings the bell and your saliva starts to run just thinking about the community property split. She's got you by the proverbial balls, and she'll squeeze them—until your eyes bug out.

This type of situation also perpetuates infidelity. You feel trapped so you must also find a sympathetic ear. She finds out, so the ante is raised. Not only will she take the community property, she'll take the business, your Jeep, hunting dog and all your toys.

I have met many men who I believe would divorce their wives if they wouldn't have to pay through the nose, and wifey-poo knows this, so she immediately lays on the pressure.

It's a sick game where both players need a shrink. However, the mere fact they stay and play must mean they like it. I have no tolerance for men and women who create such a situation and call it marriage. Nor do I feel sorry for either party. Life is short and it's only money. But maybe these types of people need the excuse to stay together.

One such male did get out, but he framed her canceled alimony and community property checks in the family room for all to see. He never did get over the amount of money he lost to her. And wouldn't you know, he's started to play tennis with Alimony Alice from the beginning of this chapter.

Maybe these people attract defeat on purpose. They say misery loves company.

Test & Review

1. How secure and independent is the woman you are seriously dating? Chances are if she isn't, you will have a problem if and when you marry. Most men dislike secure and independent women. This is where men miss the boat. When a woman is dependent, you are in for it. Much as she makes you feel like Rambo, darling, you'll be fighting like Rocky if things don't work out.
2. When the little woman informs you she's going to take your old tie-dyed T-shirt and jockey shorts if you file for divorce, wrap them up and give them to her. Stop the game before it starts or you won't be passing GO and collecting $200. She will.
3. Plan on choosing your type of woman in the beginning, then play it straight. You won't have to worry about divorce or alimony.

21

Know Your Rights,
Then Find a Lawyer Who Does

Some of you have already been fleeced by either your ex-wife and/or her attorney. Let's not discount the fact that maybe you were taken by both, hers and yours. The rest of you divorce-game novices might be considered virgins. Take heed, if you are; you might save yourself time, heartache, money and emotional problems.

When a man is involved in a divorce litigation, the biggest problem arises when he relies on an attorney to protect him from Alimony Alice without really researching the lawyer's background.

Another problem is that most people have little knowledge of their rights in a divorce transaction, thus having to rely on the attorney's suggestions without question. Unfortunately, the scales of justice, blindfolded since birth, really don't give a damn. Unless you have a crack-shot barrister and one who has your best interests at heart, you'll probably be taken down the primrose path of financial ruin.

In my estimation, California and a few other states have the fairest divorce laws. The no-fault divorce, along with community property split, seems to be the most equitable way of handling a divorce. All money and joint community property that has been acquired by both parties is split and equally divided. If that doesn't work, then all property is sold and the money divided. If there isn't a child custody contestment, then all should go well and fair.

Several states still have very antiquated divorce laws, and most favor the women. These states allow the bloodsucking types of females, you know them now, and their attorneys to have a financial ball, and we know with whom.

However, with so many men being taken to the cleaners, a special group was formed exclusively to protect a man's rights while he is going through the throes of divorce. It's called America's Society of Divorced Men, Inc.

Since its conception in 1969, ASDM has made courageous headway where men's rights are concerned. The Illinois office alone has won over 65 child custody cases and six where the man received custody, alimony and child support. Quite an attainment in a state like Illinois.

This progressive organization provides the most positive assistance for the man contemplating divorce. No longer does he have to be at the mercy of bad legal counsel that steers him sideways and cons him into signing the papers that might financially bury him, sometimes forever.

The society is a non-profit organization, so they charge $40 to each member and, believe me, it's the best $40 you'll spend if a divorce is in your future. Your initial fee entitles you to unlimited hours at any time with a counselor, your first appointment with an attorney and a year's membership.

As part of your membership, this society researches divorce laws, observes divorce attorneys at work in court and checks their references. Also, extensive research is done on your individual case and men's rights in general. They also take an active interest in your emotional and financial status. In other words, neither dear little wifey or her lawyer can hassle you. The society does everything it can for you, including holding your hand if it has to.

If there isn't an office in your city, the nearest office handles out-of-town clients and will work diligently to see that you get the right attorney and more than a fair shake.

Mr. D. R. Templeton, president of the American Society of Divorced Men, says: "We believe responsible men have an inalienable right to be secure from every unreasonable loss of their children, property, money, their good name, and that marriage must be a viable contract wherein both spouses may be held accountable."

Notice how Mr. Templeton refers to "responsible men." That is the key. This organization was not designed for men to take women. There are plenty of male barracudas around and they need no help. That is the other side of the coin. Help is needed for responsible and interested men who have been de-checkbooked, de-pantsed and generally wiped out by devious, vulturous females.

If you have ever been through a divorce, you know it is an emotional and guilt-ridden time. You are thinking emotionally, not rationally. That is why it is imperative to acquire the correct information concerning your rights. Too many men want out of the arrangement so badly that the spouse and lawyer know just how to back them up against the wall.

You already know what you're married to or you wouldn't want to dissolve the union, but you can't run scared or believe misinformation.

Don't ever take a friend's advice or think you can outwit the law without the help of an excellent lawyer. Beware of friends who are attorneys or friends who "know a good one."

Many experts say divorce laws haven't kept pace with the changes in relationships. More couples today are dividing household responsibilities, including earning the income. But divorce statutes in many states still consider the woman financially dependent, whether she is or not.

Forden Athearn, author of *How to Divorce Your Wife* (Doubleday & Co.), lists several pointers on how to divorce her and protect your joint assets. He suggests before you've told her that you've decided on divorce, ask yourself how she is going to react to the news. If there is any doubt in your mind that she will be fair and objective, take these steps:

1. Close joint bank accounts and put all funds in your name; take possession of all stocks, securities, bonds, and notify all charge accounts, in writing, that you're no longer responsible for any charges your wife runs up. These are defensive, not vindictive actions. You're simply putting everything in a safe place until the assets can be divided. (But if your wife decided to get back at you by charging up a storm or cashing in your savings bonds, you're protected, too.)

2. Be sure to make a list of all the assets you now have in your name and their values. You're not trying to be secretive and you'll need it later on when settling who gets the property.

3. Tell your lawyer (it should be someone with successful experience in divorce cases). Give him a complete rundown on yourself, your wife, your children, your marriage (and what you think happened to it) and your economic situation (your list of assets helps here). Be open. Don't hide anything. Your lawyer must have the complete picture. Your wife can involve you in some nasty legal hassles if you have concealed some assets.

Ask your attorney about his fees. Time involved and difficulty of the case alter the going rate. Check with the bar association if you feel the fees are out of line.

Then you tell your wife. Be sure and duck to avoid flying objects. Explain that you want a divorce. In that discussion (I would prefer to call it a brawl), tell her about the arrangements you've made to pay the bills. Discuss (there's that nebulous word again) what you've done about your joint checking accounts, securities, etc. Give her a copy of the assets list (then be prepared to eat it) and let her know that any future personal debts she incurs are hers alone to pay.

Well, I think Mr. Athearn has some excellent ideas, but he obviously hasn't dealt, or maybe he has, with the mad Tarantula. The above would make her furious and I think she would stop at nothing short of killing you. But you can try it, with the assistance of several bodyguards.

I think my suggestions are a little more subtle. As you will see in the following, I suggest freezing all accounts. That way little Miss Cushion-Sitter won't be offended if she thinks that neither of you can touch the goods. But you know the little missus better than anyone. After all, you made her what she is—confident.

There are ways to protect yourself, emotionally and financially, before going to court. If you don't, you could be wiped out of many financial assets that you have jointly. Put a freeze on any bank accounts, stocks and bonds, joint property, and the like. I have known of women who literally wiped out checking and savings accounts before any court litigation was constituted. You can have an attorney put a restraining order on accounts and insurance policies, preventing Helpless Hanna from changing the beneficiary, borrowing against it or cashing it in. During the time of an upcoming divorce suit, deal in cash, allot so much for the household bills and spending money and keep the holdings frozen. Don't you cash them out because that shows bad faith and you might look like that bum your wife will try to convince the judge you are. Emotionally, try and remember she will soon be your ex-wife. There are many ways women use men and their emotions. You've read the book; have you learned anything so far?

I once knew a man who was really taken, and while he was being ripped off, the Belle, a real bitch in crinoline, was using him to the hilt. While they were legally separated, she bounced him out of the house, which she eventually sold, pocketing the proceeds. She called him to baby-sit the kids anytime she desired. She called him at work every time one of the kids whimpered, saying they missed dear ol' dad, and by the way, would he mind coming over that night to fix the plumbing? After she sold the house and was moving to a townhouse, she had him move a desk for her, claiming she didn't know what to do with it. By the time they went to court, she had him convinced she wouldn't, and couldn't, make it alone with the wee ones because she was alone and helpless. He felt like a complete heel. She got everything and managed better than he financially.

The best advice while separated, if there is no chance for reconciliation, is stay away, and I mean far away. If you're through buddy, be through. The types of women I have described in the previous chapters don't stop playing the game—ever. Remember, if they have someone to play with, the game's won and in their favor. There are many situations like the above, so wipe the guilt out of your mind and disentangle yourself emotionally before leaving.

Test & Review

1. Before any litigation, protect yourself emotionally and financially.
2. Check your directory for an organization that handles divorce rights for men.
3. While you're still acquiring legal advice, work on yourself to avoid possible guilt feelings attached to the divorce stigma. Develop an outside hobby (not women dummy, haven't you had enough for the moment?). You will be surprised what an interesting hobby can do for you—less time to think about your problem.
4. Keep your mouth shut, unless you're talking to your lawyer. Any other advice can be confusing. Don't talk to your mother, mother-in-law or her. It's none of their business and they won't know yours if you keep your mouth shut.
5. After you're divorced, and if you're paying alimony, make sure your lawyer has worked this particular situation to your advantage. Many attorneys have advised their clients wrongly as far as IRS deductions go. If you have to, have a sharp tax consultant work with your attorney on this matter.
6. Pray like hell.

Male Liberation
(Chauvinistic Pig or Slaughtered Lamb)

When the females bared their chests and marched to Washington screaming for "equal rights," guess who they really liberated? YOU!

Equal rights? They didn't get them, they gave them. Now as a result of their much sought after liberation, these women are experiencing the same anxieties that besieged males for eons: burnout, stress, heart attacks, high cholesterol counts, drug abuse and alcoholism are prevalent in females now. Ah, liberation!

Lately, articles are flooding the market explaining why the sexes are avoiding each other. Men are becoming recluses, choosing to go out with their buddies instead of pursuing the female. They claim it's not worth the time.

Now isn't that just great? Women have progressed from having been knocked over the head with a club and having our hair pulled out by the natural roots, to knocking him over the head and not getting laid. Are we smart or what? Next we will be tying crystals all around his penis to see if it will improve his erection. Now instead of women complaining about "equal rights," they are bitching about the lack of male virility.

Why all the fuss about "liberation" and women's rights anyway? "Behind every successful woman, there is a man." "What?" women scream. "Never!"

Let's take Jacqueline Susann, one of the most successful contemporary writers of her time. Did you think Jackie just wrote a book and it hit the best-seller list? Wrong. There was a husband very much in the forefront. She admitted she couldn't have done it without Irving.

Irving Mansfield was very connected in New York and Hollywood, having been a successful television producer. When Jackie wrote *Valley of the Dolls*, it cost hubby approximately $400,000 to get it published, promoted and distributed. He also devoted his time, effort and expertise to help Jackie accomplish her goal of becoming a best-selling author. This doesn't detract from Mrs. Mansfield's talent, but without Irving's contacts, knowledge and total commitment to Jackie's goal, Ms. Susann might have remained obscure.

In his book *Jackie*, Irving informs the reader of the many obstacles they both had to overcome so Ms. Susann could make it to the top.

Helen Gurley Brown, the illustrious editor of *Cosmopolitan*, became a household word. Did Helen just happen to march into the offices of *Cosmo* and inform them she was ready to put the magazine in the top ten publication list? Hell no. Helen had the good sense to marry her boss, David Brown, editor of *Cosmopolitan* before Helen. When he tired of the job, he possibly turned over in bed and asked Helen if she'd like to take over (something like that). Well, she said, "You bet," and the rest is history. When David was running *Cosmo*, it was a homey pub. Helen, of the *Sex and the Single Girl* fame, decided to run it like a companion to *Playboy* and blew the socks off of all the other mags on the newsstands. She sold sex, sex and more sex. Society was ready for that topic. *Cosmopolitan* began running in the black.

However, regardless of her talent, without David's contacts and support, Helen couldn't have reached this zenith in the publishing world. Again I am not knocking Helen, just proving behind every successful woman there is a man.

Would there have been a Cher without Sonny? I doubt it. Do you think Bo Derek would have become a "10" if husband John Derek hadn't been pulling the strings? The answer is no. Mr. Derek was an old-timer when it came to playing Svengali to some now famous ladies. His first wife, Ursula Andress, became a sex symbol, thanks to Johnny's suggestions. Linda Evans can thank John for her sultry, low, soothing voice when he taught her to scream her head off in the California hills so her vocal cords would become damaged, thus lowering her voice.

Go back in history. Mary Magdalene had Jesus, Cleopatra had two men in her life pushing her towards the throne of Egypt—Antony and Caesar. No dummy Cleo. Queen Isabelle of Spain had ol' Chris

Columbus sailing the ocean blue acquiring more land for her and Spain, thus making her a famous monarch.

Every First Lady of the United States has enjoyed fame, prominence, perks and money because of her husband's position. Do you think the public would have known Jackie Kennedy if Jack hadn't been President? This executive title enabled Jackie to enjoy international prestige. Jack made her a star and because of her fame, she was able to marry one of the richest men in the world and socialize with kings and queens.

Jackie would have remained an obscure socialite if her marriage to Jack Kennedy didn't happen. But it did, and she benefited in every aspect, far beyond her dreams.

Get the point? Men have been climbing the ladder of success since cavemen were competing on who could kill the biggest boar. The knowledge and drive for success is inbred and naturally inherited while women have evolved with unrelated attributes.

That is why women find the drive toward attaining status in the business world frustrating. They figure by verbally demanding their "rights," success will be handed to them on a silver platter. What a misconception.

Men instinctively know how to cut through the crap in business. They also network with each other where women don't. They claim they do and form all these business women's organizations, giving lip service about networking with each other. But I happen to know why they are playing at it.

Women are at a disadvantage, especially if they are married or have children. They are working, raising children, and taking care of a home and husband. These are tremendous responsibilities. Not much time is left to dedicate to a career.

Women should wise up and align themselves with men who can assist them toward their goals. It's much easier, quicker and less stressful in the long run.

I know from experience. If I had found a male partner, I would have saved time, effort and money, accomplished my goals three times faster, and not had an Excedrin headache most of the time.

When women are alone in business, they are game for every supplier in their field. Bankers treat a female business owner like she has leprosy, accountants act as if she is a mongoloid idiot, and most of her suppliers pad the bills.

I haven't totally figured it out yet, but I sometimes think these male suppliers subconsciously feel they hold the key to her success and unknowingly harbor some resentment toward all women. You pay for these quirks.

In order to be successful in business, women must develop a hard exterior—in other words, be a bitch. If you're not, plan on being taken by everyone you come in contact with, including your employees. A smart man once told me, "Don't ever be nice in business, because people mistake niceness for weakness." He was so right.

Women, biologically speaking, are less forceful in business than men. Yes, there are exceptions, but generally speaking, women are not as powerful as their male counterparts. This, of course, is unladylike. So women are at a disadvantage in business when dealing with men. A man will always have the upper hand simply by being male. He is always supposed to be the strong one.

Why should women liberate themselves from the greatest asset they can have in the business world—a man?

Keep on Truckin'

Well guys, have you learned something about how to figure out a woman? If the topic has interested you enough to pay attention, you now have more insights on how to deal with the female and her trickery.

You should be better equipped now to keep your head above water, your brain and pocketbook intact, and, yes, even enjoy the challenge of dealing with women on a day-to-day basis. Forewarned is forearmed and, buster, you have been forewarned.

There is no easy remedy or solution for figuring out a woman, but with some awareness of their cunning tricks, the game won't be so one-sided.

Men and women were meant to live, date and love one another. However, God had a great sense of humor when he created both sexes. This distinct biological difference between men and women sometimes makes it difficult for the two to live harmoniously.

You see, women know all about men and what makes them tick. They are taught from childhood how to manipulate their male counterparts. Men, on the other hand, aren't instructed in such nonsense because they have to make a living in order to support Priscilla Pilot Fish in the manner and style to which she has become accustomed. From the time a man is born, he is taught to use the tools of survival. By the time he has matured and thought of marriage, she is a master, having practiced on her unsuspecting prey along the way. He is totally in the dark.

What happens, you ask, if you become attached or infatuated with a Tarantula? My advice is to date her long enough for that infatuation to wear off, then drop her like the poisonous spider she really is and find a working Showdog or Worker Bee.

Many men marry Tarantulas when all the time they really love Southern Belles. Know yourself. If watching the calla lilies bloom turns you on, then by all means admit it and head for the Mason-Dixon line and find a Belle to ring yours.

I am not saying it's a sin to be married to a Showdog or fall in love with a Femme Fatale International. What I am saying is, you have to know the players in order to play the game correctly. I know many men who are married to Liberated Lenas when indeed they would be happier with a Showdog.

Now that you can detect the type of women you're dealing with, you're better educated on who would be a better partner for you.

Keep on truckin' means keep aware, alert and on your toes. You don't have to be paranoid and cynical, and miss out on all the fun. Many men who have been used, abused and misused take it out on other women. This isn't fair to the woman or yourself. You'll never find your perfect soul mate.

I have met many men who have been devastated by a divorce. After paying through the nose, they develop a caustic attitude toward women and they lose out on a lot more than sex this way.

The trick is to figure out what type of woman you are dealing with and go from there. First you have to know yourself and what kind of female makes you happy. You can't wear blinders and refuse to see the writing on the wall. Many men tend to categorize all women as "no good." These are usually the macho types who are insecure. When a female doesn't immediately jump to their demands, she's unacceptable.

In order to find your perfect mate, a man must first bury his ego. This is difficult because that ego is the hardened exterior that protects you from your vulnerabilities. To be sensitive isn't setting yourself up to be hurt; to be stupid is! Men tend to be "stupid" about women.

Read the unauthorized biography of Frank Sinatra by Kitty Kelley. He had the perfect wife, Nancy. She would sew her own clothes, make his silk ties, cook, take care of the children, save his money, etc. But something told him he needed a glamour gal. So he chucked his family life for a string of wild and disastrous relationships and marriages. He finally settled down to marry a blonde Showdog. This is evidently what he needed; he's still married to her.

Often men have a preconceived idea of who they should marry. These images come from society, movies, parents and books. Because they follow other's ideals, chances are they miss a perfect mate who just didn't fit their fantasy.

The first step in finding your counterpart is to be totally honest with yourself. In order to accomplish this, you must first know what and who you are.

If you have "found yourself," then search for someone who complements you. The mistake everyone makes in choosing a partner is looking for someone who will make him complete. This is impossible. We are all diamonds in the rough. It merely takes effort, time and knowledge to make carbon sparkle brilliantly.

Men and women also get trapped in "no win" relationships because they think they can mold their partner to suit their needs. Won't work. Start taking inventory of yourself as a person. Be honest. Look in the mirror and give yourself a sincere appraisal. Write down a list of your attributes, positive and negative. Plan to improve the negative aspects of your personality.

For instance, if you possess a great personality and a tremendous sense of humor, but are overweight and hide these traits with a caustic attitude, go on a weight-reduction program and develop a self-improvement regimen. Mentally see yourself trim and fit with a pleasing, outgoing attitude. Women will respond positively.

Men sometimes have a tendency to use the put down approach towards attractive, intelligent women. Maybe this is their protective shield. However, all this does is turn off the type of female you're probably looking for.

Men have been raised to accept a challenge. This is great in the business world, but can be risky in a relationship if you don't know what you want. This is how the Tarantulas of the world trap you in their web. Make sure you know what you'll be having once you've conquered the challenge.

The old cliché, "if it's easy, it's not worth having" is bullshit. Inherited money is easy. It spends and you don't have to lift a hand in order to enjoy the benefits.

It's the same with a relationship. Sometimes people come into our life and the relationship is easy. It's enjoyable with no effort. That is when it's right. But how many times do you see men screw up these partnerships, only to trade them in for a difficult one.

This makes no sense, is totally illogical and many times costly because if they marry the wrong person, and divorce isn't a feasible solution, soothing one's nerves with shopping and spending money follows.

Many men program themselves to be losers. They marry the wrong mate, then spend their lives bitching, moaning and running away from the situation, but usually never divorce themselves from the little woman. They feel they got what they deserve. This type of relationship perpetuates misery for both parties. So you've got two sickies feeding each other's inadequacies.

Life is short. The natural state of man, as God created him, was to be happy. Unhappiness creates ill health, stress, drug abuse, alcoholism and sometimes death. Who needs it?

Bury that high school mentality and develop a mature and realistic approach in your request for the right partner. Would you go into business with a game player? Hell no! Then why try marriage with one. Ask yourself, would you want an associate who was mysterious and unavailable? Not on your tin-type.

Approach marriage and a relationship as if you were going into business with that person. Brother, you are. Take a long look at your choices.

Can you communicate? Do you have goals in common? What type of childhood did she have? Is it compatible to yours? Does she like sports, or is she a shop-a-holic?

Experts who research why some marriages are successful and others fail have found you have a better chance if you come from similar backgrounds, possess the same values, principles and ethics, and are interested in similar long-term goals, hobbies, child-rearing concerns and financial arrangements.

Why try and fool "Mother Nature?" She always wins. Go with the flow and keep on truckin'.

Test & Review

1. Don't immediately fall for the mysterious damsel who appears to be such a challenge because she's always unavailable. If you're already infatuated and want to see who's really hiding under the mask, plan a week-long vacation and ask for her company. No one can masquerade for an entire week. Try Tahiti or Bora Bora....no costumes here.
2. If you are the type who thinks you don't deserve a "10" or a partner, call your local shrink immediately.
3. If you are with a Tarantula but love Southern Belles, give the spider the boot and take a trip to New Orleans. Your Belle will be ready to ring yours.
4. If you have a history of choosing the wrong woman, read this book again.
5. Never quit dancing, honey, keep on truckin' and eventually you'll find the right partner.

CHAPTER 24

What Do Women
Really Think About Men?

For eons men have professed they couldn't figure out women. Well, I have a news flash for you guys; women are just as confused about men.

They are also perplexed about what a man wants in a relationship. Because of this frustration, they resort to head trips and games (at least, let's give them that excuse).

It has always been my opinion that women don't really like men. There's the old cliché, "You can't live with them and you can't live without them." The apparent reason for this subconscious dislike is women don't really know men.

During their childhood, women played with Chatty Cathy and Barbie, while in their teens they buried their heads in Seventeen and Glamour magazines. As children, men and women were separated by their perspective activities imposed on them either by parental authority or society. They played different games and most of the time associated with the same sex.

Boys talked and interacted with each other and so did girls. This perpetuated the "mystique" between sexes that continues through adulthood.

A few fortunate girls, who were tomboys, played with boys as children thus learning their lingo, thoughts and better still, their macho games. These girls acquired men as friends early in their development and have maintained their male friendships at maturity.

These types of females are few and far between and they really like men. They want something from them—security, money, attention, sex, material goods, something.

Since this book is written for you, the man, I decided to ask women: "What do you really think about men; do you like them?"

Here are some examples:

"My grandmother told me there is no such thing as a good man," says Mary Lee, seventy-plus, of California.

Dolly Countryman, fifty, says: "Behind every successful woman is a man who tries to hold her back. Maybe two men."

Sybil Station, fifty, California artist: "I have been surprised by a few and disappointed by many."

A forty-plus former flower child, raised in Beverly Hills, says: "Oh, I like to use men for sex. They're really great for that. My friends use them for money. I don't need money. I have that."

Stacy, twenty-three, advertising executive from Florida. "They are frustrating because you really never know where you stand with them. You are expected to play the game, but they are the only ones who can change the rules. How can you play when the rules are constantly changing? One day they like you to display affection, but you tell them you love them and they bolt. That's frustrating."

Teresa, twenty-one, manicurist, Florida: "If every man was like the guy on that TV show *thirtysomething* it would be perfect. He's soft, gentle, he loves his wife and kids, and their relationship never gets boring.

"If men could be half the man he appears to be, I'd be happy. They say men are only good for one thing and sometimes they aren't good for that."

Valerie, twenty-eight, manicurist, Pittsburgh: "They are a nuisance. If you don't want them around, there they are. They are slobs. They don't pick up their own mess. I live with a man and I suppose he's got good points, but I prefer good female friends to men in general."

Michelle, thirties, manicurist: "They like me more than I like them. They come on like gangbusters. Yesterday for instance, I met a guy in the parking lot and he approached me and said how pretty I was and what did I do for a living. I told him I did nails. He showed an interest and asked for my card. That afternoon he called for an appointment today.

"I called to change the time of his appointment and the person who answered the phone said he's at the hospital, his wife is having a baby.

"I just left my boyfriend of one year because he was too possessive, but he could look at other women. Men like to make women jealous."

Vivian, late twenties, cosmetics, Latin decent: "I love men. However, I won't date a Latin man, they are too macho. They flirt right in front of you. My mother was married to a Spaniard and she is Puerto Rican, and that marriage didn't last. For the past fifteen years she's been married to an Irishman and they have a good relationship."

Faye, late forties, receptionist: "I'm not even thinking about men. I'm trying to get rid of the one I've got."

Sheila, late forties, real estate salesperson: "The bigger the better."

Linda, mid forties, secretary: "I always thought I liked men, but after my divorce I started dating, and discovered in a very short period of time that I don't like men. I prefer my own company rather than the sexual harassment and generally boring times I've had with men.

"It's all just game playing. They are all just sharks out there and I feel like a minnow."

Jacqueline, late forties, Palm Beach: "I am attracted to men with power and money. However, it's better to like a person. When you're between the ages of eighteen and twenty-four, you experience this blazing passion. But as one matures, I think men and women should be friends.

"Another thing that I feel is terribly important is personal hygiene for both men and women. We are in a new sexual age where oral sex is so predominant. This, and any intimacy, requires extra attention to our bodies. I don't know if men realize how important this is."

Johanna, Florida business owner: "I like men. I was a tomboy as a child and played mostly with boys. When I became an adult and started my businesses, I dealt with both men and women. I prefer men.

"They are more professional, direct and to the point. They usually don't have time to be pretty."

Rene, real estate developer, Florida: "If men can learn to look at women as individuals and forget their misplaced egos, it would be much easier to develop a relationship. They must put their egos in proper perspective. This ego sometimes blinds their intellect and emotion."

Claire, owner of several retail and wholesale marble stores, from Ireland, transplanted Floridian: "I love men. I forgive them because I don't expect perfection. They are only human, like women. Maybe I understand them, therefore I have no problem dealing with them professionally and emotionally."

Amalia, Spanish-American, New York/Florida: "Men suck and I don't mean it that way. They stink. Latin men are jealous and possessive, and American men are passive. I wish there was a man somewhere in between."

Jane, thirty-five, developer-planner, Miami: "Why can't women be totally honest with men? It galls me when we, the woman, have to resort to keeping our mouth shut because we might upset the relationship if we confront him with a brutally honest question and expect an honest answer. All the books you read on keeping a relationship afloat advocate the same drivel. Don't confront him with commitment, he'll run. It isn't logical that you can be totally intimate with a man, but you can't be honest."

Nancy, mid forties, artist, California: "Men love bitches. If you try and be fair and nice in a relationship, he seems to lose interest. A man has to have several bitches before he appreciates a good woman."

Ardis, early forties, salesperson, Chicago: "Men are never satisfied. They are always looking for that better bust, ass and legs. They are so stupid. They will have a great relationship and fuck it up with some busty bimbo."

Diane, late twenties, housewife: "I don't know many men. I have been married since 19 to one man. They just don't seem too considerate, kind of selfish."

Colleen, early forties, business owner, St. Louis: "I can't figure out a man either. I devoted my early years to one guy, lived with him and thought we'd get married. Forget it. I had to sue him at the end of a ten-year living arrangement because I had no money to move out. Big deal. I got $5,000 for all that time. I would have married him, like an idiot."

Women are totally confused and frustrated about what men want. The reason this happens is men are very clever at hiding their real feelings. This art is learned from childhood when the man learns he must be strong. He learns to hide his emotions, protect his freedom and keep his sensitivities under wraps.

A woman can cry, be weak, piss, bitch, moan and show every emotion known to the human race. This is just "being a woman."

In the beginning of a relationship, women want romance and men want sex. For the past several years, romance novels have far outsold the how-to-do-it books. That should tell you men something.

Women tried "free love," uncommitted relationships, quick sex and every other conceivable means to stay abreast of their male counterparts. It didn't work emotionally for them.

Biologically speaking, men are not as interested in the romantic venture of the conquest as they are in the sexual challenge of the hunt. Men are raised with challenges; women are not. This explains why men bore more readily with the same partner than women do—the old monogamy routine.

This is what perplexes many women in their relationships with men. After a man accomplishes his goals (women, job, acquisitions, etc.), he's ready for another challenge. This explains why so many marriages go sour after a couple reaches financial security. Therefore, the older-man, younger-woman syndrome.

Usually when a woman attains what she wants, she is more complacent. When women tried to fight fire with fire, it backfired. They wanted liberation, freedom, independence, and with those came the price tag. After several years of their new found liberty and competing head to head with men in a man's world, they said, "Wow, this isn't any fun."

So re-enter romance and marriage. Gone is pseudo-liberation and penis envy. Women live vicariously through romance novels, romantic mini-series and those damn daily soap operas, trying to capture the romance missing in their partnerships.

Many single women have the same complaint. "He's afraid of permanency and a commitment scares the hell out of him." Well, a commitment means responsibility, loss of freedom (the shackles of marriage), and, yes, possibly boredom.

As psychologists will say, mention marriage to many men and you'll see skid marks, because they feel they are losing control.

If we were brought up with loving, demonstrative and emotionally healthy parents, there is not that much to fear. Chances are that is how we will be in a relationship—loving, secure and emotionally well-rounded. However, many people raised from the sixties didn't come from a loving, caring, healthy environment. There's a set of luggage that will be opened and dumped on an unprepared and unsuspecting partner.

On top of all this, confusion arises because timing is crucial in making a relationship gel. One person could be madly in love and ready for a total commitment while the other isn't near the commitment stage.

There are those who say, "You must be at the right place at the right time with the right person." This isn't an easy task. Many of us have been at the wrong place with the right person at the wrong time, and so on. It's timing, my dear Watson.

In order for all those components to be working properly, you'd have to have the gods on Mount Olympus in your corner working overtime.

What is the solution? There are several, depending on the situation. For example, if you are in a relationship and you are ready for a commitment but the other person isn't, don't rush it.

It is difficult to find a compatible partner. Usually the one who wants a commitment makes the mistake of giving the other guy an ultimatum, and this can ruin an otherwise good partnership.

A good man is hard to find and so are good women. Why botch it up just because the timing is off. However, some people are masters at stringing along a relationship with no intention of getting really involved.

You men have to get off your egotistical high horse and accept a few blunt and honest questions, and be prepared to answer them.

Honesty doesn't ruin relationships or marriages. Lack of creativity does. You men like to fantasize. Get with the program and become more romantic and adventurous. Women like exciting men, especially men who take the initiative.

If you, the man, won't accept "game playing" by the female, she will not be able to manipulate and will have to resort to playing it straight. This works both ways.

Don't be so inhibited. Express yourself verbally and emotionally. Don't ever be afraid to ask a woman, "What do you really want from me and this relationship?"

God made men and women to live together in a pleasurable manner. In fact, the ultimate relationship is a combination of companionship, compatibility, fabulous sex and adventure. Why wouldn't everyone strive for this type of nirvana between the sexes?

Is it attainable? Yes. But only by correct "ego" placement, non-game playing and communicating on an honest level.

We can't expect to nurture loving relationships and solid marriages by constantly battling each other.

The truth of the matter is you might love a Showdog but are involved with a Southern Belle. You know the difference by now, so it's up to you to make the transition.

As Socrates stated, "Know thyself."

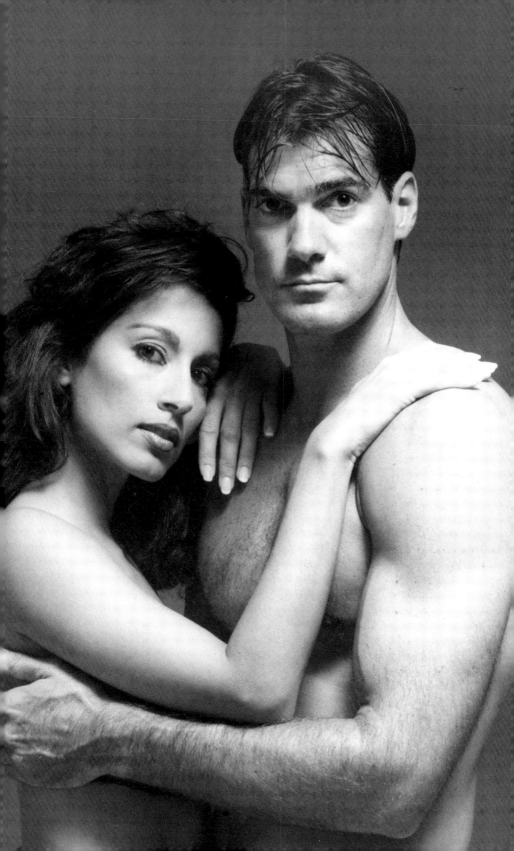

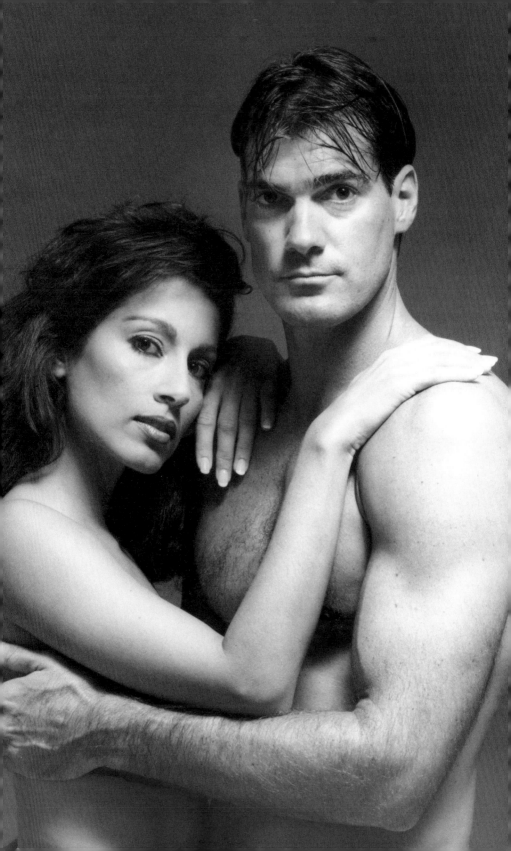

How to Figure Out a Man
The Games Men Play

joella Cain

COOL HAND Communications, Inc.
BOCA RATON, FLORIDA

ISBN: 1-56790-118-2

First Printing

COOL HAND COMMUNICATIONS, INC.
1098 N.W. Boca Raton Boulevard, Suite 1
Boca Raton, FL 33432

Printed in the United States of America

Book design by Cheryl Nathan

Illustrations by Stephen C. Left

Cover and inside photos by Michael Davidoff

Creative concept by Peter Ackerman and joella Cain

Cain, joella, 1944-
    How to figure out a man : the games men play / joella Cain ; [illustrations by Stephen C. Left].
        p.   cm.
    Title on added t.p. : How to figure out a woman : the games women play.
    Two works published back to back, inverted, with separate title pages.
        ISBN 1-56790-118-2 : $17.95
    1. Man-woman relationships. 2. Men--Psychology. 3. Women--Psychology. I. Title. II. Title: How to figure out a woman.
HQ801.C263   1994
305.3--dc20   93-46072
                                                            CIP

This book on men is dedicated to my mother, Ella Cain, who knows more about men and people in general than an army full of psychologists. Unfortunately, I didn't pay attention to her advice in this department and had to learn the hard way.

Contents

Special Acknowledgments

Without the tremendous support of COOL HAND
Communications, Inc., this book would have languished
in a rusty, antiquated file cabinet, honored with an award
of obscurity, along with the rest of my pearly words of
wisdom. Thanks to Allan Weiner, director of sales, for
finding me and the manuscript. Thanks to Chris Hedrick,
publisher of COOL HAND, for agreeing to publish them.
Thanks to Gerald Shaw for his painstaking editing. And
a special thanks to Bunny Hedrick for signing my first
advance check and supporting one of her feline sisters.

Foreword

This is not a book written for women only. Like the sassy, sometimes giddy *How to Figure Out a Woman*, *How to Figure Out a Man* is an insightful and timely look at a microcosm of a world gone mad.

In case you didn't notice, romance is "in." Couples are everywhere. People are in relationships of all sorts, and those not in relationships are on the outside looking in.

How to Figure Out a Man is a book for "real" people. The trend-mongers will find it too provocative. Those of us who glean our insight from the *Cosmopolitan/New Woman* "How to Love a Man Who Hates You" type of article will cringe at the honesty of this book. Figuring out our man/woman/companion/significant-other is not the priority of the "truly enlightened."

During the so-called sexual revolution, commitment and monogamy were bad words and it was horribly wrong to want to be in love. This left many people confused, groping and empty. Those of us not in love wondered if we would ever be again. And, those in love worried about whether commitment would ruin the chance to get out of a relationship should something better come along. Married people envied single people and vice-versa. All the anxiety and euphoria spent chasing prospective mates suddenly didn't seem what we had bargained for when we decided to grow up.

The nineties will be for adults only. It is a fact of life that love is complicated. We have to be almost clairvoyant to evaluate the directions our relationships are taking. Reading self-help books isn't a panacea for a world "gone mad," but it is a good starting point. Whether you are a woman trying to size up a prospective mate or a man trying to improve his character defects, *How to Figure Out a Man* is a sensitive but humorous look at a very delicate subject: love.

The nineties are about commitment, monogamy, honesty and integrity in relationships. Sodom turned sacrosanct? Read on and see.

Paul Wallace, M.S., M.B.A
Intake and Evaluation Specialist
South County Mental Hospital
Delray Beach, Florida

Introduction

Since I wrote the book *How to Figure Out a Woman* for men, I think it's only fair I give them equal time. Both of these books are meant to inform, entertain and educate the opposite sex about the tricks, games and little nuances used upon each other, to either captivate or decapitate the opponent.

I've tried to write this exposé with humor because if we can laugh after we've been hit with a sledge hammer, we can heal quicker—and possibly be healthy enough to create some clever revenge. However, as the experts claim, "the best revenge is living well."

It is easy to figure out a man, if you have the tools and some insight into his "brain scramblers." The difficulty arises in how to figure out what a particular man wants from you, the woman. But before you begin this course, I must inform you: I love men! Many of my friends are men and I trust men more than I do most women. However, there are exceptions in every case and the categories are the exceptions rather than the rule (I hope). You be the judge.

Basically, there are two types of men with numerous deviations. One type is good (the Abels); the other bad (Cains). Abels aren't the problem as they are straight, honest, ethical, principled and goal-directed. They know what they want, pursue it and rarely deviate from their main objective. You, as a woman, know what they're thinking. These men are scarce in the nineties. If you've been blessed and have one of these types, guard him with your life.

The "Cains" are a different bailiwick. They are more common—regretfully—than their "good brothers" and can be categorized by their game plans. They are the Non-Committal Normans, Marvin the

Manipulators and Cheatin' Charlies. These types of men are somewhat impossible for women to figure out because they send mixed messages while disguising their hidden agendas behind an otherwise normal image.

Dealing with these men can land your rump in the poor house, the nut house, or no house depending on to what degree you buy their program. They wreak havoc with your emotions, sanity, pocketbook and self-esteem.

Hopefully, this book will assist you in figuring out a man, but more importantly you'll know what it is he really wants from you.

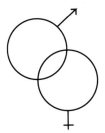

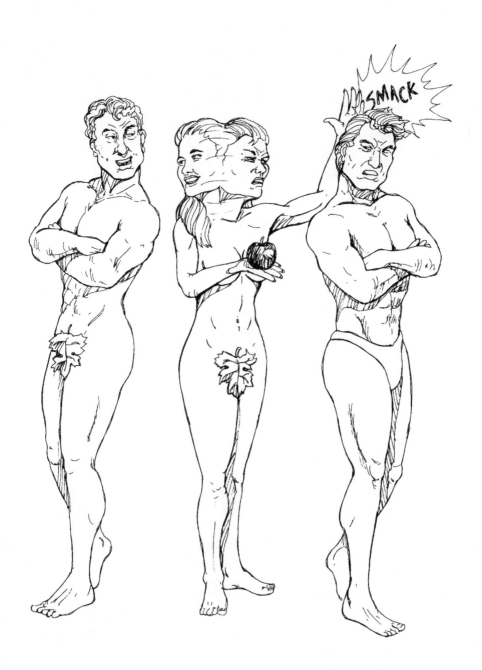

CHAPTER 1

ADAM

"So God created man in his own image," according to Genesis in the Bible. And God named this man Adam. Today's Adam is the personification of what man did with his marvelous birthright, a gift from God. Obviously, he blew it.

In order to figure out man, you must understand the evolvement and past of the species. With this knowledge, you'll be able to proceed forward. In other words, you'll know the hot buttons and be able to play the sucker to the hilt.

Man, himself, is so confused about who and what he is, it's easy to sway him. After all, didn't Eve, mother of all women, bamboozle Adam? Did he pay attention to his maker, his inner self? Hell no. He listened to Eve and got both their rumps kicked out of the garden.

The modern-day Adam isn't a smidgen different from his prototype. He will listen to the right Eve—you—and again get his ass kicked out of Eden or a tract home with a high mortgage.

What I'm trying to tell you Eves is this: You've got the power (what's left after the "liberation") to control Adam, man. You have always possessed it. You just couldn't totally figure out the man of your choice so you could wield that control.

Life in the nineties is and will be different from the existence of Adam and Eve in the Garden of Eden. However, the problem is our social structure has changed drastically since that time, but people basically and biologically haven't.

This causes much confusion between the sexes. The much touted "liberation movement" didn't help matters. It added to the already conflicting circumstances surrounding men and women.

In Adam's day, life was uncomplicated. Both he and Eve knew their designated roles that complemented one another. Neither was playing a game. They were surviving.

The Neanderthal Man was hunting boar while Nancy Neanderthal kept the cave comfortable. While he took the risks fighting off predators, she remained secure and protected.

The Pilgrims suffered hardships but man and woman knew their appropriate positions. Again, this was to protect her from harm so she could take care of his home in Plymouth. They worked together to build a new life in a new country.

The first liberated female was the pioneer woman, and she sure didn't need a movement to garner her freedom. There is not a woman alive today who could nurse an infant while dodging arrows. Women were strong back then—strong enough to be liberated without a damned group doing it for them. You had the Miss Kittys of the Long Branch Saloon, the Anna Helds of the theater, the showgirls and the dressmakers. At no time in history have women been stronger.

And necessity is the mother of invention. These women had no choice. They had to be creative, industrious and tenacious. However, they were still protected by the male and thought of as feminine. Men treated them as partners, working together to achieve a common goal, not as an adversary competing with them.

The First World War placed women in different roles. Yet, men did not view them as a threat. Again, in the Second World War, women had to work outside the home doing a "man's" job. Rosie the Riveter wasn't thought of as a rival. They were working together toward the same goal: to win the war.

Until the late fifties, women were reasonably happy keeping the family unit intact. With the sixties came the sexual revolution, psychedelic drugs and the deterioration of morals and ethics. Increased inflation and government taxation of the seventies, not the women's movement, forced women to work just to make ends meet.

Now, in the nineties, with three out of five marriages ending in divorce, you have an abundance of single people attempting to form stabilized relationships. But men and women are different in the nineties. Women finally have their much desired "freedom." But then they started paying the price. Yes, there is a price tag on everything! Women are now acquiring all the diseases that have plagued men for years: anxiety, heart attacks, ulcers, stress and burnout. Finally, women looked in the mirror and said, "Whoa! Is this all there is?" Now they want marriage, the white picket fence and a committed relationship.

But the single men are saying, "Wait a minute. You wanted liberation. So you call us for dates, pay the ante and as far as committed relationships, well...we'll see." These new-wave Adams are subconsciously retaliating against women.

I am sure Adam is still perplexed about why his ass was kicked out of the Garden of Eden. Well, we all know why. Eve told him to eat the apple and the stupid fool did. He could have suggested chomping on an available pear, but he didn't. And, with the birth of Cain and Abel, came the first chromosomal split, which added unnecessary complexity to an otherwise basic man.

Through extensive research, careful observation and numerous hours researching with a psychologist, I have managed to categorize the many mutations of the original Adam. This information will help you figure out a man.

Cain & Abel

enerally speaking, most women want a permanent relationship or marriage with the right man. Some "luck out" while others trudge through life continuously involved with unsuitable partners.

In order to find an appropriate companion, the Abels if you will, a woman must first know what she expects from this association and then find the type of man who can provide her with these expectations.

By placing a man in his designated category and exposing his modus operandi and hidden agendas women can save precious time, emotional devastation and sometimes money, by quickly evaluating whether he is a Cain or Abel.

In the beginning of any relationship a woman must pay close attention to habits and patterns of the man she is dating. This observation will serve her well when it comes to making the right decision to continue or reject the partnership.

Psychologists claim that a person who is being deceitful can maintain a facade for almost one year. However, after that length of time their true personality will emerge. That is why long engagements or arrangements should be the rule before committing to someone on a permanent basis.

One mistake many women make is they think their intended will change with time, through love or constant bitching. "The leopard doesn't change his spots" is one cliché that happens to be partly true. There are some rare exceptions where a man will change as he matures but this usually takes an insightful person with great initiative.

Another reason women get involved with the wrong men—the bastards so to speak—is, let's face it, they are more exciting than their nice counterparts. Or at least they appear to be. They are usually different, erratic, off-center and of course keep their partner/opponent confused. Women mistake this type of lunacy for excitement. But a committed arrangement with these types can end up disastrous.

Women who continually choose the wrong man usually possess a low evaluation of their own worth. If we transported Ayn Rand's theory on why men pick certain types of women, the puzzle to this problem will be solved: "...a man's sexual choice is the result and the sum of his fundamental convictions. Tell me what a man finds sexually attractive and I will tell you his entire philosophy of life. Show me the women he sleeps with and I will tell you his valuation of himself....He will always be attracted to the woman who reflects his deepest vision of himself, the woman whose surrender permits him to experience—or to fake—a sense of self-esteem. The man who is proudly certain of his own value, will want the highest type of woman he can find, the woman he admires, the strongest, the hardest to conquer—because only the possession of a heroine will give him the sense of an achievement, not the possession of a brainless slut....There is no conflict between the standards of his mind and the desire of his body. Love is our response to our highest values—and can be nothing else."*

Now the key to this philosophy is know your own worth and never prostitute it by casting your pearls to the swine.

Hopefully, forewarned is forearmed. The rest is up to you.

*From *For the New Intellectual* (The New American Library).

Marvin the Manipulator

This is the vulture-like male who controls his prey—you—through assorted tricks, games and situations in which he takes charge. In the beginning, he will pursue you with a vengeance, never deviating for a moment. You will mistake this pursuit for his desire and commitment. This isn't always your fault because he will repeatedly profess his undying love. He will tell you what you want to hear. He knows his victim well, being a master of female psychology. His act is so perfect he will even be able to control you from afar. When he finally has you hooked, he then keeps tabs on you through subtle, calculated chicanery. You will be totally unaware of this flimflam until you begin to get the picture. By then, it's too late. You are trapped.

Marvin utilizes a variety of methods to regulate you and your activities. The phone is one of his most indispensable instruments, used brilliantly for "control purposes" (husbands who are having affairs burn up Ma Bell's lines). He must. It's imperative that he knows your whereabouts, so he will be safe to take "Deceitful Donna" out to your favorite haunt for a romantic dinner.

One woman I interviewed dated a man who worked until one in the morning. He would call her at 11:30 at night to make sure she was home. This, of course, was conditioning, like Pavlov's dogs. After he was assured she was home, snug in bed, he was free to make the rounds of the all-night lounges. His favorite nights out were Wednesday and Friday.

She never knew when he was going to "pop in" after work. Often, he'd wait until the last minute on a Saturday evening before he'd inform her of his impending arrival. The maneuver was done so he could see what action was available before committing himself to little loyal girlfriend.

Another manipulative trick he used was to never ask her out on his days off in advance. Why? Because, again, what if Miss Easy Action just happened along? Why should he be prevented from taking an immediate shot? This also precluded, so he thought, the girlfriend from making other plans.

Now, the manipulator doesn't like a fair game because he must be in control. When you—the manipulated—cease to follow the program, the relationship usually goes sour. Manipulators are users. They want something from you. You are never really sure what that something is because they don't play it straight. Be prepared to get hurt if you fall in love with one of these devils of deceit.

Before they have you hooked, they will go to any extreme to capture (trap) you. After they have succeeded, and the challenge is down to a roar, they begin to lose interest. However, they will continue to lie, professing their eternal love and how much they miss you that evening. The entire time, they're planning a night out at the local swinging singles club to do some cruising for new prey.

These guys are always cruising. The play never closes for the night. If you have a girlfriend you've introduced them to and they like what they see, they will even ask you more about her. They think they are so clever.

Years ago men of this nature manipulated their wives by monetary strings. Now, with more women in the world of commerce and controlling their own finances, it's difficult to use the ol' money caper. So they use sex. One of the greatest games is to get mad at you (for nothing really significant) just to pull you back in tow. You are totally perplexed by this ploy because it's difficult to communicate with a manipulator. They use anger to avoid any sexual contact. This again is control.

Men control women because they must have power. If they feel they are losing their authority over your actions and activities, it's a blow to their egos. In every relationship, there is a power struggle going on. When a man can manipulate you he has the power. This puts him in control. Smart women always make their partners think they have the power.

A manipulator is a taker. Now, you can't have a taker without a giver. One personality is strong, the other weak. A taker is inner directed: his world, his feelings, his ego. Everything is "me" and "my." Manipulative people intimidate and bully their mates; thereby keeping them on the defensive. Mature love excludes manipulation. It should be based on reciprocal respect.

Manipulators seek out weak people. So, if you find yourself being controlled by someone, you have no one to blame but yourself. A victim of a manipulator should make every effort to build the necessary strength to avoid being used by "M.M." Usually, women who marry or have relations with these users have a low self-image.

The first step to breaking out of the manipulated mold is to recognize that you're being controlled. Second, take measures to increase your self-confidence and image.

It's not a positive element in building your self-esteem to be involved with this insecure coward. The longer you stay with him, the more you will question your positive attributes. Manipulative people devour their prey, only to leave them emotionally destitute. Then they're on to another unsuspecting martyr.

How can one avoid a manipulator? Be aware. There are different types of control. A manipulator can be blatant, which is easier to detect. Or he could be subtle and more difficult to recognize.

There are certain tactics a "user" employs in order to manage his prey. Guilt, moodiness, physical attacks, emotional abuse and intimidation are all forms of manipulation.

Addictive people, alcoholics, drug abusers, etc. are masters. They transfer guilt to their mate/spouse and hide behind their addictions.

The minute you find yourself in one of these "sick situations," get out.

Test & Review

1. Don't take the blame for anyone when you know you are right.
2. Form your own opinions and have the confidence to stick with them.
3. If you disagree with someone, say so.
4. Be direct; manipulators aren't. They are cunning, conniving and deceitful.
5. If you won't allow yourself to be manipulated, the user will leave. On to greener pastures.
6. When someone becomes moody or sullen, don't take this personally, let him wallow in his own misery.
7. Be independent. This means physically, mentally and emotionally. People can't use you if you need nothing from them. The minute you become dependent on the other guy, you've placed yourself in a weak position.

CHAPTER 4

Romanticist or Rogue

ost people, including men, will place their best foot forward in the beginning of a relationship. Some can continue the masquerade, even up to a year, depending upon the carrot (reward). However, if you're perceptive and not "ego blind" you can usually tell within three months whether he is an authentic romanticist or a raging rogue.

"How?" you shriek. Pay attention! Awareness of everything this guy does, from the initial first date, is crucial. You'll have to read between the lines if he's a good actor, but usually even an Academy Award winner will make a mistake. And, of course, a lot depends on your inner security. If you're needy or desperate, with an unstable ego the length of Route 66, you'll miss the telltale signs.

I personally knew a very clever rascal, who passed himself off as an incurable romantic, when indeed, he was a dyed-in-the-wool rat. His apartment was filled to capacity with inspirational sayings, posters and poetry depicting love, life and the pursuit of happiness. He sent Susan Polis Schutz cards to all his new paramours, leading them to believe he was hopelessly in love with them and an extremely sensitive guy. This was of course not true; it was a contrived act. But he was aware that women are "suckers" for the sentimental types.

Rogues aren't stupid—they know what "hot buttons" to push. Romance is just one of them. They are aware that romance novels have been best sellers for years, signifying women are hungry for that ingredient in their relationships.

An international rogue who really uses the romance gimmick is the Southern European male, especially the Italian Stallion. This sagacious sorcerer is a master rogue when it comes to his polished manners, slurpy hand-kissing techniques, sexual antics and teary-eyed emotions. The same is true of gigolos. Italian gigolos are the very best at their craft—the epitome of the romantic rogue.

Another angle the rogue will use in conjunction with romance is possessiveness. This is a trait that bewitches women who often confuse jealously with love. In truth, possessive and jealous men are usually insecure as hell and use these pseudo emotions to keep their opponents off-guard. A woman dating an extremely jealous man never thinks he'd cheat on her. Usually, they do.

Now, there are truly very romantic men out there but you must learn to discern between the diamond and zircon. This again takes time. Women make a gross error in judgment by taking a man too literally, and hopping into bed with him too quickly. Then they are emotionally shattered to find, after a couple rolls in the hay, he's on his way. You must take the time to get to know the person before you get intimate, if you're interested in a long-term relationship. If not, take it like the rogues, a quick lay and what the hey!

More heartache has transpired (for women) from the hands of these romantic rogues. They can sweep you off your feet after several dates—and you're hooked! But they aren't. It is a game where they know the rules but forget to tell you.

Remember this: Men send flowers for one of two reasons. They really do care and are considerate, or they're guilty. How do you know?

Again, I say, it takes time. Go slow. If the guy is for real, he'll respect you and stick around. But if he's a rogue, he won't waste much time. He knows there's plenty of needy suckers out there who will take the bait.

Women who fall for these Satans in satin will lose more than emotions. Relationships from hell can cost some ladies thousands of dollars.

Every day you read or hear about some unsuspecting female who has had her bank account fleeced by a wolf in sheep's clothing.

One lady, looking for love in all the wrong places, met her Waterloo at a local watering hole and thought she had hit "pay dirt." Dirt was correct and pay she did. This lethargic Lothario had run the gambit with several previous conquests and, having just divorced one, had enough change (hers) in his jeans to romantically wine and dine the next sucker.

He checked around and knew she had some bucks stashed from her interior design business and several condos. She didn't check a damn thing but took him at face value, she thought.

Within several months, this romantic rogue had his name on a marriage certificate and all her goods. When she found out, much too late, what his game plan was, she was lucky to end up with a Town Car and one condo. He got her Mercedes, and the other condo (she signed a quit-claim deed), plus most of her money.

She now admits desperation for a companion was the reason. She didn't suspect a rogue in action. After the fact, she found out this was his modus operandi. In fact, one of his ex-wives agreed to be a witness against him in the new divorce. However, damage control was too late. He got to keep the condo, car and money. He's now off to greener pastures.

In the nineties, it's de rigueur to "check out" a potential husband. Many women, especially those who can't trust their own judgment, should hire a private detective to run a check on any man they are serious about. This is certainly acceptable and makes damn good sense. Unromantic and non-trusting, you bet. Smart, definitely.

If this tactic is too drastic for you, then meet his friends, business associates and family (and for damn sure introduce him to yours). Socialize with this guy. Oftentimes, a rogue can't cut the action if he thinks someone is watching his play.

Place him in every situation possible and watch his reasons closely. Men are great at ferreting out another man's ploys. Better than women. So use your men friends to help analyze the situation for you. And don't be so proud or stupid not to take their advice, especially if they care about you as a friend. Don't ever use another man who has designs on you for himself. You won't get a proper evaluation. Don't use your mother. Even if she's right, you won't admit it!

Test & Review

1. Don't be a sap. In the beginning let him treat you to dinner, gifts, vacations, etc. The biggest mistake women make today is immediately paying their own way and his. You'll know quickly whether he is a true romanticist or a rogue. Money is the humbler. A true rogue will take all the goods with a smile. A romanticist won't.
2. Beware of the man who "comes on" too fast. Sincere men don't compliment often, but when they do, it's usually sincere.
3. Ask questions. Then ask the same ones over again at a later date. See if the answers jive. Usually rogues are accomplished liars, but can be caught by a crafty lady.
4. Treat this category like any other group: be cautious, take it slow and, for God's sake, keep your Victoria's Secret underwear on, at least until you know who you're dealing with.
5. Don't be afraid to hire a private detective if things aren't making sense and the relationship is serious. Most agencies do this sort of work now. Just to conduct a personal background check isn't expensive. It's worth every penny.
6. Don't be greedy, needy or desperate, or you'll be the perfect target for any con artist.

Non-Committal Norman
and Other Crazies

If you are dating a Non-Committal Norman, life can be sheer hell. Many women I've talked to, who were involved with this type of man, almost ended up in the loony bin.

Now, most non-committals are a mutation or mixture of other categories. One particular woman dated such a combination. He was a Non-Committal Norman, Cheatin' Charlie (whom you'll read about in Chapter Six), pseudo-Gigolo (Chapter Seven) and Rogue all rolled up into one very contrived package. What you must understand before getting involved with a Non-Committal Norman is that every member of this breed is a FUBAR (Fouled Up Beyond All Recognition—or choose that other popular adjective for the first word).

One lady's true story will give you some insight into a real FUBAR. Before starting, a little background on both characters is important. The victim was bright, educated, attractive and talented, but extremely vulnerable. It was her first experience with such a scoundrel. So if it appears she was easily duped, beware—wolves enter in sheep's clothing.

We'll call the FUBAR "Norm" and his victim "Vi" for short. These two met, quite unexpectedly, but probably for a reason. You figure it out.

One evening, Vi and a gal pal had dates. They were to meet them at the Brazilian Court Hotel Lounge in Palm Beach. The men had suddenly returned to the West Coast for business reasons. This left Vi and her gal pal sitting at the Rio Bar, alone, having cocktails.

Enter Norm. He was alone and on his way to a concert. Of course, what he was really doing was hunting for another victim. He had recently discarded one after using her to the hilt.

Vi and friend were chatting and Vi, not interested in the least, had her back to Norm. He stood beside her and eavesdropped on their conversation. Vi's buddy, "Jane," noticed him and began to include him in their conversation.

He asked Vi to dance, bought them drinks and proceeded to pick up the tab. Jane decided he wasn't her fish and she joined another acquaintance having dinner in the restaurant.

Vi continued drinking, dancing and chatting with Norm. She wasn't overly impressed, but she was having fun. The evening came to an end and Norm offered to take her home on one condition—that she have dinner with him the following Saturday. She agreed.

A synopsis on both people is important at this point. Norm: looking for a woman with money to take care of him. Vi: not looking at the moment because a complicated business transaction occupied most of her thoughts. If she were looking, it would be for love (I didn't say she was brilliant).

Norm was a bartender on the verge of bankruptcy and divorced for 15 years with four grown children. He recently tumbled, by choice, down the corporate ladder. He left the wife to play bigshot with younger women, moved in with a hairdresser and lived with her on and off for seven years. He relocated to Florida to manage a bar which closed after one season, then lived the lazy life for a year of decadence and had been gainfully employed for six months.

Vi just sold her business the day before she met Norm. She had owned her own business for fifteen years and had been divorced for the past ten. Always a workaholic, this was the first time in her life she wasn't working on a project. She hadn't been emotionally involved for years. She was driven to succeed by her own talents and extremely independent, both financially and emotionally (or so she thought).

Back to the story. Saturday arrived and he promptly picked Vi up. Off they went to an elegant ocean-front restaurant. Vi still had no idea what he did for a living, but he appeared to know just how to impress a woman.

Dinner was terrific, dancing was exciting and the web was being woven. But Vi had reservations and particularly wondered why this guy felt so compelled to "sell" her. Unfortunately, Vi didn't listen to her inner voice.

Ol' Norm was really in hot pursuit by now because he knew she had recently sold her business. In fact, Ms. Naiveté showed him the sales contract. His eyes dilated, and not because he was dazzled by Vi's beauty. He saw dollar signs. Maybe this time he could hang in there for the crap shoot and just maybe his number would come up. He was sure he wouldn't crap out this time.

Norm continuously called for dates, but she declined. Her woman's intuition prevented her, for awhile, from accepting. Eventually, she agreed to go out with him and every time they did, she had a great time. But she still questioned herself why she couldn't relax and enjoy this guy.

By now she knew he was a bartender and had been for the past ten years. He claimed he had been suckered into this occupation when he was married and working for a large corporation. He began bartending after work for extra money. At least that's what he told his wife. In reality, he was more attracted to wine, women and song than the cash. He had been a real whoremonger where women were concerned. But Vi wasn't paying attention. The time was right for Norm because Vi was vulnerable.

He began professing his love for her early in the relationship and pushed for a commitment. He asked numerous questions about what she wanted out of life. This wasn't because he actually cared. He was formulating his strategy for the kill by uncovering Vi's "hot buttons."

It took him about four months to get her hooked and in the habit of seeing him. The fifth month he started working on her pocketbook. He grew moody, and compassionate Vi asked what she could do to help. He had to file bankruptcy, he told her, but didn't have the $800 for the attorney. Little generous Vi romped to the rescue and immediately lent him eight big ones.

Score one for Norm. Now he had established that he didn't have the money to continue wining and dining her first class. He also, indirectly, made it clear that if she wanted his company, she might have to pop for a buck or two.

Norm's birthday arrived and by now, Vi thought she was in a committed relationship. Wrong, darling. She was duped, but only because she was primed. She bought him a $150 shirt, Cartier cologne and decided they should go on a three-day excursion to a remote island in the

Bahamas. She would foot the bill, because, after all, he just filed bankruptcy and couldn't afford it.

This little sojourn cost her about $2,500 plus $500 in cash for him to gamble. Was she still the adorable one? Hell, no! He was moody, unromantic, sullen and, in general, an unappreciative bore. Little Ms. Spendthrift was perplexed and confused. Now, this was the time for her exit. The writing was on the wall, but she wasn't reading.

It was September, six months after she first met Norm, and it was beach-front condo hunting season for Vi. Of course, she took Norm along for his opinion. The unspoken words were saying, "We'll move in together." Never believe unspoken words.

Again, she noticed incredible mood swings and changes in attitude from him. But she dismissed it. One morning, over coffee, he even unwittingly verbalized his motive: "I should make you fall in love with me and then leave you." She told him that was a very strange thing to say. He quickly retaliated with, "I'm only kidding. I love you too much to do that." Sure, Norm.

Nefarious Norman was a womanizer from the word "go." He used them for anything they had to offer: money, sex, love, a place to live, bank loans, you name it. Nothing was sacred where this rogue was concerned.

By the end of September, he had started going out to late-night bars after work without her knowledge. Brainwashed Vi felt insecure within this pseudo relationship. Because she was committed, she assumed he was, too. Never assume anything.

Non-committal men never want to socialize with other couples or be placed in a social situation where people might assume he is part of a twosome. Vi got a sample of this when one of his married co-workers invited them over for Sunday dinner.

Norm was talking to Vi from work when the co-worker grabbed the phone from Norm and asked Vi if the two of them would like to come over for dinner. Vi, who thought they were a couple, readily accepted. Norm was furious. Again, Vi was confused.

The Saturday before the dinner, Norm was out romping at one of his all-night bars, unbeknownst to Vi. That Sunday, however, Vi was given a clue as to how this guy was keeping himself in circulation.

The dinner hostess innocently asked Norm, "Well, where did you go all last night?" Norm gave her a if-looks-could-kill look and lied, "Nowhere." Vi quickly picked up on his body language and attitude, and wondered why he was so upset if he hadn't done anything wrong.

After this and other subtle indicators, Vi began to pay attention. However, she was in the dating groove with this con too long and wasn't going to rock the boat. Wrong move! She should have immediately jumped ship.

Another reason Vi was having such a difficult time logically analyzing the situation was because this particular Non-Committal Norm was extremely complex. His objective was to live off a woman with money, date bimbos on the side and use both women until a better deal appeared. Now all of these traits come from gigolo tendencies. His non-committal problems may have been a smoke screen to cover his real motives.

Noxious Norm was a true hybrid of several types. But he used the non-committal act in the end, possibly to keep Vi off guard so she wouldn't see the real scoundrel. It doesn't make any difference whether he was a real non-committal or a counterfeit. The act is the same. If we were to cut through the psychological drivel, we would recognize that most non-committals are merely dyed-in-the-wool bastards.

Vi was still ignoring her inner voice as she vacillated between buying an ocean-front condo or a yacht to live in. In the fall, they began looking at motor yachts. She really needed him for the boat project because he was an all-round Mr. Fixit when it came to plumbing, air conditioning, electrical wiring and general repairs. Vi was hard pressed when it came to changing light bulbs. They spent the next three months boat hunting.

Norm seemed excited about the prospect of living on a yacht in Palm Beach. Vi was thrilled because this was one of her long-term goals. But every time they looked at boats, she would get a disturbing feeling in the solar plexus, which resulted in a severe anxiety attack. She had difficulty breathing and would occasionally hyperventilate.

The subconscious origin of these outbreaks was his remark months earlier: "I should make you fall in love with me and then leave you." Vi subliminally played that tape in her head. Fleeting thoughts told her he would live on the yacht for about six months, then leave her high and wet.

She was smart enough to realize she couldn't navigate and maintain a boat that size herself. Norm kept pushing her to make a decision. Every time she ignored her intuition and got ready to make the down payment, her trepidation grew stronger. By this time, the attacks were occurring regularly, but she still couldn't pinpoint their source. She just knew something wasn't right.

One day, they were driving along the ocean and he remarked, "I'll probably screw up this relationship, but so what?" Again, he was thinking aloud and Vi was shocked by this admission. And this time she paid attention. Did he want to sabotage this situation? The answer was "yes," as Vi would soon find out. At the moment, though, she loved him too much to rationally analyze his remarks and actions. Of course, what Ms. Vi thought was love was indeed nothing more than habitual lust. Norm really didn't possess the integrity and ethics Vi wanted in a partner.

His amoral attitude was evidenced by his negligence in paying back Vi's $800 loan. This omission puzzled Vi. She knew he had money. She'd watch him blow bills at the local bars like a drunken sailor. Not once did he offer her even a token payment. To Vi this was unthinkable. Especially since she knew his bar bills ran over $200 per week, not including his lavish tips.

Another one of his "ill-bred" antics was to talk about other women to Vi as if she were a male buddy. When he saw an attractive woman, he'd turn to Vi and ask if she knew her. Was she married? What did she do? Vi was appalled at his transparency and crudeness.

Vi was cognizant of the insensitivity he displayed and she realized it was a direct put-down towards her. However, what she didn't realize was ol' Norm was just getting cranked up in the game of "dump present gal for new one."

Robert Ringer, the author of *Looking Out for Number One* (Fawcett), calls this the Better Deal Theory. Ringer states: "The better dealers are those persons in whom the better deal inclination is totally out of control. It's human nature, once you have a 'deal' sewn up, to wonder about the possibility of there being a better one down the road."

Tracy Cabot, in her book, *How to Make a Man Fall in Love with You* (Dell), calls them wafflers. A waffler never makes a date in advance because he is afraid something better might come along and then he couldn't take advantage of this opportunity if he were committed to a previous engagement. He would then spend all night despondent over the date he missed. This guy is never satisfied. He is always looking for a better deal.

The waffler description fit ol' Norm to a tee. He worked in a bar, where women were in an abundance and the chances of a "hot number" sauntering in were high. He wanted to be available. That's why he never made any concrete dates with Vi beforehand.

Vi began to realize Norm wasn't long for this relationship. This made her glad she had decided against buying the boat. However, she was still in a state of confusion. Normie was giving her mixed messages. In one breath he would profess undying love and in the next, be pulling away. This guy was loaded with so many complexities, he would have had Freud in a strait-jacket.

Around this time, Norm, who had once been pushing Vi with a vengeance, stopped calling in the mornings. Naturally, he had some new victims spending the night. He also stopped calling every day. Sex was doled out stingily. Nights out became infrequent.

This Emily Post reject didn't have the common courtesy to communicate his true feelings to Vi. He had to play the game of cat and mouse. Our victim was beginning to catch on to some of his tricks and became more observant. She compared how he had been in the beginning of the relationship to his present state.

Initially, Vi had been just what Norm wanted: adorable, terrific, just perfect. Now everything was wrong with her, according to him. Her physical appearance wasn't up to par for him and her verbal abuse intensified. He figured if he put her down enough, she would leave. Obviously, he didn't possess the guts to communicate his feelings in a mature manner. But Vi wasn't moving an inch until she had more facts about this creep and he grew frustrated. He really had to get mean.

Christmas rolled around and the "bastard" gave Vi the performance of a lifetime. Two days before the 25th, Norm took Vi out to dinner. They had returned to her place and Norm was undressing. He informed Vi that he couldn't exchange Christmas gifts because he was broke. Vi knew he was full of baloney because he had been blowing money every night at the local pubs. In the nine months they had dated, Norm had never given her anything, so she really wasn't shocked.

Since Norm's statement didn't get a reaction from Vi, he jabbed from a different angle. "I'll bet you wonder how I can blow all this money in bars and not buy you a Christmas gift." Vi smiled and said, "No, I didn't wonder. I know why." This retort went right over his thick skull. Again, Vi didn't get mad or react the way Norm expected.

Christmas Eve arrived and Vi had been invited to a lovely dinner party. She, of course, foolishly asked Norm if he'd like to go. Norm, by the same token, because of guilt, suggested to Vi that they have a drink at her friends' home and then have a nice dinner out.

What Vi didn't realize at the time is that Mr. Norman had no intention of taking her out on a sentimental holiday dinner (pre-meditation, not spontaneity, are these rat's call letters). They agreed to have a drink at her friend's house first. Norm gulped down a glass of champagne and off they went to his friends' house, fifty miles up the road.

They arrived, but dinner was over, and he proceeded to drink for three hours. Vi kept waiting for Norm to suggest they leave to eat, but he never did. Finally, around 11:30, they left. Obviously, it was too late for dinner. When they arrived in Palm Beach, Norm proposed they go out for one drink at a bar around the corner. Vi was furious, but said nothing.

Since Vi was unusually quiet, Norm asked her what she was thinking about. "Nothing," she replied. They went back to her home together, but Vi slept on the sofa.

Two days later he took her out to dinner (even bastards feel guilty sometimes). He assumed this little outing would eliminate his guilt from Christmas.

They were sitting at a little Italian restaurant and he asked Vi what kind of wine she would like. He was fully aware that Vi never drank wine, but insisted on ordering a bottle. She remarked, "You are always bitching about money and how broke you are, so why waste the money if I'm not going to drink it?"

"You know, Vi," he replied. "You should take a lesson from younger women. I could bring them in, order a bottle of Dom and have them eating out of my hand." Vi grinned sardonically and answered, "OK, if you want that attitude, I can smile sweetly, act impressed and spend your money." (You've had it now, dear Vi). He leaned forward and said, "Frankly Vi, no disrespect, but you are too old to pull off that act."

Vi felt as if she'd been slapped in the face by this ball-less wonder. She managed to retain her composure, but filed his remark in the "Justification for Leaving Norm" section of her brain.

Since Vi didn't react the way Norm had anticipated (all previous prey had either slapped him in the face or poured a drink on his head when he displayed these tactics), he knew he'd have to get really mean.

Several days passed and they were having drinks at Nando's restaurant. Norm made a remark about a younger woman and an older man who had walked into the bar. Age was becoming a thing with Normie. After this minor interruption, he continued on his usual kick of how he hated working and was tired of his job. Vi turned to him and said, "You are always talking about how you want to take time off and how tired you are of working. If I said to you right now, let's buy that boat and sail the Caribbean for three months, you wouldn't do it."

He looked her directly in the eye and smiled, "That's impossible because you are too old and too poor." Vi's drink was poised in mid-air and she fought for composure. At that moment she began her plan of escape from this vicious, insensitive, insecure sewer rat. She said nothing. But she thought, "OK, you son-of-a-bitch, I'll beat you at your own game—a game you have played, by your own admission, for years on women."

When January arrived, Norm was still playing his games and giving Vi mixed messages. If he only knew she was on to his facade. She was still emotionally involved with the bastard, but knew that to salvage her self-esteem, ego and emotional well being, she had to end the quasi-relationship. He certainly wasn't in it for the long haul. It was all short-term as far as Norm was concerned.

Deep down, Vi knew it was a matter of a few weeks before she found the strength to call it quits. Her feelings jumped from love to hate and, ultimately, to sadness. She had fallen in love with a well-played image, not a real person. The real person was a bastard. The image was contrived. At times, it was difficult to differentiate between the two. But in the end, the preservation of her self-esteem won.

Vi went out of town for a week in mid-January for some minor surgery. The three days before she left, she heard nothing from him. Against her better judgment, she called him. He was pleasant, but cool.

While she was gone, he took a female bartender he had been seeing on the sly into a bar in town. The owner was a close friend of Vi's and he knew it. (Ah, the games people play!) He knew the friend would tell Vi—the final straw.

He never did call her the week she was out of town. Vi thought this was highly insensitive, especially since he knew she was having surgery. You'd show a friend that much consideration. She was hurt, confused and, mostly, angry. It was enough to prompt immediate action upon her return.

She called and told him she was home. He stopped by on his way to work. She offered him a drink and before the bubbles hit the back of his mouth, she informed him he had his much wanted freedom. He was genuinely shocked (she beat him to the punch).

She also mentioned that a $3.98 phone call to her hospital room could have prevented this entire conversation. Vi must have been feeling bold, because she then brought up the fact that Norm owed her $800 and that she expected every single penny back. He wasn't overly elated with this news, but figured he better make the effort. (And Vi still didn't know about the bartender he had been dating behind her back).

Norm left. Vi cried. Norm's ego and vanity were bruised. The loss experienced was not for a person whom he had loved, but for his own machismo.

Because Vi lived in a small community, she decided it would be best for her to at least be nice to Norm. After all, everybody knew everybody else's business and she chose to maintain a pseudo-friendship with Norm in hopes of curtailing the gossip. Instead of matching her maturity, Norm continued sending Vi mixed messages. He would ask her out, under the pretense of friendship, without Vi realizing he hadn't told anyone they had broken up.

He didn't want her, but couldn't stand the possibility she might date someone else. He certainly didn't want his cronies to see her out with anyone but him (bad for the macho image). He didn't make any attempt to put the relationship back together. He had no desire to.

Vi realized, after awhile, that in order for her to truly regain her self-worth, she'd have to cut Norm out of her life completely. She gradually accepted what had happened and, with a lot of soul searching, grew from the experience. She's determined to never become involved in a similar relationship again.

There is an old cliché some people believe in: "If something is too easy, too right, it must be wrong." This one statement is so incorrect, it's almost laughable. It causes more problems and heartache than all the others combined.

If a relationship is right, it is easy. It's almost effortless. Sure, it has it's ups and downs, but it's not like a full-time job. Most men and women are under the mistaken impression that if something works, you should still try to fix it.

Ringer, in *Looking Out for Number One*, declares, and rightfully so, "Cherish the relationships that seem easy and right. They are the ones that are." However, Ringer is talking about real honest partnerships, not those of the game-playing variety.

After extensive research into the Non-Committal Norman's games, I've come to the conclusion they are just plain bastards. In the book, *Men Who Can't Love* (Berkley), authors Steven Carter and Julia Sokol claim this is a phobia, somewhat related to claustrophobia. But there are men out there who, for whatever reason, don't want marital commitment.

Perhaps he's been married, is supporting an ex-wife and children, and has too many responsibilities to enter into another commitment. Maybe he was badly taken, financially or emotionally, in a previous relationship. Once stung, twice careful. Men who have never been married are also gun-shy because of fear.

The commit-phobics that Carter and Sokol expose are not only afraid of permanency, they are downright mean, game-playing, underhanded creeps. Most of them had another woman in the picture before dumping the one they supposedly loved. They have a strategy from the very beginning, starting with the hot pursuit. They "fall in love" almost immediately. After they have the victim hooked, they become phobic. Bull crackers!

The truth is, the challenge is gone and the game is won. Now, let's drop her on her royal arse. Let's use another woman to tear her self-esteem to shreds. This is a sick person all right, but I'll be damned if I'll compare him with a claustrophobic.

These men basically don't like women. If they did, they would just leave her and not start a personal attack or rub her nose in her already damaged ego via another female, often a close friend. Some psychologists say these men are sociopaths.

Women become addicted to and obsessed with bastards. It has something to do with the excitement, intrigue and mystery. It's the same reason that men love bitches—the challenge. You can never quite figure them out. But when you love yourself unconditionally, you don't allow another person to take control of your life.

The most difficult part about being involved with a Non-Committal Norman is letting go. In their book, Carter and Sokol recommend these women seek professional help. Why does the commitment phobic, if there really is such an animal, cause such havoc? Because the woman is totally in the dark about the games and mixed messages he is using on her. She is playing it straight and he isn't.

She is perplexed about why he won't commit and his reasons for leaving. She takes it personally. Who wouldn't? If she can face the fact that he is just a bastard, a womanizer, a liar, a cheat and not "phobic" in the least, she can get through the ordeal without dropping thousands on a psychologist.

Test & Review

In the beginning, it is difficult to know when you have a Non-Committal Norman in hot pursuit. However, there are some rules to follow that will help you uncover this taker.

1. People don't basically change. Once a bastard, always a bastard. So, number one, check this guy out. Find out how he treated his wife, children or past girlfriends. Their modus operandi follows a set pattern.
2. I highly recommend, before getting emotionally involved with any man, you hire a private investigator to pull some data on him—past and present. It won't cost that much and it will save you time, possibly money and emotional devastation. This is especially true if you're living in any resort area that attracts this type in droves. They are all running from a sordid past.
3. Observe this man closely. All want something from you; either money, a place to live, an image builder or ego booster—at your expense.
4. Never, and I mean never, stop dating other men until you have a very firm commitment.
5. Go very slowly in the dating and bedroom processes. Don't be available.
6. Do not change your life. Most women involved with these types of men acquiesce to their every whim.
7. Don't give up your friends—women or men.
8. Changing plans to accommodate him won't endear you to him and it doesn't ensure his love.
9. For God's sake, never call him or ask him out. And please don't pay for dinner or buy him gifts.
10. Check out everything he tells you. This "master of deceit" lies very convincingly.

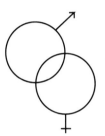

CHAPTER

Cheatin' Charlie

Cheatin' Charlies have been cruising around since God created man. The lines haven't changed one iota over several centuries. However, women are smarter and more independent now and more apt to call a Cheatin' Charlie's hand in the nineties.

Years ago, women turned their heads when ol' Charlie was found with his pants down, but not now. They don't have to tolerate philandering fellas just to keep a roof over their heads and Gerber's on the table.

In fact, when women find old Charlie the Tuna flipping around the mermaids nowadays, they use some innovative and creative tactics, either to get rid of the fish or keep him in a holding tank.

There was one terribly controlled and clever lady who knew her husband was seeing another woman and was also aware they were meeting during their lunch hour in the couple's camper. They all lived in San Francisco, where the terrain is hilly at best. Finally when the wife had enough, she followed her husband to where he and his amour parked for their lunch break.

She waited until they were in the heat of passion, then hopped into the cab of his "nooner schooner" and took-off at a rapid pace up one hill and down the other, interspersing this joy ride with a few speed bumps just for variety.

After much howling and begging from the surprised lovers, she acquiesced and drove directly to their home, backed the camper parallel to the garage door so they couldn't escape, and phoned her lawyer.

The lawyer arrived with divorce papers in hand as the disheveled and angry cohorts in crime disembarked. The husband was served and, to add the icing on the cake, the wife even asked for the camper in the settlement. The judge gave it to her!

Roaming Romeos do get their comeuppance when they're dealing with cunning mates. A couple managing a posh resort in the Caribbean had been experiencing marital discord because he, a Cheatin' Charlie from way back, couldn't keep his hands off the single "cosmo cuties" on vacation. He was so stupid, he'd play right in his own back yard by using any available room right at the resort where they lived.

His wife, onto his schemes for years, decided she would call his bluff. She informed him she needed to make a shopping trip to the mainland and would be gone a week. The hotel was filled with several willing playmates and she had no sooner left (he thought) for the airport when he was ensconced in an available room with a buxom guest. His first mistake (well, second; his first was thinking his wife had really left) was taking the phone (it had a very long cord) into the available accommodations right next to the office.

When his wife returned, she just followed the cord. Of course she had a pass key and she literally caught him with his britches around his ankles. The guest, who was naked as a jaybird, ran for the bathroom.

The wife, being a quick thinker, grabbed every stitch of clothing in sight and dumped it all in the pool. She then returned and proceeded to bang down the bathroom door. The female guest managed to run past her but not fast enough. Customers, who were sunning by the pool, watched as the wife chased a hysterical, bare-assed, island visitor off the island.

Ivana Trump should have taken a lesson from this next scenario. A very rich socialite (she married extremely well) suspected her hubby of cheating on her. She, being very civilized, hired a female private investigator to follow him. I must digress a moment. Before he would marry her, he demanded a prenuptial agreement, which she reluctantly signed and in their five years of marriage, she tried every trick in the book to get him to rescind it. He wouldn't.

On with the story. The detective did get the evidence. It turned out he was keeping a much younger playmate in an apartment not too far from their home. The wife sprang into action and asked her attorney to draw up papers, nulling the existing pre-nupt. With papers in one hand and a martini in the other, she approached Cheatin' Charlie with a gleam in her eyes.

Handing him the detective's report and, of course his martini, she asked politely if he would please sign the papers voiding their prenuptial agreement. Turning green and gulping down the gin, he reluctantly did the deed.

It was either sign the papers or run the risk of being hauled into court by a very irate wife, and losing more money than he'd originally anticipated. Now they are both happy.

Men aren't the only ones who cheat in the nineties. *Cosmo* did a sex survey and found 39 percent of married women have cheated on their husbands. Two out of the three mates weren't aware of the infidelity.

Men don't possess that sixth sense that women have, especially when their spouses are being perfidious. Women just seem to know these things. Why? I think the female species is more suspicious of men. For years women have been the brunt of male tricks and possibly it's genetic, handed down from woman to woman.

If you don't possess that sixth sense there are some telltale signs that could alert you, like a bright red flag, whether your husband is a Cheatin' Charlie or just thinking about it.

People are creatures of habit, especially men. If your hubby doesn't give a fig about clothes, then suddenly looks like he hopped off the pages of *GQ*, you'd have to be blind and a little stupid not to think someone at the office (a client, customer or that cute little waitress) hasn't caught his eye. A radical change in dressing, up not down, is the clue.

Men notoriously don't pay attention when women talk. They tune out, so this next clue will be difficult to detect. A dead give-away is when a man appears to be off on another planet. His mind and body aren't with the program; he isn't responding; his attention is elsewhere.

Money or the lack of it is a real tip-off. A man who is tight with his funds is usually the same with his emotions and compassion. You, as a partner in a marriage commitment, should be kept aware of all money matters. Many women don't want to be bothered with this issue and are kept in the dark until Harry kicks the bucket. Then the banker, lawyer, stockbroker or town gigolo takes them to the cleaners.

Also, it takes money, lots of it, to conduct an affair properly. Make sure you're aware of the financial end of your marriage, and when something appears suspicious in the "money department," you'll be able to spot the problem quickly.

Many men have been able to keep two households going financially, just because the wife was kept in the dark about their financial status. One Cheatin' Charlie kept his wife and present mistress in grand style. They conveniently took separate vacations and all was copacetic until the trips to Mexico and the Caribbean for the affair, coupled with the jewelry bills, got a little too much for the hassled hubby to bear. Something had to give, and it was the wife's trips, charge accounts, etc.

When push came to shove (and the wife found out about the mistress, who was still flying to romantic places and dressing like Mrs. Astor's pet horse), she came unglued. This added insult to injury. She demanded all the mistress's jewelry, clothes and furnishings be returned— to her. Well, the husband ended up in the hospital with a horrible case of stomach and intestinal problems, along with being tranquilized to the hilt. Another way to curtail his philandering.

Witnessing many of my friends' affairs, I've never seen a positive thing about them. Both partners are miserable because the jilted mate can never totally trust again. Even if Cheatin' Charlie comes to his senses and becomes completely faithful, the wife keeps his past performance hidden somewhere in her mind and soul, and this suspicion detracts from both parties getting on with their lives.

"Open Marriages" are a sham, a crock. I've never seen one of them work. It is used between two people to offset a total commitment. Take the couple that made national headlines in Fort Lauderdale, Florida. The husband, a policeman, was prompting his wife to entertain men and charge them for sex in their home during the day, while he watched and even made videos from a closet.

To hear them tell the story, they were a happy couple with this arrangement, totally well adjusted. Further into the story when the truth emerged, he beat the hell out of her, she fell in love with one of her clients, and they ended up splitting.

Marriage is a tremendous responsibility and if your intended hasn't "sown his wild oats" yet, don't enter this institution with him. Allow more time for the guy to get it out of his system. The divorce rate has skyrocketed. Why be a statistic?

Test & Review

1. You've got three phones, a fax, car phone and all means of communication in the home, but he's got to run to the store for something, any trumped-up product. You can bet he's making a phone call to his present beloved.
2. You tell him the house is on fire, and he says, "Huh?" He's thinking about something or someone else.
3. He's been a slob since the day you married him, but suddenly he's "Mr. Gentlemen's Quarterly." He's got something, or someone, on his mind.
4. When men are having an affair they want to smell good. Double deodorant and tons of men's cologne. Give him the "sniff test."
5. The old "work late at the office" is so trite, but they still use it. Watch his work habits. If they change drastically, beware. Make a surprise visit to the "place of business" and check out all the "sexataries."
6. Money and credit cards are fabulous "tell-alls." Check those receipts and bank statements, along with the canceled checks.
7. If it's his first affair and he's truly sorry, chalk it up to "Male Menopause," curiosity, a mistake, whatever. But if it becomes a habit, you've got a Cheatin' Charlie on your hands.

CHAPTER 7

Just a Gigolo

Webster's definition of gigolo is "a man paid to be a woman's escort."

Well, ol' Webbie should have elaborated on this subject. Gigolos are men who play for pay. Not only are they paid to escort a young woman, they also pocket the cash for having sex with them. They entertain and live with or off these desperate ladies. Sometimes they marry them, for money.

You will find more gigolos in Los Angeles, Palm Springs and Palm Beach than anywhere else in the United States because this is where the women with money reside. It's a toss-up which location houses the majority of these womanizers, but I'll bet, per capita, Palm Beach, Florida wins.

They fare well in this haven for the rich and famous because men are at a premium in Palm Beach, and the social scene is more intense there than other areas. From January through May, the Polo circuit is in full swing. About 200 formal balls, several hundred cocktail parties, private functions and numerous gallery openings create the social circle in a short time.

Women just can't appear unescorted to a formal party, so short of hiring an escort, they must comb the area for an available male. Gigolos know they are in demand, so they usually get a position as tennis or golf pro, bartender, maître d' or some flunky job where they meet wealthy women, and they are set for the season.

Years ago, these "men of the evening" were suave, debonair, classy and could certainly tango. They were classified as "playboys." Even though they dated and married wealthy women (even accepting a settlement when the marriage disintegrated), they had more class than the current gigolos. They flew private planes, played polo, cruised onto the scene with their yachts and drove vintage cars.

That era is long gone and has been replaced by men in rented tuxedos, or ones purchased by their keepers, who drive an early model Cadillac and certainly can't tango. However, many are "well-kept" and enjoying "la dolce vita" without costing them a cent.

These masters of deceit are determined to get something for nothing. They think all play and lots of pay is de rigueur for the kept man. They don't realize they must pay the price and usually the price is even too high for these dirty, rotten scoundrels. "We earned it the old-fashioned way, we worked for it," isn't in their limited vocabulary.

However, they are conditioned to easy come, easy go. They never feel bad over a broken marriage or relationship. As one gigolo put it, "I lived the good life for awhile. It was an opportunity I wouldn't have otherwise enjoyed." He is back bartending, looking for his next bank account.

Some don't fare too badly. After years of practice, they usually become masters of manipulating their female customers/acquaintances into their web and collect a few shekels if only for a short time. This is their real occupation. In fact, one gigolo reported he approached each relationship in just that manner. It's going to work eight hours a day.

Gigolos are the takers of society, the users. They are vacant, possessing neither depth, soul, emotional attachment or feelings. They are inner-directed, selfish, transparent and self-serving.

All gigolos share the same goal: marry or date a woman with money who will keep them in the manner they *think* they deserve. And what do these unoriginal users have to offer women? Not an exceptionally high IQ. However, women want men, particularly one she can dress up and take out.

Bartenders are in the best position to survey the situation as women talk to them, often on an intimate level (and let's face it, women talk about their personal business). So these "cocktail hustlers" can really hone in on an available wealthy meal ticket.

There was the gigolo who was cruising the California coast for a wealthy playmate and found a sucker he could con. He put on the "show" and she wanted an encore. She offered to keep him in the manner to which he had become accustomed, by someone else's money. He demanded his male friend move with them to Florida and share their apartment. She balked at this idea, but he refused to budge without his chum.

She bought the program, hook, line and stinker. The trio moved in and all was well until he wanted his freedom. True to form, he started a horrendous fight which culminated in her moving out of her own apartment. Dumb he wasn't. She gave him money and he paid the rent. He had the lease changed to his name. She furnished the place, paid the bills and literally kept his ass on a silk cushion.

Several months passed and one evening he and his male friend decided to go out cruising for another meal ticket. As they were leaving the complex, he thought he saw her car, but foolishly dismissed the thought. When they came back in the wee hours of the morning and opened the door, they got quite a shock: no furniture, television, stereo, etc. She and Daddy (who talked some sense into her head) had rented a truck and hired some movers. Well, the two gigs had to scramble for some quick money. Gigoloing isn't always a "day at the beach."

Many relationships between gigolos and "sugar mamas" are consummated with the woman putting her gigolo in business. She's indirectly making him an honest man. He's making a living and, first and foremost, she's got him by the balls. He can't or won't leave his own business. However, most of these broads who are so free with a buck used men (their husbands) to acquire this money and time is running out for them. Very rarely have I heard of a woman who had to work nine to five for her paycheck keeping a house gigolo.

Most women, however, who put their paramours in biz hold the trump card. Everything is in their names: corporation, the lease, the bank account. Of course, this is if they are smart. If not, they have no ace in the hole.

If he is an equal partner, he has a couple of angles to use. If the bank account is in both names, he can skate and wipe out the funds. And if his name is on the corporation papers as equal partner, well she's going to have to split the profits.

There are very few professional gigolos left in the business, as the amateurs have taken over this field. Nowadays, most older single men want women with money, so they are following in the footsteps of their professional brothers, and vying for the loot.

I've known many women who have fallen for these "preying mantises" and have been taken to the cleaners, when just an ounce of prevention or some intelligence could have preserved their inheritance or trust fund.

One victim, who naturally attained her money in a divorce settlement, lost $500,000 playing with one of the vultures, who was a member of the Gigolo Club. These men aren't stupid when it comes to conning a woman. First they are aware they have a stupid woman in tow, because if she had an ounce of brains she wouldn't be associating with him or paying his way. So, they have the upper hand in this relationship from the beginning.

Many a prominent socialite or celebrity has succumbed to the advances and ploys of a gigolo boyfriend and then has been left financially lighter, but a wee bit brainier.

Anytime a man is more interested in your financial status, bank accounts, trust funds or divorce settlements, you're probably dating a gigolo or wanna-be play for pay man. Dump him pronto.

Test & Review

How do you know you have a gigolo in residence?
1. Gigs "come on" quickly—somewhat like their twin, the hustler. They immediately turn on the charm. They are in lust, then the big "L" by the fourth date.
2. Your reaction should be slow, slow, slow. Never, and I mean never, stop dating other men.
3. A gigolo will let you know, after he has you hooked, that he's financially in the hole. He plays on your sympathy.
4. Don't lend him money. Don't buy him dinner. Don't buy him gifts. And keep your bank statements hidden. Don't let him know you have a red cent.

After the last piece of advice, the gigolo will leave of his own accord very quickly. If a gigolo thinks he can't extract anything from a woman, he's on to easier prey.

"Mommy's Dearest"

This is one of the most important chapters in the book if you really want to "figure out a man." Let's face it, his mother is the first person in the universe a man feels, sees and is aware of, from the time he emerges from the birth canal until he is weaned. She's closer to him than ham and cheese pressed between two slices of bread.

Mom's psychological make-up and how she relates to him from birth through puberty will determine how he treats the women in his life. The old wives' tale of "watch how a man reacts to and treats his mother and you can tell whether he truly likes or detests women" is true.

Other factors play a deciding role in his behavior. How does the father, if there is one, communicate with the mother, his wife? Is respect and love apparent or is he a mean, domineering son-of-a-bitch who beats the wife and kids?

My father used to say, "Marry an orphan, then you won't have to deal with his family." Another one of his famous quips was, "Children grow up in spite of their parents."

Psychologists claim that a child's personality is developed by the age of five and those formative years a boy spends with his family, or more specifically, his mother, will either taint his attitude toward women or he will respect and love them. Some men simply love women, all women. This is a direct compliment for "Mommy Dearest."

Truman Capote, the famous writer and notorious character, by his own admission was a mess because of his mother. Nina, who was somewhat unbalanced, would lock him in a closet or room as a child and go out for the evening. This caused tremendous claustrophobic tendencies in little Truman and he never forgot Nina's horrendous treatment, even on his deathbed. Her disregard for his early psychological welfare caused Truman to be chased by imaginary demons his entire life.

The hand that "rocks the cradle" makes the person what they are, man or woman. And if you bother to observe how a man communicates with his mother, you'll have a better insight into how he will treat you in a relationship.

Fathers play an important role in the formative years, whether it be overtly or through subtle suggestions, by their actions toward the mother. Little boys emulate the male parent and during the early rearing this is their only "role model."

The "good ol' boy" who treats his wife as a chattel will demonstrate to the male child how he should treat women. This son, most generally, will grow into an adult version of the old man, unless he sees his friends' parents reacting to each other in a different manner. Early schooling with understanding teachers may off-set an otherwise imperfect parental emulation.

Abusive parents usually produce abusive children, who grow up to become abusive adults. Sometimes they go to the other extreme and can't bear to reprimand their children, thus producing a "Dennis the Menace" type.

If your husband was lucky enough to have had a reasonably stable and normal childhood, you'll still have to be on your toes where "Mommy Dearest" is concerned. The quickest way to alienate your spouse is to bitch about his mother. And the easiest way to insure peace in the family is to praise his mama and try your damnedest to get along.

Unless she is the "Wicked Witch of the West," this shouldn't be too impossible or unbearable. Positive actions breed positive reactions and niceness perpetuates the same. So begin your relationship with her on the right footing and you'll have an ally, plus reduce undo friction in your immediate household.

Mothers can cause havoc on the minds and emotions of their female children the same as the male child. However, girls mature faster and as children are more precocious and emotionally independent. They sometimes avoid problems the female parent can create.

Men grow up with an inbred competitive nature which causes anxiety even into adulthood. Unable to fully relax and enjoy the adventure of of life, they must constantly be on guard in school, the work place, leisure and love. This competitive nature places an extra burden on them emotionally. Even post-menopausal men can be witnessed throwing horrendous temper tantrums on the tennis and golf course.

I play tennis with three men, four times a week, and this time has given me great insight into how these guys react. All are college educated, reasonably intelligent, but brutal when it comes to an inconsequential game such as tennis. I often wonder if they take the rest of life that seriously. These men will cuss, scream, throw racquets, hit balls out of the court and literally slam tennis balls down your throat, if they miss a shot or lose a point. Luckily, I can duck quickly.

Mothers can be a source of tremendous support to their children, especially men, due to the stress placed on them by society and peer pressure. They need assistance both emotionally and intellectually. It is particularly important in the father-and-son relationships where the adult male is jealous of his off-spring.

Many times, men aren't terribly supportive of their male children, placing unusually high standards and expectations on them at an early age, especially where sports or business is concerned. Couple this with an already existing competitive nature and you have one stressed child/adult. If the parent didn't "hit the mark" in his own life, he transfers his goals and aspirations to the son, placing an extra burden on the child. This is when the child or young male adult needs nurturing by a compassionate and intelligent female. This is when strong mothers can make the difference between success and failure in their youngsters. Milton Berle, the famous comedian, was blessed with a strong, dedicated mother who prodded young Miltie onward toward a successful career. Without her, he admits, the going would have been tough and quite possibly he wouldn't have climbed the ladder of stardom. Jackie Stallone was a domineering force behind her son Sylvester. And the list goes on where mothers of famous men were the catalyst that propelled them forward along the path of much adversity.

(A wife, who is supportive can assist a man in becoming successful, even if it's just by being a good human being, as in the old adage, "behind every successful man, there is a woman.")

Even though Truman Capote had an insensitive and selfish mother, he was supported by several aunts and female childhood friends. In the beginning and throughout his early career that foundation gave him some stability in his otherwise unbalanced life.

Of course, the reverse is often a deterrent when the mother is too possessive and stunts the emotional growth of her "little darling." These

"Mama's boys" can make terrible husbands, never accepting responsibility or commitment because Mommy always handled their problems or ran interference for them in the early years.

The best advantage a mother can give to a male child is to teach him independence, ethics, morals and manners, and just be there with the iodine, Band-Aids and a tremendous amount of reassurance.

Children who are overprotected can't develop emotionally enough to handle life's harsh realities. Parents should always be there, even if it's as a sounding board, and even if their child is a sixty-year-old codger with a problem. However, they must give these people "tools" to grow and mature.

Never forget, if you have a male child, you will someday become a mother-in-law too. And "what goes around comes around," that old law of the universe. So treating your husband's mother with as much kindness as you can muster, regardless of circumstances, is the best advice.

Test & Review

1. Would you like to place his mother on a skateboard and take bets on whether she's alive when she hits the bottom of the hill? Then you probably have a "Mommy's Dearest" in residence.
2. Would you rather have Macy's "shoved up your arse sideways" than have lunch with your mother-in-law? Yep, you've got the "Mommy's Dearest disease."
3. Do you gulp several tranquilizers when you know his mother is coming for dinner? You have it.
4. When your mother-in-law visits overnight or for an extended stay, do you place her on a cot in the basement next to the furnace? For shame, Mommy Dearest deserves better.
5. So you have a "Mommy Dearest" for a mother-in-law, but love your husband. Slip her a double vodka and tonic on her next visit and hope she snoozes most of the time away. Do a triple at night.

CHAPTER

Cinderfella or Gay Blade

I chose to combine these two categories for simplicity's sake, not to imply they are similar. A Cinderfella is not always gay, he is just a man who wants to live the "good life" while a woman pays the rent. The Gay Blade usually attaches himself to a woman, most generally of financial status or celebrity, becoming more of a companion or friend. This connection, he hopes, will further his career or social standing in the community.

Many women have "gay friends." They can make acceptable escorts, be great gossips, assist in decorating, shop, help to create that "drop dead" image and be there when you need a shoulder to cry on.

Sometimes, especially in resort areas that attract the rich and famous, Cinderfella is a gay male who makes a business out of escorting divorcees, widows or single heiresses to social functions in exchange for important career or social contacts. Unlike the gigolo or professional escort, who enjoy their occupation for money, the gay blade is a modern-day walker.

In the thirties, forties and fifties, escorts were called walkers and, as their name implies, they escorted prominent ladies to certain functions, without pay. However, I'm sure they were handsomely rewarded.

Now in the nineties you have Cinderfellas who actively pursue women of means for their money. Men have been "marrying up" for centuries. Ari Onassis was one such scion who always believed you married above your station. However, many Cinderfellas are dirt poor and really have nothing to bring to a relationship but that rarity of being an available male.

A gay blade who signifies the personification of a Cinderfella was our friend Truman Capote. In the late sixties and early seventies, Truman was every socialite's date and traveling companion. Escort to Lee Radziwill, Jackie O's baby sister, and a gaggle of other internationally famous people, Truman traveled and house-guested in style. From "21" in New York to Harry's American Bar in Venice, Truman enjoyed "la dolce vita" with the jet set. Every prominent lady he escorted or traveled with thought him a wonderful companion, choosing Tru over most of their busy and boring husbands any day.

However, all the time Truman was being charming, he was taking notes for his "tell all" book, *Answered Prayers* (NAL-Dutton), which were thinly disguised stories about the "swans," as he called his ladies. "Little T" became persona non grata within the social cadre. He was somewhat perplexed when he tearfully lamented, "what did they expect, I'm a writer, that's what I do for a living. I'm not here just to entertain these people." Following the publication of that book until the day he died, his lovely swans never spoke to him again and his days of being "Cinderfella" were over.

There are heterosexual males who are wanna-be Cinderfellas—and don't possess creative talents, their own money, or anything unusual to add to a relationship—but are just plain disgusting, bordering on the gigolo category. In fact, I have more respect for a gigolo, who knows what he is and plays the game accordingly, than I do some of these men trying to grab a free ride.

Usually you can find a bevy of Cinderfellas hanging around like "lounge lizards" after a rain in resort towns that attract wealthy women. Palm Springs, Palm Beach, Scottsdale, La Jolla, Los Angeles, Miami, the French Riviera, are just some of the locations these "play for pay" pseudo gigolos congregate.

They most generally live on the edge financially. They are on fixed incomes, small trust funds, Social Security checks, or, if they are a young Cinderfella, in a commission sales position.

Women with money often know they have a Cinderfella or gay blade on the string and don't care. It's worth every penny to have companionship and they can afford the expense. It's the women who are taken in by these freeloaders and can't afford them I worry about.

For example, one school teacher had saved about forty-thousand dollars toward her retirement when she "fell in love" with a yacht captain who had designs on her money.

Eventually, he lightened her bank account of the forty big ones and had the balls to ask her to borrow more money so they could go into business together. When last seen, he was sailing off into the sunset, without a word, toward greener pastures. Not bad for six months work.

Many women who marry a Cinderfella end up paying alimony when they divorce this pilot fish. In the "Showdog" chapter in *How to Figure Out a Woman*, I name some of the women who paid outlandish settlements to their Cinderfellas. Joan Collins, socialites too numerous to mention and a myriad of everyday women have paid to play. Money is the aphrodisiac, or the deodorant as one lady so aptly put it. She claims it covers up a lot of stinks you'd rather not handle. Men are mesmerized by money as rapidly as women and these types of men have no compunction about dipping their hands into your gold.

Test & Review

1. Never, and I mean never, give a man money. If he is still around after six months of paying his and your way, you probably don't have a Cinderfella.
2. Women make the mistake of talking too much about their finances. How do you think these gigolos and Cinderfellas know you have it? Of course, it doesn't take a mental giant to surmise as much if he picks you up in a million-dollar mansion on the ocean. However, you can downplay the financial aspect of your life by conning him—touché. Tell him you're living on a small trust and, by the way, you're short this month; could he loan you a couple of thousand. If he is a Cinderfella, he'll be down the highway without you.
3. If he asks for a loan, inform him you'll have to talk to your accountant, then graciously tell him your old mean business manager won't advance any of your allowance. Of course, he'll hang in there for awhile, just knowing you have a buck or two. However, you'll sleep easy, knowing he doesn't have it.
4. If you're desperate for "male companionship" and want to marry a Cinderfella, pre-nupt, pre-nupt, pre-nupt. This could backfire, as you have elevated his standard of living and when he goes to divorce you, the judge, who could be a Cinderfella himself, might decree alimony payments. Talk to a lawyer!

CHAPTER **10**

What Makes Sammy Run?

Why do men run from committed relationships and marriage? Let's first assume we are dealing with a normal man. You've established, beyond a reasonable doubt, that he isn't a Non-Committal Norman (or another type of crazy), a gigolo, or just another neurotic nincompoop. First, we'll examine the unappealing characteristics a woman can exhibit that influence a man's decision to run. Secondly, we'll look at how events in a man's life may also cause him to flee.

Men run from possessive, obsessive, desperate and neurotic women. They will also run, fast, from addictive women. There are plenty of women out there who have lost men because they've shown too much of the insecure side of themselves. There is another reason, however, a much more common one, that makes Sammy run. If the female is too easy, sexually, chances are he'll bolt like a bat out of hell. You heard me. You believed the opposite. Wrong, darlings. To prove it, I will quote from several books on this subject. Check out "Roll Over Baby, I Think I Love You." It gives detailed descriptions of women who "rolled over" too quickly and didn't even get a phone call.

An old book, called *The Anatomy of a Love Affair*, written by Evelyn Bourne in 1965, states: "Regardless of how broad-minded a modern woman's attitude is toward sex, the man involved would still prefer to put up a fight of some sort with the girl he's got his sights set on, whether for purposes of matrimony or seduction. A man's a man and a woman's a woman and in spite of the vote, nothing basic has really changed since grandma's time."

A woman admits to a man she's physically attracted to him and she's baited her hook properly; he's flattered enough to become interested in this paragon of good taste. But if he makes a pass at her and she answers, "Why not? I'm a big girl now," he's going to back away...emotionally, if not physically, for she's taken the pride of accomplishment out of the affair in one fell swoop. And unless she's unusually cold-blooded, what girl wants an affair that's lacking in emotional rapport?

Another quote supporting the same theory is from a book called *No More Lonely Nights* (St. Martin) by Dr. Stephen Price and Susan Price. It says: "A man is delighted to be seduced, but that's not going to make him want to get you to the altar. The woman who obviously maneuvers a man into a hotel room or her apartment is sending him unrewarding messages about the nature of their relationship. She isn't stimulating his desire to get to know her as a person, but is letting him put her in a quick, convenient category: someone to sleep with when he feels horny."

In their paragraphs about coming on too strong, they say: "If he is genuinely reaching out to her, his initial gestures are usually subtle, even tentative. You will scare him away with strong or demanding responses just as he is beginning to make himself vulnerable. When a man feels attracted to you, he is in a state of emotional arousal, and you want to keep him in this active mode, not to reduce his passivity by a barrage of energy. There is truth in the cliché that a woman who is somewhat hard to get is appealing to a man. He must feel that the pursuit is his idea."

Relationship Sabotage, by the same authors, states very simply that, "Through the stages of courtship rituals, which are usually very romantic, people learned how to love. Unsophisticated earlier generations knew something the swinging singles do not: If you have sex too soon, this romantic phase never gets fully developed...

"Women must realize that many men tend not to integrate love and sex in the way most women do, and that men will easily disconnect from their loving feelings when they feel vulnerable. In the early stages of a relationship, a man might press for sex as an avoidance of getting emotionally involved, actually using sex as a defense against real closeness. When you exercise your power to withhold sex, you allow a man to get in touch with his deeper needs for you as a whole person, rather than merely as a sex object."

OK. You've gotten past the problem of sex and when to have it in a new relationship, but somehow, he just doesn't act like he feels the same way. First, you need to stand back and consider if you're pushing too soon for a commitment. Women are notorious for prematurely expecting a man to dedicate himself to a serious relationship. This step inevitably backfires and he usually splits. Next, you must ask yourself some questions. Is he the primary focus of your existence? Does your life revolve around him? Do you associate with people other than his friends? Do you do everything for him? Do you have interests besides his hobbies? What have you done lately that was just for you?

Men have enormous egos. And, in the beginning of a relationship, it massages their egos to have a woman exhibit dependency. However, this grows old. The man might begin to feel smothered, or that the relationship is becoming too much like a responsibility, or that his freedom is somehow being impaired.

When he begins to feel this way, he'll give you clues. But you need to pay attention. He may start picking fights over absurd things. He may criticize you for no reason. He may not call as often or perhaps break dates. You need to recognize this as a red flag, signaling that he is not happy and may be thinking of running. Examine your actions and reactions in the relationship. It's quite possible he feels that you're acting obsessive, possessive or neurotic. If you believe you are, after analyzing the situation rationally and objectively, then maybe it's time to look for a new relationship.

If you realize you've been exhibiting some of these characteristics, then it's time to develop other interests. Start looking for other outlets so your life is more balanced. Take a class, join an organization, learn a new sport. Do something for you.

This will give him some relief and allow you to gain the self-confidence and security necessary to stop acting the way you have been. Chances are the relationship will improve with your new-found independence. If it doesn't, like they say in the used car business, "get a new customer."

There are many situations that occur in a man's life that influence his actions in a relationship and his decision whether or not to commit. There are tons of single, divorced men. Believe it or not, a divorce affects a man as much as a woman. If he feels he's being taken to the cleaners, financially, emotionally or both, by his ex-barracuda, he's going to be very hesitant to commit any time soon. He's going to be guarded to say the least. He may also be paying a fortune in alimony or child support, which will have an impact on his dating availability and budget.

If a man has spent time in an unhappy relationship, he probably isn't chomping at the bit to get seriously involved again. Yes, men can get hurt too. Men can also become extremely involved in their careers while climbing up the ladder and simply not have time for a serious relationship. The most obvious reason a man is reluctant to commit is that he is just having too much fun playing the swinging bachelor. He's out dining and dancing several nights a week, each time with a different woman. He sees no reason to settle down with just one.

If you really want to get a clear picture about whether a man is likely to run, you must look at his childhood. How does his father treat his mother? Are his parents divorced? Did he have a reliable role model, teaching him how to act in a committed relationship? His father and mother's relationship is of the utmost importance because it was his first experience with male/female interactions and probably the one that will have the most impact in his adulthood.

When you desire a committed relationship with a man, you must examine both you and your actions as well as his history. Then, and only then, can you make an intelligent decision about whether it's the real thing. If you decide it is, then it's going to take a lot of work, for both of you, to sustain it. If it doesn't work, and he still runs, it wasn't meant to be. And you really don't want a man who's that intimidated and threatened by a commitment, do you?

Test & Review

1. Get to know the man. If possible, meet his family. This will tell you if he has healthy-relationship role models.
2. If he's divorced, inquire about what type of marriage he had. Depending on the answer, you'll understand a lot more about his attitude toward new women in his life.
3. If marriage is your goal, keep your mouth shut in the beginning. Men are allergic to the word.
4. Remember, don't be possessive, obsessive or neurotic. Control your jealous emotions.
5. Cultivate outside interests. Keep your life balanced.
6. Don't be a mommy; be a mistress.
7. If Sammy does run, don't waste one minute suffering or working your brain overtime to figure out why. Get a new customer!

CHAPTER

11

Penis Power

Since the birth of mankind, women have controlled and manipulated men with sex. Throughout history, women have been able to de-throne, decapitate and destroy the male species via sexual manipulation.

The world was ruled through vagina power. Entire civilizations were brought to their knees by man's sexual vulnerability. Let's take Samson and Delilah. Not only did he lose the hair, he lost his power and eventually, his kingdom. While Salome danced for King Herod, John the Baptist forfeited his head.

Cleopatra ruled two men, Caesar and Antony, indirectly giving her control of the Roman Empire. Napoleon couldn't even get through a bloody battle without penning love notes to Empress Josephine. And in a more modern saga, Jackie O seduced Aristotle, not only with her powerful image, but with her femininity. But, after several years of marriage and many millions of dollars, Jackie's breathless little girl act grew stale for Ari and he couldn't get out fast enough. However, he died before the ink on the new will was dry and Mrs. O ended up with $20 million.

With "women's liberation" came true liberation for the male and total loss of control and power for the female. Women fought against being sex objects, thus bestowing their sexual prowess upon the male. *Cosmo* jumped on the bandwagon, informing women it was time to start looking at men as sex objects. Their centerfold of Burt Reynolds was the first male pin-up. At least then the strategic parts were covered. Then came *Playgirl*, exposing man and all his glory in full color. The tables had been turned.

While women bought less make-up and reduced their trips to the hairdresser, beauty salons were filled with men getting their hair styled, colored and permed. The cosmetic and jewelry counters at Bloomingdales were overrun by men experimenting with everything from skin toners and creams to facials to gold bracelets.

With men's new found beautification came their renovated sexual image. They were now the pursued. Women became the aggressors. Now women had to put up with, "Not tonight, honey." He could now give the century-old headache excuse. And she had to buy it. After all, hadn't he?

For the first time since the creation of the human race, man, not woman, possesses the sexual power. He didn't take this power. It was given to him freely by the "New Woman."

Single women find themselves relegated to making the first phone call, initiating the first date, picking up the first dinner tab and making the sexual overture. Are they liking this position? My research proves they don't. However, they feel compelled to be the initiator. Thanks, Ms. Friedan.

Men, on the other hand, are elated. They love it. They can sit back on their lazy asses, waiting for the phone to ring and for her to arouse their lackadaisical libidos. If they're interested, they'll take the bait. If not, they know the phone will ring again.

The more passive female, not yet equipped to be the aggressor, sits at home reading her Harlequins and living in a fantasy world. Patiently she awaits the once aggressive Prince Charming mounted on his white steed. Her odds have to be a hundred to one that this longshot will make it through the starting gate. Get with the program! Men are no longer romantic or assertive because women have laid everything out for them on a silver platter.

Numerous men have told me that women, nowadays, will do anything in bed, even on a first date. There is no challenge left. And why work for something when you can get it free?

But with this new-found power have come complications. Picture this: Assertive Alice calls Blasé Ben. She asks him out; picks up the dinner tab. They go to the theater; she pops for the tickets. Now, it's back to her place for some night toddies. Alice expects a roll in the hay. Naturally, she just spent $200. Sound familiar, guys? Ben breaks out in a cold sweat. His brain has clicked on, but his penis hasn't. He feels used. But it's OK, he rationalizes, he wasn't planning on going to bed with her on the first date.

By now, Alice has stripped down to her knee-hi's and wonders why Ben is putting on his blue blazer and preparing to hightail it home. "You bastard!" she says, "What the hell is wrong with you?"

Ben wakes up the next morning in his own apartment, of course. He immediately makes an appointment with the nearest impotence clinic. He has no difficulty finding one as they are more plentiful than service stations.

The doctor reassures Ben he's under strain and stress and can't expect to perform on a dime. It must have been Alice's approach that made him question his sexuality. "Now Ben," says Dr. Feelgood, "if you want to eliminate this problem, then you initiate the date, pick up the dinner check and make the sexual overtures. You'll pole vault all the way to the bedroom."

This little scenario shows what can happen with the role reversal in the dating game. Society is playing with fire. As Margaret Mead explains in her book, *Male and Female: A Study of the Sexes in a Changing World* (Morrow), "...if the culture is patterned so that men are required to make love to a particular woman at a particular time and place, then rebellion may set in....The male can maintain, in all honesty, that a culture which does not protect his spontaneous sexuality will in the end perish, because there will be no children conceived to carry it on....This is perhaps one reason why men are so often regarded as the progressive element in human history."

Dr. Herb Goldberg, in his book *The Hazards of Being Male* (NAL-Dutton), states: "I feel strongly that a man only has sex under conditions of genuine total spontaneous excitement and full arousal. With anything short of that reaction, he may be setting the groundwork for impotence."

If women insist on taking the aggressor role with men, they better be prepared to live in an Amazon society. Plan to have a large stock of vibrators and plenty of batteries.

Sexual desire is one of the greatest motivators. Whoever has the power to generate this erotic desire ultimately possesses power and control. And whoever has the most power, rules the world. But women have relinquished that power and are now complaining that men are wimps; that they are not assertive or aggressive. Well, why should they be? Women have seized their role.

What's left for the male? He can now sit on his silk cushion and eat his bon bons, have his bills paid and be the eunuch you've always wanted.

Test & Review

1. Don't ever call a man you would like to date. Exceptions are men who are friends.
2. Don't be aggressive or assertive.
3. If a man doesn't call or pursue you in any way, it is just this simple: he doesn't want to.
4. Leave the sexual pursuit up to him.
5. Don't feel guilty and offer to pay for dinner, lunch or any function. Pay him back with a picnic on the beach, a candlelight dinner, a special art opening or social function.
6. In the beginning of a relationship, don't give too much. Be mysterious, intriguing and not so available.
7. Save any gifts for him until you've dated him for at least six months. And then give them just for his birthday or possibly Christmas.
8. Again, I suggest don't stop dating other men. Not until you have that forty-carat engagement ring on your left hand.
9. Clever ways of ferreting out that shy man: Throw a cocktail party and send him an invitation; fix him up with one of your girlfriends, then double date (this could backfire, but who cares?); find out his field of expertise. If he's a master electrician, have him wire some special lighting, offer to pay him for this service. Chances are he'll decline and maybe even take you to dinner.
10. Be relaxed, calm, self-assured and secure with yourself. Men can sense a desperate woman across a crowded room.

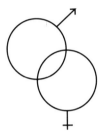

CHAPTER

12

Grandpa and Babycakes

"I'd rather be an old man's darling than a young man's sweetheart," seems to be the motto of many young women who are dating and marrying older men. There is an obvious explanation for this type of union.

As one man, who was enjoying a relationship with a "nubile nymphet," explained, "Younger women are not as set in their ways. They are more spontaneous, eager to please and harbor no sexual hang-ups compared to their older sisters."

Continuing, he further expounded the fact that women his age were too rigid, sexually and socially, and not at all adventurous with that uninhibited "joi de vive" that men find so stimulating and appealing.

However, another man who had participated in the "Grandpa-and-Babycakes" game, had this to say: "I tried dating younger women but finally wised up when I started reminiscing about my combat in Korea and she brought up *Star Trek*. I knew right then and there, we were dancing a different tango."

He explains his folly as a stage men experience when they need reassurance and certification that they still possess the power to attract a younger woman.

In order to create a "macho image" when a man is more mature, the woman must be younger. It's a feather in his cap, when impressing his cronies, that he has this young girl on his arm and in his bed. They think if an older man has captured the fancy of a "bimbette" he must have machismo.

Men attracted to young ladies who are still wearing their patent leather "Mary Janes," fool themselves into thinking their *Cosmo* girl is in love with them, not their money. After interviewing and observing many of these mercenary madonnas, I noticed the same golden thread of similarity...money, running through their veins. When one tyke was asked why she was dating her Daddy Warbucks, she bellowed, "Get real lady, it's the money. If you think this old codger turns me on, you're crazy. The money does and I'm treated like a queen. Sex and massaging his ego are small prices to pay for the return on this investment."

Older women who marry men twenty to thirty years their senior aren't as pliable as their younger counterparts when it comes to the bedroom scene. They resent the sexual antics and attention they have to dish out to the old goat. Middle-aged ladies who trade "lay-downs" for a bank account are often incensed when they have to participate with Daddy-O in a horizontal position. "I can't stand it," one woman whined, "I have to fortify myself with a double martini and tons of Valium before I climb between the sheets with *him*." One older nymph avoided these sexual sessions by cruising the world at least four times a year. (He was too old to make the trip and hated ships). Several years passed and when he wised up he cut off her travel allowance. By the time they divorced, she had a ship's captain on the hook, closer to her own age and anchored him on one of her previous Atlantic crossings.

Just because old Grandpa has the bucks, doesn't always mean his little darling is going to get any. Those wealthy octogenarians who appear to be easy pickings aren't. They didn't acquire all that cash being stupid. Many times they are cheap, possessive and terribly unreasonable with their younger wives.

Historically, men begin to stray, mentally and physically, when approaching their late forties and early fifties. Referred to as "male menopause," this difficult passage leaves men bewildered, frustrated, insecure and restless. A man feels lost in the shuffle somewhere between the pet parrot, family dog, cat, kids in college, dirty laundry, and his spouse's change of life.

During this time, if the opportunity presents itself in the apparition of a flat-faced, virginal looking blonde with an IQ smaller than her bust size, he seizes upon the occasion to flee from the responsibilities of the family, and fulfill his fantasies before it's too late.

Men change, as do their female counterparts, when they approach that magic age. Whatever that mystical age is to them personally, they assume, somewhat correctly, life has passed them by.

At this time a man is most vulnerable because of divorce, death of a spouse, old age, menopause or whatever the cause. During this period of insecurity and readjustment, a male is easy prey, especially if his wallet is fat.

Unfortunately, the ratio of available men to women in the nineties is about seven to one. This presents a problem for more mature women who are looking for a mate or companion in their age group. And if these men are attracted to younger women, it really throws a monkey wrench in the dating game.

Women in the nineties, who are competing with the Babycakes, will have to become more inventive, resourceful and creative. Our man in the beginning of this chapter gave us the secret. Remember he explained younger women were more resilient, adventurous, playful, less rigid and, of course, sexually exciting.

Today, there is no excuse for a woman not to look attractive. Plastic surgery is an option for anyone, and the costs aren't exorbitant. A personality transplant might be in order if you're too staid, uninteresting, non-stimulating and living a quiet life of desperation.

One "ace in the hole" a mature woman has over a young girl is experience. If she is smart she will combine this with panache, style, wit and some brains–and wham-o–the Babycakes would be obsolete.

I've seen young virile men go bonkers over sharp older women. (Check the next chapter for more information on this category.) Just for an example, Colette, the famous French writer and poet, wowed men way into her twilight years. Old men, younger men, all were enchanted and mesmerized by her charms. The same goes for Mae West, Elizabeth Taylor, Mary Tyler Moore, Angie Dickinson, etc.

I had the pleasure of observing firsthand a personality totally captivate a room full of grown men. Peggy Lee, who is now in her seventies, was about fifty years old when she closed the showroom in the Palmer House in Chicago. Peggy was the stunning blonde songstress who recorded many top hits, but was known for her famous "Fever!"

At the time I was a reporter/columnist for the *Chicago Tribune* and the press was invited, along with other personages, to attend a private cocktail party in Peggy's suite before the final show.

Now, Miss Lee was quite heavy but very blonde with a peaches and cream complexion, and a recently lifted beautiful face. She reigned supreme over all of her male fans. (I witnessed these men standing in line to meet Peggy and ask for her autograph. They were mush and putty in her presence.)

I, myself, was fascinated with this scene, and decided to just sit and observe the actions. I'll admit I wanted to know her secret of seduction. She spoke very low and modulated her voice to an alluring pitch. Her flowing caftan, clung to just the right areas of her chunky body, creating a feminine, soft line, disguising any figure flaws. Her suite was bathed in scented candles providing the perfect lighting for a romantic setting, even though there were at least one hundred people in the room. Beautiful music played in the background, further stimulating good conversation. A master stroke addition to an otherwise fantasy creation. All types of men from all age groups hovered around her aura just for a glance, a word, a smile from the illustrious Peggy Lee.

Since I wrote personality sketches for the newspaper, I had the pleasure of meeting many celebrities and famous people. I've never seen another famous woman create such an impact on men as Peggy Lee, including Elizabeth Taylor (and she's one of my favorites and certainly not a piker, in the seduction of the male species). Miss Lee wasn't thin. In fact, she was pounds overweight. She certainly wasn't young by today's standards, but she had these men on their toes and knees, slobbering, stammering, and hopping to attention. I would venture to guess most men in the room were college educated and upper echelon businessmen.

So you see, darlings, with a little smarts, a lot of work, a tremendous amount of foresight and a great image, you too can be a young man's sweetheart or an old man's darling!

Test & Review

1. You'll know when your husband or boyfriend is getting ready to stray when he: Pops all the buttons off his shirt and exposes his chest, even if it's at a "black tie" function.

   You get the American Express bill from the local jewelers, and all you have is one gold wedding band. This doesn't mean his girlfriend is wearing these gems, he is.

   He spends twice the amount of time at the hairdresser getting his hair dyed, permed, transplanted or styled. Plus, a facial and manicure. His cosmetics bill is higher than yours.

2. You're widowed/divorced father is trying to understand the words to rap music. He's leaning toward the Grandpa/Babycakes syndrome.

3. Your grandfather is trading his orthopedic "ground-grippers" in for a pair of Italian leather Ferrengarmo pointed-toed loafers and wears them sans socks...you've got a Grandpa/Babycakes scenario in the making.

The Graduate

The younger male/older woman relationship is somewhat complex. Is he a younger gigolo in disguise, suffering from an Oedipus complex, or just plain more mature and likes an intellectual and sexually experienced companion?

The European male has always sang the praises of the mature female, comparing her to the aging of a fine wine. However, this trend is wending its way into American relationships and becoming quite de rigueur.

Cher, now forty-seven, after dating, marrying, then divorcing Sonny Bono, started and continued dating younger men, sometimes twenty years younger. Angie Dickinson, according to the "smut sheets," was dating a twenty-four-year-old and supposedly happy, despite the tremendous age difference. She is a ripe sixty-one.

A forty-eight-year-old divorcee, who entered into an affair with a much younger mate after divorcing her older husband, enthusiastically raves about the benefits of dating her boytoy. "The sex is fantastic," she beams. "Also, he is ready for any adventurous challenge and our dates are never boring." Sound familiar? Read the "Grandpa and Babycakes" chapter again.

When last I heard, they were both skydiving, wind surfing and burning up the quilting in their double sleeping bag, while camping in the Carolina Hills.

The Graduate and Grandpa/Babycakes syndromes are actually one and the same with the partners switched. Older women gripe, groan and complain about the sexual prowess of the mature male, claiming he can't "get it up" and if he does, he can't keep it there for long. The older man is not with the program, they claim, and his limited sexual attempts are uneventful.

Older women who date younger men, like their counterparts, are interested in the "spice of life," especially when it comes in a younger package. They don't give a fig if Pampers, pablum and a pacifier are part of their new dating accouterments. To them, it's a step up from oat bran, Tums, denture grip and the late show. Old Homer is too much of a liability. More mature women today aren't smitten with men, whose conversations center around prostate problems, hip replacements, or dental and penile implants. If you have to press a button for an instant erection, the older female would rather babysit with a younger stud, who can pole vault around the room on his own speed.

No longer is it "not acceptable" for women in society to date younger, much younger men. The old dictum of "growing old gracefully" is passé. In fact, no one wants to even grow old in this day and age, much less do it with a partner.

Of course, our society has been on a "youth-oriented" trip since the sixties and totally preoccupied with lean, hard, muscular bodies and butts that stand to attention, to the point where intellect, class and humor are left in the dust.

Granted, the media has played an important part in spoon feeding the American public into believing youth and beauty is the ultimate turn-on. This shallow attitude probably explains why our social mores, ethics, morals and virtues have become almost non-existent.

The line, "I'm not growing older, I'm just getting better," is a crock of crap, created by a Fifth Avenue advertising whiz-kid, probably in his twenties, to lure women into thinking the magical cream will make it happen. Not on your tin-type, buster. Drastic measures are needed, or you'll be left in the dust for more attractive competition.

Unfortunately, nature has a sick sense of humor because just when a woman has gained some experience and cultivated some class, her body falls apart. As my mother says, "It is a shame a woman isn't born forty with a twenty-year-old body, she'd be dangerous." Doesn't work, Tonto! So if you want to stay in the dating game, you've got to accentuate the positive and eliminate the wrinkles. Thank God for Retin A and gycolic acid.

Men get handsome and mature as they age; women get old. If you believe this, being forewarned is forearmed. Instead of going to night school, buy a Stairmaster and rowing machine, and then get yourself a young one. Body, not brains, gets them every time.

Test & Review

1. Work on your personality. You'll find men love happy, upbeat, positive ladies. This applies, regardless if the man is eighteen or eighty, when dealing with a man, any man.
2. Work on yourself, mentally, physically and financially. Yes, Virginia, men love successful women, women who can take care of themselves. Success is a strong aphrodisiac and this is a great turn on for both "Grandpa" or the "Graduate."
3. Spontaneity is another attraction. Rigidity is not. Learn to be flexible...this trait implies a youthful spirit.
4. Mystery is a cultivated charm that lures all men. Keep an element of mystery about yourself. Women who tell all aren't exciting or interesting.
5. A physical female has a better chance of meeting then keeping a man. Take up a sport–golf, sailing, tennis, etc.
6. As a woman thinketh, therefore she becomes. Think young, walk young, live young. Laugh! Happiness is another magnet.

A Good Man Is Hard to Find

Yes, there are men in them thar hills, but are they good men? By now, you should have more insight into differentiating between a "Cheatin' Charlie" or "Marvin the Manipulator."

But in order to meet men, you must be where the men are. You can't barricade yourself in the house or apartment every night and expect Prince Charming to come riding by on his white charger and carry you off into the sunset.

As they say, to win, you must be playing the game; be at the tables. I wouldn't suggest local watering holes, as you meet too many losers. However, out of all those frogs, there might be a prince. So, if you feel comfortable, try an occasional visit. But never, and I mean never, become a regular at any drinking establishment. This is death. Familiarity breeds contempt and if the waiters or bartenders don't get you, the butts warming the same bar stools there every night will. Remember, they are men and it's called a reputation. You might be innocent of any wrongdoing, but being a woman, a regular woman, will brand you every time.

Liberation didn't address this age-old problem and you aren't going to change this situation. Double standard, yes. But know the rules, keep your mouth shut, and obey them. There is a way around this situation. Choose five "hot" lounges in your area, and keep rotating your visits. Never twice in the same week. Do not become "one of the boys." This will curtail any further dating activities. I don't care if you're a female

"Minnesota Fats," don't shoot pool, tell jokes, use profanity, or play liar's dice. Play up your feminine side.

Sooner or later, the ol' prince will lumber in and ask about you. Guess what? The regulars and help will be only too quick to defend you as a "nice girl" who just happens by occasionally. See, you did it...and the prince will be only too eager to ask you out because, after all, his peers have already given you an A plus.

This also applies to your associates. You can't be too careful. "Tell me who you go with and I'll tell you what you are," was an old pearl of wisdom my father used quite frequently. You are judged, unfortunately, by your friends. Be selective.

I've dated some real frogs in my time (haven't we all?) and this can wreak havoc with other available suitors. They think, if you are that stupid, what do they want with you? You can't afford to be seen with a less than desirable escort. Sorry, that's the program, folks.

Where does a "good man" hang out? Don't laugh, but church and related functions are great places to meet eligible mates. So are art museums, openings, shows and art galleries. Join the local museums and place your name at all the local art galleries so you'll be on their mailing list for upcoming shows.

Join some local charities, Cancer Society, Heart Association, etc. They all have fund-raising activities, cocktail parties and balls. If you're really desperate, and could tolerate dating an attorney, hang around the law library—men, men and more men. Just a tip: lawyers are notorious for being frugal with a dollar. Theirs.

First, you must know what kind of man you're attracted to and the type of profession he is in. This is a must because if you want a show-dog owner, you're not going to meet him at a church social. Try the race track.

If doctors fascinate you, then become a volunteer several days a week. You're bound to run into a single MD making his rounds. Then you're in a better position to cultivate this type of union.

You get the picture. Finding a good man is a full-time job that takes energy, inventiveness, creativity and tons of persistence. But it can be accomplished. Meeting a man, especially one who is marriage material, isn't easy in the nineties. But with a lot of planning, I have no doubts you'll dig up several candidates.

Broadening your social circle, especially with the opposite sex, is tantamount if you want to meet, impress or hook a husband. Entertaining is an excellent vehicle toward this goal. Plus he'll get an opportunity to see you in action in your own environment, where you are in control.

It's easy to invite a man you are smitten with to a party. A hell of a lot easier than calling him for a date. (Don't try this one, it places you at a disadvantage. Regardless what men say, they don't like to be put on the spot.)

Parties are casual, fun and can show off your creative talents. For instance, my Cinco de Mayo parties are always successful. It's the fifth of May and a Mexican holiday. In the beginning, people say, after they receive the invitation, what's Cinco de Mayo? I explain and go forward. I serve Mexican cuisine, margaritas and sangria, purchase some Latin tapes, decorate the table (buffet style) with colorful plates, napkins, candles, etc.

Invite another couple plus *him* for dinner. Put on the dog for this one, and make sure your table setting is to "die for"; ditto the meal. Entertaining on this scale is an excellent way to get to know your good man and gives him an opportunity to see you at your best.

If you're on a limited budget, then necessity is the mother of invention. Be creative. You'd be surprised at the grocery chains that cater small parties, for little money. Where there's a will there is always a way. Atmosphere is the key when entertaining, and so is the guest list. Interesting people make a party. And by now you should have collected a barrage of these types who will be perfect. He'll enjoy meeting your friends and this will directly reflect on you.

It takes time to cultivate a friendship and a relationship. Most people aren't patient enough when it comes to the time and effort required to hook a husband or good man.

We are an instant-gratification society wanting the golden ring without paying the price of the piper. Women and men become too impatient if the ball doesn't move quickly, thus throwing in the towel just when the bait is beginning to entice the fish.

The more you include these eligible men in your "social soirees," the more comfortable they become, letting their defenses down, so they can enjoy your company. Don't worry or fret if a relationship hasn't evolved as yet. Remember, men have male friends and, who knows, he could be just that good man you've been hunting for.

Test & Review

1. Be the hostess with the mostest! Gain a reputation for throwing the best parties in town. He'll be begging for an invitation.
2. Work hard at creating a social life for yourself. The more people you know, the more people you'll meet. Develop a social circle of male friends. Play tennis, golf, sail, etc. These men have other male friends.
3. Make finding a good man a project. Create a plan of attack. Your blueprint for finding the right man should be creative and exciting. Persevere.
4. Get off your duff and plan an outing several nights a week. Join clubs, organizations, charities, church socials. One inventive lady I know visits AA meetings once a week. You'd be shocked at who belongs to this group. Attorneys, doctors, several millionaires and a gaggle of available divorcees.

CHAPTER 15

Marriage Material: Where to Find Him

Not all available men you meet are going to be good marriage material. But it's just like sales; it's a numbers game. In other words, you may have to kiss a lot of frogs before you find your prince. A discerning woman should be able to intuitively know whether the man has the attributes she is looking for. We've already exposed Non-Committal Norman, Marvin the Manipulator and all the other rogues, some under the "hustler" category. The hustler is not husband material. A sharp female can spot him quickly. Number one, a hustler will approach any woman who catches his fancy because he knows if he's rejected, it's just a matter of time before he scores. Again, he knows it's a numbers game.

He's not interested in a specific type or anyone on a permanent basis. It's the chase, challenge and conquest. After he conquers, he's off to another challenge. This man is a taker from the word "go." If you choose to get involved with this creep, it will be short term and you will be left a blathering idiot when he dumps your fanny for another conquest.

How can a woman recognize this womanizer quickly? He's cocky, forward and is in hot pursuit immediately upon meeting you. He is a visual man. His attraction is based on how you look. He is not interested in your inner qualities or depth of feelings, unless they are for and about him. Selfish is his call letter.

His image and how he attracts women is contrived. He is a phony. He is not in possession of an unusually high IQ. However, since he is trying to close the deal with you, he gets into high gear in the flattery department just to get you hooked. He plays to your ego. In the beginning he will ask numerous questions about you and you think this is because he's so interested. Wrong. He's getting a handle on how to play you. This gives him the edge because he now knows what "hot buttons" to push.

On the opposite side is the "wallflower." He is timid, shy and appears non-aggressive. This can be deceiving though. He may be a silent type that carries a big stick. If indeed he truly is non-assertive and you find yourself smitten, you will have to plan on being the initiator in this conquest. Not blatantly, though, as this could scare him away. These men are shy and will not assert themselves, even if they are "in lust" with someone. They fear rejection more than winning a few times here and there, unlike the hustler who could care less about a little rejection from time to time, because he knows failure is only temporary.

Then there is the "observer." This is the strong, silent type who knows exactly what type of woman turns him on. He will sit in a place and intently watch the object of his desire. He is terribly astute at body language and by the time he makes his first move, he will know a lot about his conquest before uttering a word.

When you decide you're ready to find a marriage mate, you have to create a strategy, the same way you would make a business plan. You can call this unromantic, calculating and manipulative. But when you send me an invitation to your wedding, you'll call it smart.

Number one on the list is to put yourself in circulation. You have to be out to meet new people. Plan to be away from the television set at least three nights a week. Before you begin stepping out, you must make yourself appealing. Update your wardrobe, hairstyle and make-up. Many men admit they are attracted by looks first.

You must also take a long look at your attitude about men. Make sure it's positive. If you really don't like men, it's going to show. Your attitude about yourself is also important. If you believe you are worthwhile and have something to offer, other people will too. You might as well enjoy yourself if you're going to take the time and effort to go out three times a week. This is the unseen, magnetic quality that attracts men to certain women.

After you've updated your look and the attitude, make yourself as interesting as possible. You must be able to converse. Expand your intellect. Watch the news, read a paper or news magazine, pick up the latest bestseller. Also, if you don't know how to dance, learn. Then plan to go dancing two to three times a week. Not only is it a way to meet men, it's great aerobics. At least you'll keep in shape.

Now you're ready to circulate. But where do you go? There are many sports that attract men: golf, scuba diving, tennis, boating. If you have the money, buy a boat, even a small one. There are plenty of fish in the sea if you're riding the waves. You'll also meet a ton of men where there is gambling. Spend a day at the horse track, or an evening at a casino or betting on the dogs.

Join some organization in your field or one that you're interested in. There are hundreds of them: Toastmasters, Civitan, community associations, Rotary, Kiwanis, Chambers of Commerce, your local visitor and convention bureau. These are all great places to meet new people.

Singles clubs are another alternative for expanding your social circle. Many churches now have singles groups that attract good people. Single people don't entertain anymore. Throw a cocktail party and have each of your girlfriends bring a single man or two. Have the men you invite bring an available male friend.

Take weekend trips alone. Hotel lounges are great places to meet single men. Hotels are especially active when there's a convention in town. Do a little private investigating. Find out when and where mostly male conventions are taking place in your area. Join the opera or symphony association. Become a patron for an art gallery or museum. If that's not in your budget, attend free openings and preview concerts.

It's always more fun to go out searching with a friend. But it's not always possible to have a gal pal available every time you want to go out. You must learn to go out occasionally by yourself. The first few times will be horrendous because of the stigma attached to a single woman going out alone. You can't worry about what people will think. Go with a positive attitude and enjoy yourself. This will breed confidence and inner security. You'll be amazed at how proud you feel.

Above all, in your search for a partner, you must have patience, patience, patience. You want something that will last. And you probably won't find it overnight. No matter how frustrated you get, never, and I mean never, become desperate. Men will pick up on that like a bloodhound. You'll be doomed to attracting viperous men who sniff out desperate women, knowing they're easy marks. Remember, positive attitude. Your prince is out there!

Test & Review

1. Pick your sport, then join a club. If you play tennis or golf, go alone sometimes. You'd be surprised how many times I've been asked to become a fourth in tennis and golf with men.
2. Cultivate a group of all-male friends. They have other male friends and will be more than happy to fix you up.
3. Throw a party and invite more men than women, then insist your bachelor friends bring another male friend.
4. Most women won't go out alone. That old stigma, you'll look like a pick-up. Who cares? Men will talk to a woman alone before they will approach a group. The first time I tried this ploy, I chose a familiar hotel lounge but I still had to circle the block five times before I had the courage to walk, proudly, into the bar. It worked...I met a Non-Committal Norman, but chalked it up to my research.
5. Travel alone. At first take a weekend close to home (make sure the hotel has a swinging bar). I was in Miami at the Inter-Continental Hotel once, sitting at the lobby bar. A stunning South American male sent me over a drink, then asked me to join him for dinner. It was a most romantic interlude.

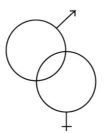

16

Men Fifty and Over: A Different Breed

By the time a man approaches the big "Five-O" chances are he's either starting male menopause, smack in the middle, or three-quarters of the way through his mid-life crisis. It's inconsequential because he has a plethora of problems.

When he reaches this difficult passage and he has not achieved some modicum of success, either financially or emotionally, he will be a mess. You can bet he's a basketful of insecurities and possesses an ego as large as the Houston Astrodome.

Men who are experiencing male menopause are pains in the ass, much like their female counterparts who are fighting with the same trauma. Granted, it's partially hormonal (his testosterone is running amok) and the rest is avoiding the aging process.

Another factor, where men are concerned, is the need to win. Since birth, men are pushed by their parents and peers to be successful in all their endeavors, thereby explaining why they have tremendous egos and cover up their inadequacies with macho tendencies.

Women fare better in this department because the pressure to win and be competitive in sports or business isn't placed upon them in their formative years. Now, when other women are on the scene, it's a different story.

After a man completes the "change of life" he usually comes to grips with his past failures, accepts himself as the person he is (warts and all), and is more rational, open and honest. He knows now he has nothing to prove to you or himself, and if he did, he doesn't possess the desire or energy to tackle this problem.

But while he is careening through this emotional tunnel, he's going to be a handful. I've played tennis with a myriad of menopausers. Believe me, they have hurled insults, thrown racquets, pouted, cussed and even quit in the middle of a game because they were losing or missed a point. You'd think an inconsequential game of tennis was Star Wars and they were losing their battle.

One 'pauser partner even went so far as to hire a championship player to play with him one day just so he could win. His ego was satisfied and he was happy as a pig in slop. It was obviously that important to him because he was living a life of quiet desperation in the other areas. Priorities become misplaced along with anger during this stage.

Now the seventy-year-old codger, who is far past menopause, just drop-shots the hell out of the ball, keeps his mouth shut and is so damn grateful just to be standing upright. He's been there and knows you can't fight Mother Nature.

Men fifty and over, who are experiencing "the change," take everything seriously and personally. Their ego and self-esteem are non-existent. Unfortunately, an inflated or deflated ego will override any semblance of intellect they possess. Couple this with loss of youth, looks and the lack of an opportunity to make their first million, and you have a full-blown complex in bloom.

A woman in a union with this type of male better be resigned to spending hours massaging his weak ego while continually walking on eggs. Their childlike behavior can run the "bad seed" a close tie for the Academy Award and it's most exhausting just to keep these guys on an even keel.

Little "Barbara Bimbo" (see next chapter) won't experience the same difficulties with this same man in comparison to the woman closer to his own age because it doesn't take a secure mental giant or a King Midas to impress her. Remember, she's only in this relationship for the goods while you, the more experienced, mature and hopefully intelligent female, want more from the association. During the time his ego rules, brains are left in his rump.

Unzip a man's pants and his brains fall out, they say. During male menopause, I believe, a man places his brains and maturity, or any semblance of rationality and sensitivity to others, under the rear tire of his car and throws it in reverse. Haven't you observed an otherwise smart man all of a sudden become a real jerk after approaching a certain age?

This trait really escalates when a younger male is on their turf. The old-bull-and-young-bull syndrome is especially dominant when a man approaches mid-life crisis and is starting to lose his hair while developing a huge middle-age spread, and his young son, with a slim midriff and tons of dark, wavy tresses, is dating young girls with slim midriffs and tons of dark, wavy tresses.

I have witnessed this type of sick competition firsthand and was appalled at the lengths these aging losers would go. One aging, overweight, pompous, insecure, menopausal bastard who ran a yacht dealership in South Florida, epitomized this type of behavior. He held his younger competition at bay by cheating them on their commission checks. He doctored their sales contracts, illegally copying client's names and different sales figures, then stole the profit, throwing them a crumb here and there.

Not only did he have the "balls," shriveled at that, to steal their paychecks, he would make them beg and grovel for their money, often stretching them past the breaking point, until they would settle for a pittance of their original pay. He was despicable, but most of his younger employees didn't have the experience, nerve or financial reserve to confront this creep. Now here was an aging sixty-five-year-old man who should have been helping his younger employees in the business. Not only was he a menopausal mess, he was a dyed in the wool con artist, especially with the ladies. He would entice them with money (paychecks he stole from his younger employees), gifts and lavish dinners. And, if I might add, charge it on his son-in-law's American Express. When he got them hooked, he'd dump them for wealthier prey.

However, as P.T. Barnum claimed, "There's a sucker born every minute," and these women asked for it. At last count, the old thief hooked a rich mama and is living on her money like an aging King Tut.

When a man is experiencing the change of life he is most vulnerable to younger women or older women with lots of money. He feels that this is the last race and in order to preserve his damaged ego, he must land a young stunner or an old money bags.

Men like this can become aging gigolos not in the professional sense, because they weren't gigolos in their younger years. But they become much like their female counterparts–desperate.

Now if you're lucky enough to find a man over fifty who has his ducks in a row so to speak, and he's reasonably secure, you might still be warding off strange behavior.

It can run the gamut of trading the family station wagon in for a sleek Jag or Mercedes convertible to skydiving on the weekends, or leaving his job, purchasing a sailboat and leaving for six months to island hop in the Caribbean. Harmless, yes. However, if you're married to this Dr. Jekyll and Mr. Hyde, it keeps your life in a shambles.

With the ratio of women to men being seven to one, depending on the area you live in, ruling out men fifty and over isn't feasible. You just have to be better prepared to deal with this age group of dysfunctional males.

This probably explains why women are into dating the younger male. However, it won't be long, depending on his age, before he starts to perm his hair, don his gold necklace, wear his shirts unbuttoned to the waist and hide his Grecian Formula under the sink.

Test & Review

1. If you're dating or married to a man who is experiencing male menopause, patience is the only advice I can give. Understanding and compassion are also useful. It beats splitting his head open with a hammer while trying to bang some sense into it. And it certainly beats doing time because you've killed the bastard.
2. If you're both plagued by menopause, check into separate resorts until it's over. This might take nine years or so. Try the St. James Club in Antigua. You might meet a younger, richer paramour, then you can divorce the old one.
3. Try a sense of humor. At least you can laugh when he perms his hair and dons all that awful gold jewelry. However, you better laugh loud because you have to be seen with him. Ugh!
4. Short of getting a brain transplant, check into the nearest plastic surgery center and have a complete body overhaul. At least you'll look good while he's looking at someone who looks good.

CHAPTER

17

Competing with Barbara Bimbo

This is a most difficult category to compete with, simply because your opponent's bust size far out-measures her IQ. I'm not implying that she's stupid; far from it. Barbara Bimbo has every positive asset (and they're sure as hell not drooping) to win the battle. The more mature woman will have to plan her war strategy like Patton attacking Rommel.

With this in mind, let's first identify the men who date bimbos or younger bimbettes and why. There's one group generally between forty and forty-five. They are the obvious menopausers. However, there are many men, struggling up the corporate ladder, who don't want to be bothered by another intellectual experiencing the same tough climb.

Why are these men satisfied with so little? Simple. By the time a man reaches forty, he's probably been married to a woman his own age, inundated with tremendous financial responsibility and his career is at a standstill. Or, he's been divorced, is paying huge sums of alimony and child support, but is still financially stable. He has all the latest toys.

There's another type of man attracted to the bimbo. He wants an attractive female, who will never question him and always adore him. She's a convenient showpiece for friends and business colleagues. His age group is normally twenty-five to thirty-nine. One astute, younger bimbette-pursuer frequented the single's bars. He was a landscaper by trade and couldn't beg, borrow or steal a date with Babs Bimbo until he cleverly ordered business cards giving him a new occupation—lawyer. After he handed out a few of these, he had to fight them off with a club!

Dating a bimbo is simple. All it takes is cash (bimbos may not be mental giants, but they know how to get the goods). They do not require a commitment. They aren't possessive. They don't need a Las Vegas headliner to keep them entertained. They are easily impressed by an occasional meal, a bottle of Dom and an Andes after-dinner mint.

It's easy to see why Barbara Bimbo is so successful. However, she also has a very powerful trump card: sex. She uses sex as her calling card—pure unadulterated, uncommitted, uninhibited, unemotional sex. She puts no emotional demands on her partner. She simply adores everything he does and lets him know how brilliant she thinks he is because he can balance his own checkbook or throw his clothes in the dryer.

I remember one quintessential bimbo who hopped around a Christmas party in her reindeer and candy cane speckled hose, making her legs look like they were afflicted with a rare skin disease. She cooed at every man at this holiday celebration. Her ultimate "brain dead" remark came when she asked a guest, who was a bartender by trade, what he wanted to drink. When he asked for vodka on the rocks, she gyrated around, wrung her hands and whined, "I'm so nervous. I feel intimidated fixing a bartender a drink."

How mind-bending can it be for one to twist off the top of a vodka bottle and drop ice in a glass? This little act served a dual purpose. She looked helpless and he looked like Donald Trump making a million-dollar deal.

An international corporation that employed two thousand people had all the executive positions held by men—who hired only bimbos as their assistants. The sole requirement for employment as an assistant at this established company was a bust size of 44D. It was a stretch for these busty beauties to find two brain cells to rub together.

One of their marketing geniuses (and I use the term loosely), couldn't understand why a colleague was having problems with a printer they both used. The business associate accused the printer of being unable to comprehend a deadline. The marketing maven opened her eyes wide with surprise and sweetly explained, "I can't believe you've had difficulties. I just go in and give him a big kiss. I always get my things on time."

As I've mentioned, bimbos aren't always young. There are plenty of aging ones in circulation. One very attractive, forty-eight-year-old New

York resident had been legally separated for six years. She never got divorced so she could continue to collect alimony indefinitely and had two steady gentleman suitors. One flew in several times a month from California to wine and dine her. She made sure there was plenty of time for a shopping spree, as she had an extravagant shoe fetish and her long-distance Romeo guaranteed her a larger shoe collection than Imelda Marcos.

Now that you're familiar with the character of the bimbo and the men who date them, it's time to give ol' Babs a run for her money. When a man gets ready to make a commitment, he wants a more stable, responsible, sensitive female. It's difficult to maintain a long-term relationship with someone whose intellectual level is Romper Room. Remember the man of fifty-five who'd been dating a young bimbo and started talking about his combat experience when she brought up *Star Trek*? It was time for him to move on to a woman his own age.

This is why the first rule of competing with a bimbo is to never disguise your intellect. The second guideline is to be more spontaneous and flexible. When Babs is asked to go to Nassau, she doesn't give her suitor a thousand reasons why she can't. She goes with the flow.

Also, recognize that ego is an integral part of being a man. A little flattery and awe goes a long way. Men also love a good sense of humor and a clever wit. Most bimbos lack both. Research was performed with college males who were shown two photographs of equally attractive women. One was smiling and the other wasn't. The consensus was that the one smiling was more attractive. So, keep smiling!

Not all bimbos are beauties, but all men interviewed for this book say that appearance is the first thing that attracts a man to a woman. In order to compete with a younger woman, you've really got to have your physical act together. This means hair, make-up, wardrobe, attitude, posture and, yes, your figure. If you have to totally revamp your image, do so. If it means hiring a professional to assist you, it will be well worth the money. John Robert Powers, the owner of the famous Powers Modeling School in New York, says: "There's no such thing as an ugly woman. With the proper instruction, any woman can be beautiful."

One final tip. The way to a man's heart is not through his stomach, it's below it. If you don't own the latest edition of *The Joy of Sex*, run to your nearest book store. Bimbos are proficient in that area. But here's how to put them out of business in this department. Most bimbos are neither creative, imaginative or romantic. Give a man a choice of a slam-bam-thank-you-ma'am session with a bimbo versus a moonlight boat ride complete with champagne, skinny dipping and passionate lovemaking on the bow, the decision is clear. Sex needs to be a happening, not a chore. Your mind is your greatest asset. Don't be afraid to use it.

Test & Review

1. Visit your local department store when there's a beauty consultant in town. Learn some make-up and hair tips.
2. Attend some fashion shows to see how the chic and sophisticated are dressing, then emulate it on a smaller scale for your budget.
3. Join a fitness center, take an aerobics class, walk, take up a sport. Whip that body into shape.
4. Quit reading romance novels and start scripting them. Don't expect the man to be romantic. It's up to you.
5. Invest in a wicker picnic basket with champagne glasses and matching linens. You can use this for a picnic on the beach or nearby lake. Plan to open the champagne at sunset. You can do the same thing on a canoe trip. Or go boating or walking by moonlight.
6. Short weekend cruises are very romantic.
7. Dinner by candlelight with beautiful music is always a winner!
8. Break out the bath beads and set up a candlelit bubble bath for two.
9. Scented candles and incense combined with exotic oil and a book on massage makes for a creative, passionate evening.
10. After you've known him awhile, take him on a glass elevator ride in a tall building. Stop the car between floors. You'll be amazed at how the excitement of getting caught arouses him.
11. Send him flowers at the office with a key to a hotel room.
12. Go to his office at noon and plan several lunch-hour surprises.
13. Rent a houseboat for the weekend. Tell him to pack a few things and pick him up at the office. Be sure you get his Visa number to pay for the houseboat.

prince would be more creative and romantic. A frog, would use any trick of the trade to get you in a compromising position.

A prince is secure with his own sexuality; he doesn't have to punch holes in his belt or bedpost, tallying up his many conquests to feel like a man. Frogs aren't secure in this department, so any game is de rigueur when it comes to seducing a woman. They must prove, if only to themselves, they've got it.

Most princes are shy around women, or at least quiet. And women are magnetically drawn to shy men. Why? Because they can't figure them out so quickly and women are used to a more aggressive type. Shy, proper men aren't always princes, but these traits are usually found in a higher caliber man.

The aggressive male might always get a date, but in the interim he could also get syphilis. It doesn't always pay to be too assertive when it comes to sex in the beginning. It takes time to meet a prince, and remember, you have to kiss lots of frogs.

Still in the class department, manners are a must. Society isn't mannerly anymore, so most people have forsaken this "lost art" of social graces for a more brusque, rude, ill-bred demeanor.

There is never an excuse for rudeness. However, people have become almost barbaric when it comes to manners. The magic words are still magic. "Thank you," "please," "excuse me," along with the basic etiquette, are still mandatory if you want to "win friends and influence people."

An unmannerly person, man or woman, is ill-bred, and if that man in question doesn't have some manners, you've got a Frog spelled with a capital "F." Dump him on his lily pad.

Also, a man who is classy doesn't use profanity in mixed company, at least off the tennis courts. Nor does he tell off-colored jokes.

Amazingly, men hate women who use any type of profanity. They can, but for you to indulge in this practice places you on their level or below, and men want women whom they can place on that pedestal. Sorry gals, that's the truth! I didn't make the rules, they did. And if you want to play ball in their ballpark, you'll have to play by their rules.

Younger women must apply this same routine when they are dating their friends and peers. Regardless what your segment of society is doing, you can't afford to deviate. If you want respect from a man, you must first respect yourself. And being one of the boys in this area isn't going to help you achieve your goal.

If a man asks you out, then he is supposed to pay. Get it! These tight drips who ask a lady for dinner then have the guts and gall to ask her to

CHAPTER

18

Your Prince Has Arrived
(Or Is He a Frog?)

Shopping for love isn't an easy task, as there are so many frogs hopping around in the market place. A prince is quite a rare commodity. However, let's try and decipher the difference between the two, then place our pseudo prince under a microscope and find out if he can really sleep on a pea and know it.

What are the main characteristics of a prince? Class for starts. A classless man is definitely a frog. One who kisses and tells, if you will. That is a frog. A prince would keep his own counsel, and not open his mouth about any sexual involvement just to build his weak ego.

I don't know about you, but I simply detest men who blab about their sexual conquests to anyone who will listen, then continue to paint a graphic picture of what transpired. Please spare me the details and topic of conversation. Frogs, like some women, talk too much about their pursuits of the opposite sex and this is "déclassé." Princes possess ethics, morals, principles and values. Frogs don't.

You can evaluate quickly whether you're dealing with a prince or frog when it comes to sex. A principled male wouldn't force his attentions upon you until you were ready, but a frog would. For starters, a share the evening's expenses are frogs of the first order. Of course, I blame women for the misconception. In another century, a man wouldn't think of asking a woman out unless he paid the bill. But now, because women pushed liberation down their throats, these men think if you're liberated, you pay. And what's most astounding is they do.

Now I am not talking about young people, in college, who are struggling for a degree, where both are working their way through four years, holding down double jobs. I am addressing the majority of single men and women who are playing the dating game.

If a prince couldn't afford the ante, he just wouldn't ask you out. A frog wouldn't hesitate to have you dig into your wallet and pay his share. You're a damned fool if you buy this one. Unless a man has to work for something, he doesn't respect, or even like it.

Human nature is fascinating. People resent hand-outs. It makes them feel inferior to the handee. The same applies in relationships.

A true man wants to protect, pay, pursue, be knight in shining armor. A prince does too, so close your pocketbook when you're out with a man, any man, and see if he's a prince or frog.

Now there are extenuating circumstances. For instance, you can't invite a man to a society ball at $200 per person and expect him to pick up the tab, unless you've discussed it with him beforehand. And you certainly can't suggest a trip to Europe or a cruise to the Caribbean and expect him to pay through the nose. You must make financial arrangements ahead of time. But with dinner, a movie, the theater, and, of course, if he asks you first, the responsibility is his, not yours.

Let me explain the word "liberation" to you. According to Webster's, liberate means "to free." It doesn't say "to pay." Got it? If not, get it!

Pigs are dirty. Frogs aren't, but they have lots of warts on their bodies and these warts are usually, in the human vernacular, mental and emotional problems. So with a frog be prepared to deal with emotional instability, mental dwarfness and insecurities.

Hopefully, the prince will be emotionally mature, rational and egotistically stable. If he isn't, you've got a frog in disguise.

If the man you are dating is a garbage can full of complexities, you're not Jung or Freud, so give it up and continue the hunt.

"Someday my prince will come," was the introduction for some shrink to develop the Cinderella Complex. This complex was designed to better explain women who were looking for the white knight or prince. I ask you, would someone in her right mind intentionally go after a frog? I shouldn't think so. However, it's not unusual to go marry a prince and then kiss him and have him turn into a frog.

Forearmed is forewarned. This means taking the time to get to know this person before hammering out a pre-nuptial agreement. Again, I say, it takes about a year before a pseudo-prince becomes just another frog.

I'll give you one better. Sports is a great leveler. You can tell more about a person's personality when you play tennis, golf, sail or interact with him in sports. Why? His true self emerges because he isn't trying to bamboozle you with fancy footwork, and you can catch him off-guard.

In tennis, I can tell who has a level temperament, or an extremely violent one. Are they selfish, are they cheats, are they immature, are they complimentary, are they considerate? These traits emerge in a game of tennis, especially if you play with the same people for quite some time. When you're playing doubles, you are depending upon your partner, so you can gather a tremendous insight into that person. You can bet your last dollar I wouldn't marry a man, even if he was a prince, unless I played some sport with him, preferably tennis, for at least one year.

Make a list of what type of man you are interested in and the attributes you'd like him to have, a goal sheet if you will. This keeps your mind focused on the type of man you'd like to date or marry.

You are going to have to make an effort. Princes aren't just sitting drinking beer at the local pub. The frogs are, so if you haven't found your prince as of yet, change watering holes and add some extra-curricular activities to your agenda.

Princes are active. They are living life, not just watching it go by. They like to dance, play tennis, golf, sail, scuba dive, travel, play the market, fish, whatever. Numerous activities attract the princes of the world. And don't forget, princes need a princess for the castle. It might as well be you!

CHAPTER 19

Roll Over, Baby, I Think I Love You

A man uses flattery to get a women in bed; he uses cruelty to get her out. The main goal for a man in the beginning of a dating scenario is to get a woman into bed. He can easily accomplish this by using his wits. Men want to challenge, chase and conquer. Today, many women have destroyed this little game by being too easy.

The backlash for this quick availability is that when a man gets what he wants without resistance, he leaves. Why? Because he has no respect for this conquest. According to Emerson, "The accepted and betrothed lover has lost the wildest charm of his maiden in her acceptance of him. She was heaven whilst he pursued her as a star. She cannot be heaven if she stoops to such a one as he."

Many women I interviewed related personal accounts of their "roll over" experiences. One very attractive gal, who met an intelligent, tall, gray-headed gentleman at a cocktail party, fell for his line. They were immediately attracted to each other. She invited him over for coffee after the party. After many hugs and kisses, she informed him that she would not hop into bed with him, as much as she would like to, before five dates. His response? "I like to hear that because it sets the tone of the relationship." Listen up, Virginia. They will tell you how to play the game. Unfortunately, most women don't choose to hear.

They had made plans to brunch the following Sunday. She was to meet him at his home and they were going to drive to a quaint place to eat. Sunday, she arrived with a bottle of champagne and a book for him. After many bubblies and conversation, she informed him she was hungry. He took her to a restaurant nearby and ushered her back to his lair for more bubbly and a steamy Jacuzzi.

Hormones were raging and the inevitable happened. She spent the night and left a nice note the next morning while he was at work. He called, of course, but didn't fail to inform her that he was expecting a female house guest the following weekend and wouldn't be able to see her. A week passed and he called. She invited him to her home for the Fourth of July weekend. He accepted. They got along famously. Again, he informed her he would be busy for the next week or so because of another female house guest was due.

Almost a month passed without a call from him and the lady was livid. Then, out of the blue, he called under the pretense that he had a call from "Jane" on his answering machine. Since she was the only "Jane" he knew, he assumed it had to be her. Well, Jane hadn't called so this must have been his clever way of getting in touch after a month. The conversation was cool. He said he didn't know when they'd be able to get together, but he wanted her to keep in touch. Jane didn't have any desire to continue such an insensitive relationship, so of course she never contacted him. She was confused because of the intense sexual encounter. He wasn't.

Women mistake the sex act for love. Men don't. They accept their lusting libidos for what they are. This is what upsets women. They think men are insensitive. Some are. But most men generally have one goal in mind in the beginning: to get her into bed.

Women also expect too much from relationships initially. If they hop into bed quickly, they want a commitment; at least a phone call. What they fail to realize is that once they have gone to bed with a man on the first, second or third date, he's no longer interested. He doesn't respect her.

Women, when they succumb to a man's advances too soon, and the man doesn't react the way they expect him to, experience anger and hatred toward themselves. It is then transferred to the male. Before rapidly donning their Dr. Dentons and going beddie-bye, women need to get a grip on their hormones and exert some self-control and discipline.

Many women I interviewed explained their "roll over" experience this way: "Well, if I didn't go to bed with him, he wouldn't take me out again." Who gives a damn? He's too shallow. Where would a relationship go with a man that vacant?

Another case history involves a woman in her mid-twenties who had set her sights on a handsome professional. A friend had introduced them when "Becky" needed some legal advice. She subtly pursued him for a couple months, talking with him only on the phone, while she worked on improving herself physically. She dropped 20 pounds, was exercising regularly and had her hairdresser give her a new look.

Their conversations during this time usually began as business, but he always managed to make them personal by the end of the call. She enjoyed him and was really hoping for a relationship, but he still hadn't asked her out.

She decided it was time to make a move, since he hadn't. She bought a new outfit and asked him to meet her for a drink because she needed some "business" advice. They talked and laughed for three hours over martinis. The evening ended with him telling her how much he enjoyed her company and asking her to keep in touch.

By this time, she concluded that they would be friends, but she was still hoping for more. A couple of weeks later, she had to drop business papers off at his house. He hadn't been feeling well, but told her it was okay for her to come over. He asked her to call when she was leaving. She wasn't looking forward to this because she still hadn't resolved and gotten rid of her feelings for him. But he needed the papers and she was going out of town the next day.

Becky called him as she was leaving the office and he informed her that he'd just taken a shower and needed a half hour to get dressed. She found that strange. How long did it take to throw on a pair of jeans and a t-shirt? When she arrived, he was dressed as if he were going out. She assumed he had a date or was expecting someone. They chit-chatted and much to her surprise, he asked her if she'd like to go out for a drink.

They got to the club to find a bachelorette party in progress. They ordered drinks and for the next two hours she listened to him make comments about every female in the room. This just confirmed her "we'll-just-be-friends" theory, although she did find it a bit insensitive of him to salivate at other women when he was with her.

When they got back to his house, she got her keys and said goodnight. He walked her out to the car and then he really surprised her with his demonstrative approach to saying good-bye—a very intimate kiss. Needless to say, hormones ruled the brain and she spent a very enjoyable three hours, prone.

A week passed and she didn't hear from him. She had called him about business and his only reference to that "passionate" evening was, "Tell me Becky, do you still respect me?" They've never gone out again. Roll over, baby, I think I love you.

These are just two examples of the "roll over" theory in action. Many women from here to Timbuktu have had at least one "roll over" session in their dating lifetime. If a man goes to bed with a woman without knowing her, it's just sex. Period. But if a man has had ample time to know the lady, he has vested interest in her as an individual and the act of sex has a deeper meaning. In this situation, both the man and the woman experience deeper feelings toward each other and, more importantly, about themselves. The respect is mutual.

Men can't use the "roll over" attitude without a partner. So you figure it out. Women since the sixties have been brainwashed to believe sexual freedom was theirs without a price. Wrong. There is nothing on this earth that doesn't carry a price tag, either monetarily or emotionally. Women have paid a terrible price for sexual freedom. They paid with loss of emotions, loss of respect and vacant sex without commitment or attachment. Since the sixties, the female population has become a society of unpaid whores. Yes, even married ones who weren't happy had affairs. One interesting study reveals that more men than women experienced guilt after having affairs.

Why do women acquiesce so easily to a man's advances? There are several reasons. Number one, they think all they have to offer is sexual favors. Obviously, they don't have enough confidence in their other attributes. They are insecure, so they are easily flattered or intimidated into a horizontal position. Some women just can't say no: to their friends, children or men. They think by saying yes, they will be accepted. Many women think they deserve less than perfect treatment from a man. A man will always treat a woman the way she expects to be treated. They follow her lead.

Since Patsy Promiscuity emerged from the sixties and romped from one psychedelic pad to the other, women placed themselves at a disadvantage to men in the sexual arena. This continued through the seventies. However, by the late eighties, women were beginning to realize their gross error in judgment. What a woman had been told was her inalienable right—sex for the sake of sex without love, commitment or romance—was unfulfilling and vacant. But, most women still refused to remove "fellatio artist" from their resumes. And they still haven't stopped bed-hopping on the first date.

There are exceptions to the rule. A few, select, sharp women have accepted the fact that men haven't changed since Adam and consider any woman who hops into the sack on the first date a tramp. And today, hopping in the sack doesn't just mean traditional sex.

Women, eighteen to eighty, have been brainwashed by some very clever men into thinking they must be highly proficient in oral sex in order to be "datable." On the first date, she's on her knees, regardless of whether she's wearing braces or dentures. Toss the walker and the lollipops, Adam has spoken. It's "penis power" in action.

This explains why fifty-year-old men have been dating twenty-year-old women. As one twenty-four-year-old explained, "Oral sex just isn't as intimate as regular sex." Another *Cosmo* convert.

By the same token, men are using oral sex as a substitute for traditional sex because even they can't get that turned on by a non-intimate quickie. So, they've figured out, satisfy the female through oral sex and then she really won't care if he can perform. Aren't they clever? And you bought it.

Single men and women are both confused. Their roles aren't defined anymore. The reason women have been brought to their knees is because they've allowed someone else to establish the rules. They haven't developed their own values. Until we, as a society, set higher standards for relationships, we'll continue to grope in the dark.

Test & Review

1. Six to ten dates before rolling over. This gives the man the opportunity to know you.
2. Keep it simple, unemotional, detached, no expectations.
3. Observe every move.
4. Listen to what he is saying to you.
5. Ask questions about him.
6. Watch his body language closely.
7. Check for inconsistencies (lies).
8. Never get drunk and let your defenses down until you know this person very well.
9. Divulge nothing about yourself. In other words, don't spill your guts; be mysterious.
10. Never change your current lifestyle. Don't stop dating other men or give up girlfriends for any man. When you are married, you can delete the date-mates.
11. Don't get on your knees unless you're in church.
12. Don't take out your dentures or throw away your lollipops too quickly.

You Can Marry More Money in Five Minutes Than You Can Make in a Lifetime

A ri Onassis claimed a person should always "marry up." His union to his first wife was a definite improvement in his social standing and financial status, as her father was a multi-millionaire shipping magnet. However, his second marriage to Jackie Kennedy wasn't as financially lucrative for him. For Jackie O, it was a clear case of marrying-up.

I am not suggesting that your prime premise for marrying should be for money. However, it's just as easy to fall in love with a man who has his financial ducks in a row as it is to fall for one who doesn't. At least find a male who possesses the potential to make a decent living.

If you think poverty is fun, try it! You can do more for the betterment of yourself, your mate, your children and society with money. You are a burden to someone without it. So, either you marry it or make it. And, darlings, you can make more money in five minutes by marrying it than struggling by on the nine-to-five work force.

Metaphysical aficionados say we make our own successes, create our own environment. People literally design their heaven or hell right where they are at this moment. With the right attitude, you can attract the positive, not the negatives into your life. So armed with this knowledge, it shouldn't be too difficult to attract or be attracted to that man with all the gold.

I advocate women start this program at an early age—and that means before marrying and having several children. Women with multiple marriages and children to raise aren't as appealing as those who have never been married. But, for you more mature ladies who have been in the marketplace before, it's not impossible to meet a "rich prince" even if you do have some extra baggage to cart along; it's just easier when you're younger.

In order to marry a man of means, you must socialize in the right circles so you have the opportunity to meet him.

This isn't impossible, but it will take some planning and work. What doesn't? You must first take stock of your assets and liabilities, then make a list of how you can turn the liabilities into assets.

Finding a man with money to marry is much like your search for the prince. However, you want a wealthy prince and, since the stakes are higher, the effort will be more stringent.

Men with money usually marry women with money, or one that looks like she has it. So your main assignment is to refine your visual image so you look like you were born with a silver spoon in your mouth.

OK, I'll admit, it's deceitful, but after he falls in love with you, and the forty-carat diamond is sparkling on your left hand, neither of you will care. He'll be happy and you'll be ecstatic as well as the envy of all your "house-mouse" friends.

Men with money can buy anything they desire, so again, your main attraction for him will be an unattainable demeanor. Not too drastic, but a little lofty. Make him work hard for this prize.

You must never forget that men of all means are already paranoid about women after their fortunes, so they will be on guard for "gold diggers" who appear too easy.

Your personality will be the magnet that cements a financially acceptable man to you, because he probably has seen it all, traveled to exotic places all over the globe and met all the "right people." So you better be able to be thoroughly entertaining.

Read everything you can get your hands on, so at least you can be a charming conversationalist, an interesting companion, and not a bore or embarrassment to his friends. Cultivate the arts. Men with money have season tickets to the opera and ballet, and purchase paintings as investments. You should be well-versed in all aspects of the cultured life.

Wealthy women now work, at least at some form of business, even if it means volunteering at some charity or hospital, oil painting or sculpting. They love and migrate toward talented people, often becoming a benefactor along the way.

Remember, Onassis thought he captured the catch of the century with Jackie Kennedy, until he got all the shopping bills totaling millions. He remarked, "Is that all she can do, is shop?" He became quite bored with Jackie, choosing to reinstate his love affair with the opera diva, Maria Callas.

Moneyed men are frugal with a buck, so be prepared to use every tactic and trick up your sleeve to extract a hefty allowance. Then when you've got him panting and ready to race up to the altar, make sure you've got the best lawyer in the business to hammer out a reasonable pre-nuptial agreement. Expect this. Every wealthy man or woman will demand you to sign one. It's the fashionable thing to do these days.

Beware when you're "rich-man hunting" that you've got the real McCoy and not an impostor. Many people pursuing a money mate have been duped. They find out too late it's all flash and no cash, all show and no dough. This happens sometimes to both men and women who hover around wealthy resort areas in search of Mr. or Mrs. "moneybags." They are both playing the game, cleverly I might add, only to get married and discover they've both been pooling their welfare or Social Security checks.

There are many proven tricks that can be used to develop the right allure to entrap your prince. If you're divorced, plan to suggest you're widowed. It's so much more acceptable in the circle of "high society." Hopefully, your ex-husband lives out of state and there are no children, or this game will be easily exposed. Also, men think widows are wealthier than divorcees, and of course, you can play the sympathy routine.

Onassis had several ploys for attracting wealth: Never pay taxes, keep a perpetual suntan and live at the right address. The suntan and right side of town we can accomplish. Taxes, forget it.

A tan leaves one with the impression you are one of the idle rich, because if you had a job, you'd sport a color created by florescent lighting. Another reason for the tan, it gives you a look that you might sail, or have a yacht, ski, play tennis, or loll around the beach club during the day.

Renting or owning a place in the presentable part of town is a great trapping that is as important as the right physical image.

There is a great book, called *Decorating Rich—How to Achieve a Monied Look Without Spending a Fortune* (Random), that is a must read if you want to create a wealthy environment. At least you'll "live well" before you really live well.

It's important for your personal living quarters to be decorated with rich overtones because you'll want to entertain your prospective "rich catch" in a romantic and comfortable setting. Remember he's been used to the best, and you must also show off your talents in the homemaking department—even though you'll immediately hire a maid, chauffeur, butler and private secretary as soon as "Mrs." is placed in front of your name.

There are many inexpensive accessory pieces you can collect and add when your budget allows, to give a monied motif. First, learn to mix an antique piece along with your ordinary furniture. For instance, a comfortable couch (use down instead of the hard, foam rubber), several upholstered chairs, an antique chest, an oriental planter placed on a teak base, or oriental screen with a matching oriental lamp could be the basics for a living area.

Plants, statuary, glass-top end and coffee tables, using faux short columns for bases, along with leopard accents, or colorful, patterned throw pillows, all combined can create a rich look. Now just add framed photos, some of the family, more of you dressed to the hilt at parties or in formal wear, sailing, tennis or horseback riding, and you have an expensive party for peanuts.

The quickest way to achieve that "look" is to use monochromatic coloring for the windows, floors and walls. For example, do white on white. White walls, carpets and white shutters, along with white chairs and couch. Then throw an oriental rug for accent and richness along with an oriental screen, lamp or chest.

Then add mirrors, several paintings, plants, a fern and some classic books on the coffee table, with of course white candles and your framed pictures, and you've created that Palm Beach or Santa Barbara decor. You can accomplish the same feeling using beige, sandalwood or any light basic color from white to beige; then add your accents.

Shop the resale shops for bargains. Even the discount stores will have your plants, frames, pillows, etc. Always remember, you must think rich before becoming rich, so everything you do with your wardrobe, yourself, and your home must spell wealth. And, yes, you can do this on a budget. It's just as easy to decorate rich as decorate poor; it's a matter of taste. And to develop this class, read the decorating magazines, pay attention to what decor attracts your fancy. Then emulate and copy it.

Do the same thing when it comes to developing your personal image. Create that signature look that always wows men, rich or poor. Again, use the same theory. Purchase a few basic dresses or suits, white, black or beige, then accessorize them to death. Did you know the famous actress Lillie Langtry captured a real, live prince and king while living in France, with one basic black dress? Lillie was poor, with little or no resources. She found enough money to have a dressmaker design her an out-of-sight black basic outfit. Of course, Lillie had more than her black basic at her disposal. She was a courtesan, but her wardrobe consisted of that one "drop dead" garment until the prince and a king started dressing her in the finest of garments and jewels. So it can be done.

After living on the west coast of Florida, where socializing consists of playing golf, bridge, and shelling, I moved onto the island of Palm Beach. I was in dire need of a totally different look compared to my khaki clam diggers.

Of course, I was on a limited budget but I had to attend many social functions and needed a new wardrobe. So I followed Lillie Langtry's game, and allotted one thousand dollars for a new outfit. That was a ton of money to me at the time, but I had to spring for a Donna Karen black basic with matching belt. Dress was $800 and the belt was $200.

The design took me any and everywhere, and to this day, it's still in great shape and right in fashion. Both women and men compliment me when I don my Lillie Langtry special.

Creating an image, the right image, doesn't mean you have to be a phony. It just means you've got your act together. Class and taste are acquired. A person isn't born with these two attributes. In fact, I've noticed the more money some women have, the more gross their taste and class becomes. It's amazing but true.

This brings me to another subject if you're intent on marrying up. Most people can spot a phony a mile away. Don't put on airs. The truly rich don't because they don't have to. They've been born with wealth, and generally the old monied guard are like old shoes, and you wouldn't know how much they had stashed. Just be your sweet, soft-spoken, clever self, dressed to the nines, with impeccable manners, and an extremely vibrant and interesting personality, and your prince will come, in a Rolls Royce.

CHAPTER

Behind Every Successful
Woman, There Should Be a Man!

When I say there should be a man behind every successful woman, don't immediately erupt into a screaming fit, protesting I've misplaced most of my brain cells. Let me explain my prognosis. After in-depth observation, plus reading about numerous successful women, I noticed men were very instrumental to their success, usually assisting them in some capacity behind the scenes in their climb up the ladder.

In comparison to the ladies who tried to do it alone, the woman with male support made it bigger and better, and became richer with less strain, stress, complications or harassment.

When I delved into the subject further, I learned that the top female producers shared a common prerequisite. They had men as partners, involved husbands or male consultants, investors or attorneys who aided them in attaining their goals.

A perfect example I used in *How to Figure Out a Woman* is the story of Jacqueline Susann's meteoric fame in the publishing world. It's worth the mention because she was the forerunner for the present types of fictional books that sell like "hot cakes." Jacqueline married well, to Irving Mansfield, a then-famous television producer and public relations man, who possessed a myriad of the right connections in the entertainment field.

Granted, she possessed a vivid imagination and was a superior story-teller, but she wasn't a writer, by trade or talent. However, she was blessed with a determination to succeed that surpassed General Patton's. But without Irving's money, contacts, and tremendous moral support and hands-on assistance, she would have remained a very frustrated Jacqueline Mansfield, wife of Irving. These facts don't detract from her success. On the contrary, she made about eight million dollars in the seventies, when eight million was eight million. It's just another piece of evidence showing that behind a successful woman, there is usually a man.

Aligning yourself with the right man can either make or break you in the world of business. Very few women have the guts, balls, stamina, knowledge, energy or negotiating skills it takes to fight all the odds a person must fight in order to win the golden ring. Plus the fact when you fuse two people of the opposite sex together with the same goal, you create a strange phenomenon called "synergy."

You also create an unbeatable combination by coupling the male and female headed toward the same goal because you combine the perfect balance of negative and positive, the yin and yang.

Roger Vadim, the French film producer and Jane Fonda's first husband, created Bridget Bardot and Catherine Deneuve and helped propel Ms. Fonda into a star. The same methodical care taken by John Derek when he re-honed Ursula Andress, Linda Evans and Bo Derek. Bo, and only God knows her real name, was just a teeny-bopper when Grandpa Derek started sculpting his masterpiece. I can guarantee you, Bo wouldn't have become a "10" without Mr. Derek's assistance.

The very popular Ivana Trump rose to the pinnacle of celebrity after divorcing Donald. With a twenty-five-million-dollar settlement and tons of international business connections generated while married to Mr. Trump, she ain't exactly pulling herself up out of the gutter by her own bootstraps. Without Donald's money, social status and connections, do you think Ivana would have become the "international star" she is today? The answer is apparent.

Ask yourself: Would there have been an Eleanor without Franklin Roosevelt, a Jackie O without Jack or Ari, or a Nancy without Ronnie? And go one step further. Who would have heard of Hillary or her damned haircut? You do get the picture. Men are extremely useful and helpful to women. So why do women place barriers between the sexes when the going could be a hell of a lot easier?

I'll go another step. You wouldn't be reading this book if it hadn't been for a man. Several men. And so you can focus on this subject matter, I'll repeat the story for you.

Several years ago I sold the *How to Figure Out a Man/Woman* manuscripts to a New York publisher, but during contract negotiations, my agent and publisher couldn't come to a conclusion on the financial end. During these meetings, the publisher, his girlfriend, myself and a friend met for cocktails. I had worn a ring that may have been a bit flashy, and the girlfriend remarked to her boyfriend publisher, "By the looks of that ring, she doesn't need the money." Thanks, sister of the skin! He shrugged off the stupid remark, but nevertheless, we stopped negotiating.

I continued sending out the manuscripts to women editors mostly, and didn't get to first base until I met a man who happened to like the *Woman* manuscript. He in turn talked to a publisher he worked for and a male editor. The negotiations went quickly and smoothly, and, I must say, I had several men in my camp. Also, women were redeemed in my eyes, through the wife of the publisher, who signed both my contracts and my first check.

In the past, men were always supportive about my work, and weren't afraid to verbalize it. Basically, women were extremely luke warm when it came to compliments.

Women have a difficult time networking with each other, that is why it's important to find a man who shares your common goal and then combine your talents.

Another reason you should employ men to do your bidding is they like to negotiate with each other. They speak the same language. Men act differently when talking business with a woman.

In sales, if men are sincerely interested in doing business, they will most likely deal better with one of their brothers. I've been subjected to so much macho crap when presenting a sales presentation to more than one man at a time, it isn't funny. They seem to feel a need to perform in front of their peers when a woman is present. This is where women in business are at a disadvantage if they haven't a man around as a buffer.

By the same token, I've worked with men where we both are making the presentation to a man, and it works beautifully.

Why fight it? Women like to deal with men, men like to deal with men, so why not cover the odds more in your favor and find a man who is supportive of your ideas, and join forces? It makes life easier.

If you think I'm barking up the wrong tree, listen to what the researchers found out when they polled a large group of women about a woman as president. The majority of women admitted they wouldn't vote for a woman. They wanted a man in that position. The Liberated Lenas can march to Washington, with their gravy-stained wraps, until they turn blue and it won't change the way the sexes react toward each other.

In fact, if you can't beat them, join them. Find a man who likes women and utilize his talents, in connection with yours, and you both have it made. I think that is what God had in mind when He created men and women. Viva la difference! They should work together in every aspect of life.

I do feel women have made great strides in the area of sexual harassment if the scales of justice don't become tipped. Sexual harassment was terribly rampant in the business community, especially in the entertainment field, until women became fed up with this weak type of behavior, which threatened their livelihood, and decided to put a stop to it.

Unfortunately, men were in power positions and misused that power in business to extract sexual favors in return for jobs. Marilyn Monroe knew the casting couch well on her climb up the ladder of stardom. It was the same with many starlets who were subjected to this demeaning piece of claptrap.

Hopefully, men and women have learned the workplace isn't the area to extract or offer these types of bonuses, just to get or keep a job. Another good reason for the male/female partnership is that you are somewhat protected from these types of advances. You can always send in your partner when things get heated or a little kinky.

Men can bring to a business relationship and personal relationship the opposite positive traits a woman needs to further her career and enhance her personal lifestyle. Marriage was designed to assist both men and women in becoming better people while forming a more reliable and unified alliance.

Men and women must re-evaluate their opinions towards each other and try to coexist in a positive manner with each other, instead of drawing the lines of battle. Both sexes can accomplish triple the amount of good with each other rather than trying to keep fighting the battle of life alone.

If there's truth to the cliché, "Behind every successful man, there is a woman," why not, "Behind every successful woman, there should be a man!"

CHAPTER 22

Laying the Trap

Hallelujah, you've now found your prince. The next segment of this scenario is to capture him; lock, key, castle and crown. This is the strategic part of the plan and if executed properly, you can add a "Mrs." before your name. If not, you might find your padded fanny out in the streets, pounding the leather off the soles of your Guccis, hunting for another royal subject.

Before you begin this program, I'm assuming you are in love. If not, all the tricks, maneuvers and game plans will eventually dissolve into a big fat zero. You can't fake love for long and the charade is easily detected, even by a dimwitted prince.

So make certain you're absolutely honest with yourself first before you lay the trap. If not, the Fairy Godmother might wave her wand called karma and turn your prince into a frog right before those baby blues of yours.

When you lay a trap, what do you need? Bait! And your bait better be of the imported variety. None of this cheap, imitation, domestic cheese whiz stuff to catch the big mouse.

In the beginning, your first tactic should be not to move too quickly, appear too desperate, act too excited or interested. Remember, you're on a bivouac, preparing for battle. So stay calm, cool and collected. You mustn't scare your sweet prince with buzz words that smack of marriage, relationship or commitment.

If a man thinks you can "take him" or "leave him," he's perplexed, somewhat confused and ego-deflated. It's a great way to keep your opponent off-guard. Therefore, he will try harder to help you catch him. In a simpler synopsis, he'll do your work for you, if you don't stir the pot. Detachment is a great enticer for both the male and female, but men usually succumb to this ploy quicker than women.

Again, I reiterate. By being or at least presenting the impression you are "luke warm" about him and the relationship places him in a relaxed position, it allows you to maneuver quickly towards your main goal while his defenses are down. "All's fair in love and war." This is both, and whether you capture your prince will depend on what kind of general you are.

Getting a man to take the plunge toward marriage is about as easy as coaxing a stubborn jackass down the side of the Grand Canyon, unless you are a master of the game. This strategy certainly isn't for novices.

No man in his right mind would get married by his own volition. You must place him in a vulnerable position. Short of using water torture, a woman must utilize every game in the book during the job, either with gourmet meals, Victoria's Secret lingerie or brilliant conversation. Money could be a tremendous aphrodisiac, but most of us can't rely on that enticement. So again we have to trudge toward our goal with such a vengeance that neither sleet, snow, tornadoes or a monsoon can deter us from attaining our main objective.

I must insert a most important warning. During the time you are "laying the trap," tell no one, especially your girlfriends. Women aren't allies of other women when one of their feline friends is on the prowl for a male. In fact, they will throw a monkey wrench in your "game plan" every step of the way. This doesn't say much for women networking with each other, does it? But face facts, women are at their most treacherous when a man comes on the scene.

I've observed two ladies out on the make and one man will appear. When one makes a trip to the ladies' room, the other will rip her to shreds, immediately informing the male about all her faults. Best friends do it to each other if there is a male within a hundred yards. So keep your own counsel and tricks to yourself if you want to win the game.

Your success in this matter will also depend on how resourceful and creative you are. Also, at this juncture, you must be willing to "pull out all the stops." If outrageous behavior is apropos, then by all means, be outrageous. If he is attracted by the demure damsel and you're a "motorcycle mama," then trade in your leathers for a crinoline.

During this time, you must be a chameleon. You want to win the prince and if you're not willing to go the extra mile, there are twenty other damsels waiting in line for your royal highness.

Communication is tantamount. Ask every question in the book then listen, listen, listen. However, be discreet with this regimen. You'll need to know every thought, desire, fantasy and goal that Mr. Prince has so you can zero in on those emotions. People, when they are emotionally involved, think emotionally and not intellectually. And sweetie, you want this guy thinking emotionally with a capital E.

Find out what kind of women he's attracted to. Then incorporate a few of those traits into your personality or image. Marilyn Monroe did exactly this when she wanted to capture playwright Arthur Miller. She became quite the little literary buff, reading *War and Peace* along with a myriad of other classics. I'm sure this only added to her charm and we know it improved her ability to become a brighter conversationalist. Read *How to Figure Out a Woman* and pay close attention to the chapter entitled, "History of Women." These ladies were masters at the game of seducing and prince capturing.

Regardless of what you think, men like attractive and sexy women. This is what first lures them into the net. Even fishermen know that in order to catch fish, certain species, they must use pretty, eye-catching lures.

Now a prince isn't going to want a scullery maid, so your image must be pulled together. It won't hurt to take a few lessons from the glamour queens of yesteryear. From the twenties through the forties, women were "hot looking." The grunge look won't cut it, so eradicate any layered, perma-wrinkle, or less than classy attire from your wardrobe. Take it down to your nearest "nearly new" shop. At least you'll make fifty percent of the selling price. And while you're at it, take a long, hard look at their merchandise.

I personally know a Palm Beach countess who dresses like a million bucks, and purchases most of her after-five wear at a resale shop. Of course, she's blessed with an outstanding body and great looks. However, the countess has a flair and men are attracted to her like moths to a flame. She's a "Hot Tomato" because she created that image for herself and plays it to the hilt. Sex first, then brains. (The countess speaks several languages and is no dummy in the intelligence department.)

Another famous Palm Beacher, known for her kinky behavior rather than her stunning attire, who married a prince is Roxanne Pulitzer. And after divorcing the heir to the Pulitzer fortune, she then aligned herself with a count. A clotheshorse or glamour queen she ain't. But supposedly she's quite ingenious.

She worked overtime promoting herself, posed for *Playboy*, wrote several books and kept her name in print around town as a sexy seductress. There must be something in seducing princes.

The "glamour gals" of the forties are the ones we should take some lessons from as they were extremely successful in seducing princes.

Rita Hayworth supposedly captured Prince Aly Kahn's eye when she arrived at a party in Cannes dressed all in white. With that flaming red hair mesmerizing him, he had to meet her. Of course she married him, but she couldn't keep him interested. I think Rita lacked personality and possibly intellect, but she knew how to get the ball rolling.

When you "lay the trap" it's a combination of things that attract a prince. Frogs will be enticed by any woman, but you have no use for the frogs of this world. It's a prince you're after, so this will take more planning.

A first-class appearance is first and foremost because you must get his attention. Secondly, a bright and pleasing personality along with humorous wit is a definite turn-on. Thirdly, keep him at arms length in the beginning, because respect is something you'll want from this prince down the highway if you want him to build that castle on the Rhine for you. Men don't marry women they don't respect unless they are desperate, you are pregnant or you're both nuts. Oh, one more deciding factor...you've got money!

Become a good conversationalist. Men aren't interested in your age, your menopause, your PMS, your kids, your ex-husband or your problems. Contrary to what has been said about successful and intelligent women, men like them.

Read something besides the *Enquirer* and *Cosmopolitan*. Men talk about politics, making money, business, playing tennis, the gold market or racquet ball, the latest best seller and so on.

Learn to play games men are playing. Men love women who are proficient at their games and if news gets around you are an excellent tennis player, men will be calling for a doubles match.

In other words, men like interesting women. Don't you like interesting men? How many times have you dated someone and all you had to say was "he's so boring." Men are no different. They love to communicate with a "hot ticket." One who is energetic and stimulating. That gets them every time.

Many women are running to the doctor, gulping prescription pills for those anxiety attacks brought on because they're alone and want a man instead of "heart attack alley" due to the stress of pursuing a career. Well, there comes a time when you must bite the bullet, then decide what you want most.

I didn't say it was going to be easy finding a prince. Frogs are easy, but landing a prince, then the castle, is going to take plenty of work. If you're not up to it, marry the frog, warts and all. It's up to you. You possess unlimited potential as a person and woman. Be the best you can be!

Keeping Him Interested,
Excited and a Little Off Guard!

This chapter should have been entitled, "The Feminine Mystique," not in reference to Betty Friedan's book about the liberation of women, but because in the past thirty years, women have forsaken one of their main attractions—mystery. Women replaced their "mystique" with a new program of "let it all hang out." And this has caused men to be less interested in women on a romantic level.

Men went bonkers over Marlene Dietrich, Jean Harlow and the "glamour girls" of the romantic period because they were mysterious and unattainable, at least from their screen persona. They didn't let anything hang out, especially their bodies and brains. They created an aura of mystery that generated tremendous sex appeal.

Today, the average mid-American females who appear on daytime talk shows are spewing out their guts and emotions, while exposing their souls along with their bosoms. There is no mystique left, as these modern-day oracles blab their innermost thoughts for millions of people.

At the same time they're beating their gums about every personal nuance; they are complaining that romance has gone out of their relationships. And it has.

Women feel this loss tremendously, as romance novels have remained best sellers for years. It's a round robin because the more they alleviate the mystique from their repertoire, the more they desire a romantic involvement. You can't have it both ways.

How romantic do you think a man would feel, communicating with you about PMS over a candlelight dinner? There is nothing sacred in the nineties, and the media is partially to blame for this faction. Commercials depicting products we must use, from the best tampons to jockey shorts, are bombarding the public by the minute with personal problems and their solutions. We, as people, desire romantic unions. We aren't animals, coupling just to procreate and proliferate our species.

Faith Popcorn in her book, *The Popcorn Report* (Harper Business), claims our society will return to nostalgia on a large scale. Businesses or products depicting a touch of yesteryear will be hot! People will want their lives to be safe and secure with some purpose and meaning. They will be attracted to "nostalgia" types of theme restaurants, clothing, films and life in general.

We've tried living the high-tech, sophisticated approach and found it doesn't work for humans, simply because we are human, not robotic in our emotions. Society is realizing it's lonely out there and people want a change. They long for love, romance, a home and family in the future.

The same will apply to relationships. Blatant and kinky sex becomes boring, uninteresting and vacant. Since the sixties, many people have been experimenting with living on the "wild side," only to find it isn't rewarding.

I predict, within several years, depending on the status of our shaky economy, this present society will return to basics, if it can. People are our most important asset, and we will begin to protect our home, relationships, family and environment.

This attitude will follow into relationships with the return of the female becoming more feminine and the male recapturing his past position of provider, leader and protector.

The pendulum will swing back, if it isn't stuck. The entire world is experiencing momentous changes, and hopefully for the better. Maybe, just maybe, the people involved will be able to adapt to these major changes. It's not the world that's gone mad, it's just the people in it, and so much depends on each human being living on this earth as to what really happens to our future.

If we continue to settle for second best in relationships, the government, our quality of living, television programming and, most definitely, the arts, we will live a second-rate lifestyle.

Everything is connected. When something is moved or destroyed, it alters the chain of life. And this chain of life is most important where relationships between men and women are concerned. Without positive and nurturing relationships, our society would be extinct. Women and men are unhappy with their present-day pursuits of the perfect mate. Dating is difficult in the nineties, so why create more of a chasm?

Unfortunately, there is no "free lunch," so if you truly want a rewarding relationship, you must meet the intended half way. The quickest way to change a man, is for you to change. Men follow your lead. As I have explained, if you want to be treated like a lady, then act like one. Men wouldn't think of treating a lady like a whore, or vice-versa.

If you want more respect, then command it. Don't demand it; that never works. The same applies to romance. You will have to start the ball rolling in this department, then he will continue.

Men love glamour and mystery. This is an easy assignment. All you have to do is set the stage and turn on the lights; he'll pay for the theater ticket.

There are the three A's in life—Awareness, Acceptance and Action. Now, if you live by the three A's I'll guarantee you won't be disappointed or disillusioned. So first be aware. If you truly want a relationship, you must resign yourself. There is work involved. Quit bitching and get on with it. Prioritize. How much effort are you willing to expend in order to have a relationship? If you shrug your shoulders and retort, "not much," you don't want one that badly. So plan to live alone and like it. Nothing wrong with that either.

Second, accept the fact you really want a man, and will allot the time needed to find one; then keeping him interested, at least enough to walk down the aisle.

Next the action part. Plan to swing into action with a positive attitude, and, yes, you will accomplish your goals.

Create a mysterious aura about yourself, and this means keeping your mouth shut about your business, personal and financial. Let him get to want to know you before you start an intimate conversation about yourself. They say if a woman will tell her age, she will tell anything. Guess what? I know every one of my friends' ages, male and female. They don't know mine.

Women love to talk, and there is nothing wrong with this but it's the topics they choose that I question. They tend to take strangers into their confidence too quickly, and this destroys any mysterious allure they may have. Plus the fact, you want this man to want to know you and to put some effort in the tribal dance of romance.

Become an interesting conversationalist. Again, this takes some time and effort and required reading but you've already taken the challenge, so make the trip to the library and pick up some reading material.

Men love gossip, contrary to what they say, especially on an international level, and some of the seducers of wealth scions, were great gossips. Many of your mistresses of royalty, spent evenings filling the old king full of the latest gossip of the court and his kingdom.

Be careful in the gossip area, or you'll get a reputation of being a "Blabber Mouth Bertha" and he won't trust you. Also, never, and I mean never, gossip about your girlfriends' personal businesses. Gossip on a national vain, he'll think you're in the know.

Keeping him excited, stimulated, interested and a little off guard, is easy, if you're exciting, stimulating, interesting and a little wacko. Don't be afraid to let your personality emerge. Men love exciting women and one who speaks her mind. At least show him you're intelligent to have your opinion. Men don't like "yes" women.

Cultivate a little bitchiness, and then add to this exciting, interesting, wacko and mysterious. I will guarantee you, you've got an admirer for life.

Mystery can be attained through actions. I watched a friend refuse to allow men to pick her up at home until about the fifth date. She knew they would stay around that long because they were dying to see where she lived. By that time, she worked her magic on them and they were pretty well hooked.

Make men want to get to know the "real you" by keeping some things to yourself in the beginning—not always being available, and certainly not informing where you're going or who you're with. These tactics drive men wild.

If a new potential amour is picking you up for an evening, have beautiful red roses, with a card attached, natch, in full view. This also speaks volumes. You have another admirer. Say nothing.

Have a friend call you at the designated time he is to arrive and chat, quickly but flirtatiously, on the phone. Hang up, prepare to leave without a word. Another brain bender. Remember, men love competition, and if you'll plant little, subtle hints (not verbal) they must be subtle, that others are interested in you, he'll think he has a star. Jealously is not the premise here; making you look popular is, so take it from there.

Women got tired of acting and playing these harmless little games. They turned in their stage performances while getting paid, I might add, for the reality of a paycheck, career and freedom; only to find the carrot at the end of this stick was loneliness, escalated medical bills for the stress and strain of making it alone, and less freedom.

CHAPTER

24

Sexual Trapeze Artist
or Circus Clown

Women misunderstand the role that sex plays where men are concerned in a budding union. They are under the misconception that if they don't "roll over" immediately, he will take a powder. So what! This is even a quicker way of exposing his true intentions. If a man is just after sex and you're interested in a commitment, why not put him through the test!

Of course, women fail to grasp this theory, so they drop their bikinis, then become emotional cripples when he leaves or doesn't call them again. In the beginning, they shouldn't succumb to his advances so rapidly, and if he still didn't call, they would emerge with at least some modicum of self-esteem. And if he doesn't call, when you've held him at arm's length, you know he was a frog, or you just didn't connect. Either way it's a win-win situation for you. You can't always be the loser.

"Men and women both tend to like and trust the familiar," says Tracy Cabot in *How to Make a Man Fall in Love with You*. "The most familiar is themselves, which is why people tend to find others who have tastes and values similar to their own." You notice the book says love, not lust. And that is what every woman usually wants. Love, committed love, not sex, is the reason women date men.

So, if we take Ms. Cabot's advice, we must first gain a man's trust, then he will relax and become more vulnerable to our feminine wiles. Today, with the sexual revolution becoming somewhat passé, a woman will have to be prepared to develop a line of communication with a man, insure his trust and know him well before trying to bamboozle him with her fancy sexual tricks. It will take practice. Practice saying no, with a smile, of course, and possibly a quip of, "I'll take a rain check," before consummating the sexual act. If you want a rewarding relationship that commands respect, true love, devotion and romance, all the trappings you read about in those novels, you'll have to take the time, effort, planning and creativity to make it work.

Women haven't been trained in the subtle "seductive technique." Their grandmothers were, but many women of the nineties don't have a clue. So with a little execution of some very old tricks, maybe you'll be able to capture that prince. Leave the sexual trapeze tricks for after the marriage. Or at least until you've got the ring.

It will be critical for a woman to develop the "art of seduction" in order to snag a man in the nineties because he's "burned out" with shallow sex and vacant partners. Remember Faith Popcorn's theory about our society returning to nostalgia? Well, that includes re-creating romance and values in relationships. Love is fashionable. A sharp gal, who adds intelligence, allure, mystery and romance with a sense of humor to her total package, will get the ring, the diamond ring.

Why do you think the lingerie chain Victoria's Secret is so successful? For several years now, women have been purchasing romantic underwear. Accessories, sheets, coverlets and decor for bedrooms are designed with a romantic flavor, and women are purchasing more glamorous types of designs.

Romance and seduction won't fly if you're a total bitch, with a less than pleasing personality. Men know the importance of living with a charming, clever, happy person, so don't neglect this part of your education. Men aren't stupid, naturally. We helped educate them, but they can be mesmerized by the right woman.

Gone are the days when you could snap your garter belt and have him do tricks. Competition is keen, and only the "girl scout" who's prepared and done her homework will get the badge.

What makes a woman seductive? Many things in combination create the end product, but confidence is the main attraction for men. Women who are insecure or inferior aren't seductive.

You radiate confidence by the way you talk, walk, look and act. That's the way you project it. How do you acquire a confident attitude?

By learning to depend on yourself. Start projects, then finish them. Each little success will improve your image of yourself. You'll be proud of your own accomplishments, and this very simple act builds confidence.

For instance, I once heard a woman, in her mid-forties and divorced, explain to me why she was afraid to drive by herself to Miami, which was about sixty miles from her home. Surprised, I asked her why. She didn't know exactly, but she was afraid. Now, this woman was insecure as hell, and it certainly wasn't an appealing trait. She could have driven to Miami, turned around and drove back, and a milestone would have been accomplished in improving her confidence. But she wouldn't hear of it.

Sometimes we must do the very things we are afraid of. This doesn't mean dangerous feats, it just means overcoming your anxieties about certain neuroses. I hate elevators, heights, driving on crowded expressways, flying and a myriad of minor dislikes. But I force myself to combat my feelings, and dive in and start swimming. This builds confidence.

Every time you overcome an obstacle, your confidence rises up the ladder and you become more secure. Tackle a sport, some avocation you'd enjoy or a problem you can't solve. Make a list of these things and when they are completed, check them off and give yourself a reward. This is building confidence. The more you attack the problem head-on, the closer you are to completion.

"I can't," shouldn't be in your vocabulary. Clinton T. Howell wrote in his book, *Design for a Living*: "You can do anything you think you can." You may become just what you decide in your mind to be. What the mind of man can conceive, the mind of man can produce.

Negative thinking produces negative living—living which is unworthy of the potential the Creator has placed in you. Let the power of positive thinking take control and charge of your whole outlook and life.

But to realize your full possibilities you must have high aims, ideals, and ambitions—all linked to an iron will. You yourself determine the height to which you shall climb. Have you the summit in view? Then start for it.

You can make yourself a towering figure in the work of the world. No one owns you. One hundred percent of the stock in your personal corporation belongs to you. Vote out the past mistakes, failures and regrets—they have no more power over your future.

You can make success sure by effort, sacrifice, enthusiasm, unselfishness and self-control. You are the master and maker of your own destiny.

Think, not merely, but *act* on the thought. This pretty much sums it up if you digest Mr. Howell's words. A positive attitude, which takes time and diligence to develop and then maintain, is a trait that men find endearing and attractive. More on this subject in "Women know Thyself."

Sex comes naturally. These other attributes must be studied, acquired, then used on a daily basis before they become a part of your total person. And in the nineties, you're going to need every attribute available in order to survive in a confused world. You will no longer have to be a sexual trapeze artist or circus clown in order to entice your man. You'll have to be the bionic woman.

Woman, Know Thyself

Socrates said "Know thyself." Therefore, you cannot be false to any man. Of course, Socrates was talking about women as well. So, I decided to tailor a chapter just for you. For only when you know yourself can you rise to your full potential, not only as a woman but as a divine creature.

We all want to be successful. But in order to be rich, young, beautiful, healthy, successful and loved, you must be unified. In other words, balanced. However, nothing comes easy. To accomplish these goals, it takes dedication, discipline and daily concentration. First and foremost, you must know yourself.

Since the beginning of time, women have been conditioned to be givers: give to the mate, the child, the community and lastly to yourself. Women feel guilty if, God forbid, they give to themselves first. This line of thinking is warped and perpetuates resentment and anger towards the recipient. We must re-program ourselves to give first to the you of yourself: the physical, spiritual and intellectual.

Every woman understands "woman's intuition." We are born with it, so therefore we think it comes naturally, and it does. However, it can be developed to a much higher degree and used as a tool to further accomplish happiness. Call it gut feeling, whatever. But in truth, it is your inner self.

We are like an onion—tissue-thin layers surrounding the inner core, the real you. As we peel back the layers, one by one, we finally find the nucleus. This is the database, the all-knowing part of you that only wants what is best for you. That is why it nudges, sends you the subtle messages we call hunches. Until you recognize this inner voice and begin to develop its potential, you will continue to lead a life of quiet desperation.

It is not my intention to go "out on a limb" and play Shirley MacLaine. We've all had enough out-of-body experiences. In fact, our society needs to get a grip on reality. But, in order to succeed in any endeavor, one must tap every available resource. And ninety-eight percent of the world population is not living up to its full potential.

These are two main reasons why. First, most of us do not realize and accept the existence of universal laws. We, as individuals have laws we live by, man-made laws. We are controlled by a government that says, "You shall pay one-third of your salary to Uncle Sam and not question it." And is there anyone out there who would dare defy the IRS? I doubt it. We've bought the program, folks. Now there is a much more important set of laws, the laws of the universe.

You can get a tan because the sun comes up every morning. Food is available because of seasonal changes and pollination. These are just a few of the universal laws. How can anyone think they aren't governed by these even more so than by man-made ones?

There are four laws that we must consciously abide by in order to achieve self-fulfillment. The most important one is, "As a man thinketh, he shall be." The other three are those of attraction, freedom, and equilibrium. Through proper use of these laws, you learn first, how to win; second, how to hold; and third, how to share without losing.

The first universal law I mentioned is the most critical. You become what you think and believe. Every one of you, right now, thought yourself into your present job, relationship and financial status. Your past thinking becomes your future. As James Allen so eloquently stated: "Man is made or unmade by himself. He also fashions the tools with which he builds himself mansions of joy, strength and peace. By the choice and application of thought, he descends below the level of the beast. Between these two extremes are all the grades of character, and man is their maker and master."

We have all been programmed, since birth, by our parents, teachers and society. If our thoughts have been programmed in the negative, we must reprogram ourselves into the positive. For instance, if you come from a poor environment, chances are your thinking is geared toward poverty consciousness. You've been conditioned to believe this is what you deserve. Therefore, you must reprogram all the negativity you've brought into adulthood. You become what you think and believe. And, if you believe you don't deserve wealth, beauty or an ideal relationship, you will never have them.

The second law, the law of attraction, is a fascinating one. It states that if you wish to make anything attractive, to yourself or others, you must make it romantic, beautiful, interesting and intriguing; that its own attractiveness is its power to attract. This applies to yourself, your environment and your personality.

The next law is the one of freedom. The urge of every living thing is to be free. The average person finds it much easier to obtain something than hold on to it. But we must realize that anything that is bound or held loses the freedom of its own nature and will therefore search for an avenue of escape. This knowledge is very important in relationships with your mate/husband, children and friends. You must always give the other person freedom of choice.

The final law is equilibrium. Science tells us that not a grain of sand shifts without the world balance readjusting immediately. Your perfect balance, or equilibrium, should be just as important if you are to have a harmonious and satisfactory life. The way you achieve this balance is to unify the body, mind and soul. They must all work in unison. If you are giving too much attention to the physical and not the spiritual, you will be out of balance, out of synch. And without balance, you have burnout.

If these laws are consciously applied to your life, nothing can prevent you from attaining your heart's desires. And the best thing about it is that you don't have to pull out your MasterCard to pay for it, attend thousands of seminars or spend lunch hour with your local therapist.

Now, let's get started on really achieving your desires and goals. First, you'll need a three-subject notebook with pockets. The first section is for the spiritual you. Use it to save inspirational and motivational thoughts and poetry, words that touch you somehow when you read them.

The second part of the notebook should be used to benefit the physical you. Outline your self-improvement and physical goals. Write down what you want to look like, your ultimate state of health, etc. In addition to writing down your goals, spend time going through magazines. Cut out pictures of clothes you want, hairstyles you'd look good in, the type of figure you're striving for—whatever you want. Find a role model you most admire, whether a celebrity, model or prominent person. If you wish, pattern yourself after this person, emulating clothes, make-up, hair, until you find your own personalized style.

The purpose of the last section of your notebook is two-fold. First, to enhance the intellectual you. When you've learned a lesson in the schoolhouse of life, write it down so you don't make the same mistake twice. They're too costly. This applies to both career and personal relationships. The second aspect is to write a complete script of your personal life: where you want to live, what kind of house you want to live in, what your ideal mate looks like, the kind of car you want in the driveway.

Be bold and daring with the script and be specific. Do not place any limitations on it. Use the other pockets in the notebook to collect photos and pictures of the things you want: a jaguar, diamond earrings, a designer dress—whatever you want. This is called visualization. And you cannot have realization without it.

In addition to assembling your book of ultimate desires, you must spend time by yourself. This is how you find the inner you, the perfect you. Set aside a place in your home where you're the most comfortable. This is where you're going to meditate, contemplate and create.

I promise you that meditation is a vital key in freeing the real you. It's an important step. Because for each man there is a place which he is to fill and no one else can fill; something which he is to do, which no one else can do; it is his destiny. And the only way to discover your destiny is through meditation.

It is also a form of relaxation and is both centering and calming. You'll never need Valium if you meditate twenty minutes a day. Many famous composers, writers, poets and inventors meditated: Bach, Brahms, Ben Franklin and Thomas Edison did this. There must be something to it.

You'll need a tape recorder and a cassette of music suggested for meditation. I recommend "White Winds" or Debussy's "Clair de Lune." Environmental tapes of the ocean, rain or mountain sounds are also very good and can be found in any record shop in the new age section.

After you've found a comfortable spot, turn on the tape. You must try to do this close to the same time every day. Let everything go from your mind. If a problem you're experiencing creeps into your thoughts, push it out. Your mind must be clear. Take a few minutes to visualize yourself already where you want to be. Actually experience the feelings that accompany the attainment of your goals. If one of your goals is to find the perfect mate, see the two of you together: eating a romantic dinner, playing tennis, sunning on the beach. Feel the elation and contentment the relationship brings you. This also applies to career goals and self-improvement.

There are many kinds of meditation and a variety of methods. If this is of interest to you, I suggest investigating a metaphysical bookstore or new age section of your local library. Meditation or contemplation will not only help you discover your inner-self, it also alleviates stress, prevents burn-out, relieves tension and anxiety. In fact, research has proven that it reduces your heart rate and decreases the need for oxygen.

Along with improving your inner-image, you must not neglect the physical aspect of your body. Exercise is terribly important, as it increases the endorphins (natural energizers) in your blood supply. And exercising for one hour per day helps increase blood flow in your body.

It also serves another purpose. Regular workouts streamline your figure and help maintain agility and prevent arthritis in advancing years. A youthful body often takes years off your appearance.

With a beautifully toned figure and excellent posture, you can be assured you'll look terrific in the latest fashions, and the ravages of calcium deficiency will not attack you as quickly as it does ladies who have let their bodies go to pot.

Organizing your life on a day to day basis (incorporating the balance of body, mind, soul, and a connection with nature or a higher being) should keep you in perfect alignment, ready to tackle any challenge.

Plan your day accordingly, so you can make time for each segment of your life. I choose to arise at 6 a.m. so I can walk every morning five days a week. Forty minutes of this type of brisk exercise keeps one in shape and is an excellent way to start the day. I walk with someone, and when we are finished, we have morning coffee at a little drugstore counter, then continue the day. I also play tennis on Tuesday and Thursday evenings and then again Saturday and Sunday mornings. With this type of exercise program, I keep my body and attitude on a positive course.

During the week, I set aside about thirty minutes of a special meditation called the five-star process. I do this with crystals, beautiful, calming music, and utilize my visualization during this time for goals I want to complete.

For years I've collected pictures of material goods I wanted to acquire, and exotic places I wanted to visit. Even the photos of what I want to look like and how I want my home decorated. I take this time to reacquaint myself with my "wish book."

I find this type of systematized regimen keeps me organized and balanced without disturbing my work schedule.

Now after you discover the inner you and really know yourself, you must love yourself unconditionally. Only then will you achieve true self-fulfillment and unlock your unlimited potential.

CHAPTER

26

What Men Really Think About Women

A thirty-two-year-old bachelor saw his last "loveship" suddenly end after the woman of his life had convinced him she was madly in love with him, only to turn around with a quick blink of her Maybellines and marry another man she had waiting in the wings. He decided to take a much-needed sabbatical from the female species. Well, maybe a tiny break.

At this writing, he's using a different tactic. "I level with these ladies, right up front," he says. "I tell them I'm not interested in a relationship, I'm just interested in sex." Amazingly, he's found more than one girl who will play for play.

Most men who have been married or stung financially and emotionally, aren't quick the second or third time around to take it in the shorts, so to speak. So they horde their money and love, avoiding the possibility of "Maria Moneyhungry" picking their pockets and breaking their hearts.

One bad apple spoils the bushel. And there are some very nice men and women out there. But by the time they meet, they are usually jaded, suspicious and extremely mistrusting, which makes it difficult to attain or maintain a new relationship. Both parties are carrying too much emotional baggage and preconceived notions about the opposite sex.

However, there is hope. Some men, even if they've been brow-beaten, financially devastated, hoodwinked, clipped, bamboozled or generally conned, still love women.

One three-time divorced male, now happily, has this to say about the female species: "I love women, all women. I love things about women they don't know exist. Everything about a woman is erotic. How she smells, looks, moves, talks, the entire package turns me on. They always have and always will!"

When asked how many women he knew intimately, he answers: "I went to bed with over five-hundred women in two and a half years." Wilt Chamberlain, move over. He explained he was the social director of Parents Without Partners and was like a kid in a candy store with his hand stuck in the jar.

A fifty-year-old man, divorced once, has a totally different observation. "They are bloodsuckers," he says. "I can't afford them." Yet, this same man admires certain women and is extremely supportive of their business and artistic endeavors.

A once-married, now confirmed (aren't they all?) bachelor in his late fifties, says: "It's tough to generalize because there is a kaleidoscope of different attitudes and personalities. Some women are sensational and outstanding, while others are mediocre. We all like to think we aspire to be the best we can be. I think if women aspired to this goal they'd be fabulous human beings. Some already are."

Another man, who puts women on a pedestal, gushes: "Women are the most beautiful creatures in the universe. They give us (men) passion, pain and pleasure. I adore women, all women." Of course this is from the lips of a forty-year-old Colombian jewelry designer. Latin men do have a healthier approach toward the opposite sex.

But, according to a twenty-six-year-old journalist, "Kafka said women are the only paradise on this earth. If that's true, I'd hate to ever see Hell!"

A sixty-four-year-old, once married and now being well-kept by a "sugar mama," humorously explains: "When I come back to this earth in another lifetime, I want to be a woman and sit on my silk cushion and eat bon bons." He's not doing too bad in this lifetime.

Then we have an eighty-year-old widower, who rather succinctly has this to say about women: "I have a theory. Own your home and rent everything else. If it flies, floats or fucks, rent it!"

A middle-aged, once-divorced male, who just ended a relationship, says: "Right now my comments aren't worth a damn. But basically, I like women. In fact, most of my friends are females. I have very few male buddies. However, I've come to one conclusion. I don't understand women and I never will." (Read the *Woman* book, buddy).

One problem men and women have is that they don't bother to bond together as friends. Some of my best friends are men, and I personally love to interact with the male species. I love to talk business and politics as well as play tennis and socialize in general with men. More women should cultivate men as friends and vice versa.

I think if more friendships were formed between the sexes, maybe the games would be unnecessary and people could communicate on a higher level. There is no room for jealousy, tricks, games, manipulation and general tomfoolery. It takes a certain degree of maturity from both parties. But I think it would be worth the effort, and just maybe it would improve upon distant relationships and dysfunctional marriages.

27

Relationships in the Nineties

Single men and women are experiencing major difficulties in finding suitable partners today. No doubt AIDS and other sexually transmitted diseases have put a damper on the romance scene. It's made some people even abstain from all sexual contact—unless they fall madly in love and marriage looks like it might be on the horizon.

It's taken us from the "free love" society of the sixties to an almost "no love" society. But it's also opened up new frontiers for the meet-marketplace. Some good. Some bad.

Some Einstein wannabes have assembled "Virtual Reality" machines, along with headgear and a lot of sophisticated electronic equipment, in the hope of simulating everything from barging down the Nile to a hot, steamy orgasm. All this without leaving home. And without fear of flying or a partner. Now single people who live alone or even married people who aren't satisfied with their sexual partners can tune into their fantasies at night and have cybernetic sex.

My opinion is that we are rapidly becoming a nation of robotic spectators and we don't need another crutch like "Virtual Reality" to take the place of involved living. People need people, and we are not an island to ourselves.

On the other hand, there are those who say computer interaction has come along at the right time and has actually enhanced single living, making it possible for people to meet new friends in other parts of the country and the world. An example is one couple once separated by

3,000 miles (she lived in California, he in Florida). They met on a computer service bulletin board, which had a club for fans of the Monty Python comedy group. They discovered they had the same interests, and letters followed. Then they sent videos to each other. She traveled to Florida to meet him in person, and today they are living happily ever after. Believe it or not, there are countless stories like this in today's computerized world.

This kind of a society has its advantages and drawbacks. Faith Popcorn, author of *The Popcorn Report*, predicts in the nineties, people will be cocooning. They will not be socializing, working or traveling far away from their homes or condos. Home entertaining will replace the neighborhood bars, and at-home food delivery will be on the rise with people opting to order in instead of gathering at their favorite restaurants.

Due to a rise in crime and a sagging economy, people are choosing to burrow into the safe haven of their homes. They soon "shop till they drop" right from their living rooms, thanks to the shopping network.

So, where does all of this leave the single man and woman, who sincerely desire a one-on-one relationship? Well, I will guarantee you they will be selective about who they are dating, and sexual promiscuity will continue to be on the wane.

Miss Popcorn also sees another trend emerging. Nostalgia peppered with romance is surfacing in music, clothes, food, etc. This may mean singles will begin to place romance back into their courtship. Instead of "Roll over, baby, I think I love you," the new theme will be, "Let's take it nice and easy."

It depends on which advertising agency has the largest budget and spends the most money on swaying the American public. The "look, don't touch" attitude might prevail with a bunch of voyeurs still catching the late show at the Kitty Kat Lounge, where they don't have to participate, while scores of singles will be home, alone, wired up to their cybernetic sex machines.

Just possibly, we will become a nation of singles, who indeed want to become involved again with another person. Of course, this requires some creativity, conversational abilities, commitment and work on the part of both parties.

Maybe it won't be too difficult to take romantic walks on the beach, picnic in the park, canoe around the lake, dance with each other and, yes, even communicate through conversation.

First and foremost in relationships, as in life in general, there are no victims—only willing participants when it comes to adults. If we want a better world to live in, then we must make it so. And the first step in accomplishing this feat is to begin with yourself. As Ralph Waldo Emerson said:

"This time, like all other times,

Is a very good one,

If we but know what to do with it."

joella Cain started her writing career as a feature writer/columnist with the *Chicago Tribune*.

In 1979, she created one of the first regional women's magazines in the United States and continued publishing women's magazines until 1992.

She is currently working on a soon-to-be-published humor book and two novels.